INTERPROFESSIONAL WORKING IN HEALTH AND SOCIAL CARE

Interprofessional Working in Health and Social Care

Professional Perspectives

Edited by

Gillian Barrett, Derek Sellman and Judith Thomas

First published 2005 by
PALGRAVE MACMILLAN
Houndmills, Basingstoke, Hampshire RG21 6XS and
175 Fifth Avenue, New York, N. Y. 10010
Companies and representatives throughout the world

PALGRAVE MACMILLAN is the global academic imprint of the Palgrave Macmillan division of St. Martin's Press, LLC and of Palgrave Macmillan Ltd. Macmillan® is a registered trademark in the United States, United Kingdom and other countries. Palgrave is a registered trademark in the European Union and other countries.

ISBN-13: 978–1–4039–1206–0
ISBN-10: 1–4039–1206–8

This book is printed on paper suitable for recycling and made from fully managed and sustained forest sources.

A catalogue record for this book is available from the British Library.

10   9   8   7   6   5   4   3   2
14   13   12   11   10   09   08   07   06

Printed and bound in China

Contents

Acknowledgements

We owe our gratitude to the students of the Faculty of Health and Social Care, University of the West of England, Bristol from whom a request for a book of this nature was initially suggested. We are very grateful to all of the contributing authors who have enriched the book through the provision of distinctive professional perspectives on interprofessional working and to our colleagues in the interprofessional teaching team and the interprofessional research team who provided support and encouragement throughout. We owe particular thanks to Caroline Lapthorn who provided invaluable administrative assistance and to our families for their tolerant support.

We are also grateful to Radcliffe Medical Press, Oxford for their kind permission to reproduce a diagram from Spender *et al.*: Child Mental Health in Primary Care (2001) which appears as Figure 7.1 in this volume.

GB, DS, JT

Notes on Contributors

Gillian Barrett MSc, DipN, RGN, Senior Lecturer, Faculty of Health and Social Care, UWE. Gillian's interests are in health promotion, health communication, interprofessional education and interprofessional practice.

Nancy Carlton PhD, BA (Hons), Solicitor, Senior Lecturer and Programme Leader, Faculty of the Built Environment, UWE. Her interests are in housing and related socio-legal topics, social inclusion and community participation.

Jan Chianese MSc, TDCR, Programme Leader Radiotherapy, Faculty of Health and Social Care, UWE. Jan's interests are in oncology, radiotherapy practice, adult education and student support.

Sue Davis MSc, PGCEA, RGN, RM, Lecturer in Midwifery, Faculty of Health and Social Care, UWE. Sue also works as a midwife and midwifery supervisor. Her interests are in public health, interprofessional working and the education of health professionals.

Fiona M. Douglas MSc, DipCOT, DACE, Senior Lecturer and Occupational Therapy Programme Leader, Faculty of Health and Social Care, UWE. Fiona's interests are in student centred learning, exploring and disseminating the concept of health and well-being through occupation, and multicultural concepts of occupation.

Lindsay Dow MB, BS, DM, PGC Med Educ, Consultant Physician in Geriatric Medicine, Royal United Hospital, Bath. Lindsay is interested in education and training, from 1992–2004 she was lead for the Elderly undergraduate programme and Interprofessional Coordinator, University of Bristol Medical School.

Nansi Evans MB, BCh, MRCGP is a General Practitioner in Wales, and has an interest in palliative care.

Stephen Evans MA, PGDipOT, BSc (Hons), SROT, Senior Lecturer in Occupational Therapy, Faculty of Health and Social Care, UWE. Stephen's current interests are in inclusive design in the built environment and the social model of disability.

Robin Fletcher, Senior Lecturer, University of Portsmouth Robin specialises in critical criminology, policing studies, crime prevention and community safety. He is undertaking a PhD in the Governance of the Metropolitan Police, where he was a Detective Superintendent. Robin's interests include theories of abolitionism, communitarianism, domestic violence, private policing and police education.

Matthew Godsell PhD, PGCE, RNT, RNLD, Senior Lecturer, Faculty of Health and Social Care, UWE. Matthew's interests are the health of people with learning disabilities, nursing, social policy and historical perspectives on health and welfare.

Rosemary Greenwood RGN, Cert Ed, MSc has been a practicing midwife for 30 years. Until recently she was Senior Lecturer , UWE. Rosemary is currently employed by North Bristol NHS Trust as a Sure Start Midwife.

Diane Hawes MEd, Grad Dip Phys, Dip TP, MCSP, Head of the School of Allied Health Professions, Faculty of Health and Social Care, UWE. Diane's interests are in curriculum development, interprofessional education and student assessment in practice.

Ken Holmes MSc, TDCR, Lecturer, Directorate of Radiography, Salford University. Ken's interests are in diagnostic radiography and nuclear medicine practice.

Celia Keeping, Lecturer, Faculty of Health and Social Care, UWE. Celia also works part-time as a social worker.

Peter Kennison BA, MA, PhD, Lecturer, School of Health and Social Sciences, Middlesex University. Peter's interests include police accountability, community safety and child protection. His PhD focused on policing diversity as seen through the police complaints system, he has published on child protection and the Internet.

Jane Lindsay MSc, CQSW, AASW, Principal Lecturer, School of Social Work, Kingston University and Treatment Manager for the Integrated Domestic Abuse Programme, London Probation Area.

Billie Oliver MEd, Chartered Fellow of the Chartered Institute of Personnel and Development, Senior Lecturer, Faculty of Health and Social Care, UWE. Billie worked in community and youth work and is Programme Leader for Connexions personal adviser courses. Billie is a member of the Higher Education Academy.

Bob Pitt MEd, Senior Lecturer, Faculty of Health and Social Care, UWE. Bob's background is in community and adult education and community work and he teaches on programmes for Connexions personal advisers and on policy issues. Bob is a member of the Higher Education Academy.

Katherine Pollard MSc, BA, Dip HEM, RM, Research Fellow, Faculty of Health and Social Care, UWE. Her interests are in interprofessional education and practice, and in professional issues in midwifery.

Dianne Rees MA, BEd (Hons), GradDipPhys, MCSP, Associate Head of the School of Allied Health Professions, Faculty of Health and Social Care, UWE. Dianne's interests are in learning, teaching and assessment, interprofessional education and neurophysiotherapy.

Judith Ritchie BA (Hons), PGCE, MCIH, Senior Lecturer and Programme Leader, Faculty of the Built Environment, UWE. Judith's interests are in housing care and support and homelessness.

Derek Sellman MA, BSc (Hons), RGN, RMN, Principal Lecturer, Faculty of Health and Social Care, UWE. Derek's interests are in education for professional practice, health care ethics, and philosophy of nursing.

Bruce Senior, Head of School of Health, Community and Policy Studies, Faculty of Health and Social Care, UWE. Bruce's interests are in public sector organisations and social work education.

Jane Tarr PhD, Principal Lecturer, Faculty of Education, UWE and Scheme Director for Continuing Professional Development. Jane is interested in the educational and social inclusion of more vulnerable children and young people.

Pat Taylor, Senior Lecturer in Community Care, Faculty of Health and Social Care, UWE. Pat's interests include community development and public involvement in public health.

Judith Thomas MEd, CQSW, Principal Lecturer, Faculty of Health and Social Care, UWE and Programme Leader for the BSc (Hons) Social Work.

Judith worked as a social worker before moving into professional education. She has researched and published in the areas of health, social care and legal education.

Mervyn Townley MA, DipN, Dip NEd, RGN, RMN, RN (Child), Consultant Nurse for Child and Adolescent Mental Health Services, Gwent Healthcare NHS Trust. His interests are the transition period from child to adult mental health services and post registration education of CAMHS professionals.

Adrian Vatcher, Senior Lecturer in Social Work, Faculty of Health and Social Care, UWE. Adrian worked as a social worker in the statutory sector. His areas of interest include working with families; care management law and policy; and social work practice in international contexts.

Introduction

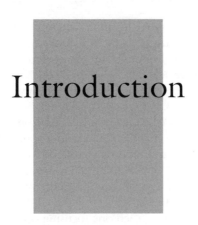

Gillian Barrett, Derek Sellman and Judith Thomas

The nature of health and social care is such that, for many, the quality of the service received is dependent upon how effectively different professionals work together. Developments in knowledge, and innovation in approaches to service delivery, have resulted in a high level of specialisation. This means that it is not possible for any one professional to have sufficient knowledge and skills to respond to the requirements of individuals, groups and communities in situations of complex need (Irvine *et al.* 2002). This being so, professionals have a 'moral obligation' (*ibid*: 208) to work interprofessionally in order to serve the best interests of the service user.

This book sets out to enable those engaged in the health and social care arena to develop an understanding of the nature and policy context of inter-professional working, to consider some of the complexities involved when professionals work collaboratively and to provide examples of interprofes-sional working in practice. The book is therefore relevant to students under-taking professional pre-qualifying programs within health and social care as well as qualified professionals working within this area of service delivery. Health and social care within this context is considered to include a broad range of professionals who work within 'the field of human service provision' (*ibid*: 207) encompassing, for example, those who work in health care, social care, education and the criminal justice service.

The content is arranged in three main parts. Part I comprises two chapters and concerns the need for interprofessional working and the processes involved. In Chapter 1, Pollard, Sellman and Senior identify a range of factors that have prompted the move from a separate, uniprofessional focus on the delivery of professional services to a more integrated interprofessional approach. Historical developments in the structuring and organisation of health and social care services are considered together with political and professional drivers for collaboration. The terminology around joint working is explored and evidence of effectiveness considered. Finally, the rhetoric around service user involvement is considered in relation to the reality of current practice. In Chapter 2, Barrett and Keeping explore some of the knowledge, attitudes and relational skills required to enable different professions to engage collaboratively. A number of difficulties that can arise within the context of interprofessional working are considered, together with a range of actions that can support those involved.

Part II includes 12 chapters, each one focusing on a particular profession. As knowledge regarding the existence and function of professions is a factor influencing interprofessional working, the authors initially outline professional roles and responsibilities before citing examples of interprofessional working through the use of case studies. Chapters cover the education setting, housing, medicine, midwifery, nursing, occupational therapy, physiotherapy, the police, probation, radiography, social work and youth work. Case studies illustrate interprofessional working within both an intraagency context (involving different professionals working within the same organisation/agency) and a multiagency context (involving different professionals working across different organisational or agency boundaries).

In the case studies fictitious names are used, except in Chapter 10 which focuses on Victoria Climbié. First names of people are used throughout for clarity and consistency. This is not meant to imply that interactions between professionals and users of services will be on first name terms. In any relationship good professional practice involves ascertaining how people prefer to be addressed. Professionals may also refer to the people they provide services for in different ways and readers will find a range of terms used in different chapters including, for example, service user, client, patient, young person and offender. The way in which these terms are used reflects the common usage within each profession.

Evers *et al.* (1994) identifies service users as experts in relation to their own needs and requirements and Tarr's chapter on the education setting (Chapter 3) illustrates the importance of involving service users within the collaborative process if a satisfactory outcome is to be achieved. Similarly Taylor and Vatcher in citing a case study around the role of the social worker (Chapter 13) highlight the need for professionals to work collaboratively with individual family members as well as with one another.

There are occasions when, although collaborative working takes place between professionals, contact with the client is channeled through one professional adviser in order to ensure coherence across different agency boundaries. This is the nature of the interprofessional working cited by Oliver and Pitt in their chapter on youth work (Chapter 14).

In Chapter 7 Sellman, Godsell and Townley cite the case of a mature male with moderate learning disabilities who suffers a heart attack in order to illustrate the need for nurses to work collaboratively with other professionals in facilitating the smooth transition of service users between primary and secondary care. Collaboration between primary and secondary care professionals also forms the focus for the case study set out by Dow and Evans in their chapter on the role of doctors (Chapter 5). Dow and Evans make the case for multiprofessional, patient-held, records as a means of facilitating communication between the different professionals involved in the care of a man with acute and chronic health problems and discuss some of the difficulties that this might present.

The theme of smooth transition between services is evident in Davis and Greenwood's chapter on midwifery (Chapter 6). The role of the midwife in supporting a 15-year-old girl through her pregnancy is outlined, together with the need for collaborative working to support Chloe in fulfilling her new role as a mother whilst at the same time maintaining her education.

Chapters 9 and 12 provide examples of interprofessional working within an intraagency context and detail the changing nature of the professional workforce resulting from the development of new career pathways. Hawes and Rees in their chapter on physiotherapy (Chapter 9) identify the need for professionals to work collaboratively in order to provide a consistent approach to supporting the recovery of someone who has suffered a stroke. The context for Chapter 12 is a specialist oncology unit and Chianese and Holmes consider the contribution of radiographers to the interprofessional team who support a woman through the diagnosis and treatment of breast cancer.

Family relationships can sometimes be a source of emotional turmoil resulting in the need to support more than one family member at the same time. One of the case studies in Chapter 7 illustrates this and Sellman, Godsell and Townley identify the contribution of those involved in a child and adolescent mental health team in enabling different professionals to work with different family members in order to avoid the possibility of a conflict of interest.

The probation service is the context for Chapter 11 in which Lindsay illustrates the contribution of interprofessional working to public safety. A case of domestic violence sets the scene to illustrate the contribution of probation and other services in developing an integrated approach to providing support to victims of abuse.

In Chapter 8 Douglas and Evans demonstrate the role of the occupational therapist in facilitating an interprofessional approach, which prevented a breakdown in service delivery to a young man with both physical and learning disabilities. A case conference involving parents, physiotherapist, homecare manager, social worker, day centre manager, health and safety officer, clinical psychologist and occupational therapist provides the means to determine a set of short-term and long-term outcomes that enable Ahmad to remain within the family unit.

The diversity of housing provision and the relationship between housing and health is highlighted in Chapter 4. Carlton and Ritchie use two case studies to illustrate some of the ways in which health, social care and housing professionals can work in partnership for the benefit of individuals with housing needs.

Interprofessional working is fraught with difficulties and the case of Victoria Climbié is used by Kennison and Fletcher in their chapter on the police (Chapter 10) to illustrate how lack of training, blurred roles, poor communication and poor quality supervision contributed to inadequate child protection. Whereas Sellman, Godsell and Townley, in Chapter 7 highlight some of the complexities associated with operationalising interprofessional working at a time when a particular nursing service is in the process of transition.

Part III includes one final chapter (Chapter 15) in which Thomas discusses further some of the issues raised in earlier chapters. In particular, the place of service users within the context of interprofessional working and the tensions associated with translating policy into practice are considered. The case is made for critical reflection as a means to facilitate the development of the transferable teamwork skills required for effective interprofessional working.

Most of the chapters include questions designed to encourage the reader to reflect upon and think critically about identified aspects of interprofessional working. These questions are designed to enable readers to develop a personal action plan to foster the development of relevant knowledge, skills and attitudes to support their involvement in interprofessional working.

References

Evers H., Cameron E. and Badger F. (1994) Inter-professional work with old and disabled people. In Leathard A. (ed.) *Going Inter-professional: Working Together for Health and Welfare*, London: Routledge, pp. 143–57.

Irvine R., Kerridge I., McPhee J. and Freeman S. (2002) Interprofessionalism and ethics: consensus or clash of cultures? *Journal of Interprofessional Care* 16: 199–210.

Understanding Interprofessional Working

1

The Need for
Interprofessional Working

Katherine Pollard, Derek Sellman and Bruce Senior

Introduction

This chapter traces developments in collaborative working and examines some of the reasons why interprofessional work has attracted such emphasis. While recognising that recent governments have stressed a need for interprofessional working and joined-up thinking, it should be recognised that collaboration and teamworking across professions is not new. Nevertheless the current emphasis on interprofessional working represents a significant reorientation of professional working practices.

The growth of the public sector since Victorian times is a history of the separate development of different professional and occupational groups. The birth and development of public sector professions and occupations may be interdependent in some ways but the rise in status of these occupational groups has not always benefited the public (Miller 2004).

Service provision across the public sector was initially organised by separate professions and agencies. In the latter part of the 20th century an increasing awareness emerged regarding the need to link services and integrate methods of service delivery in order best to meet the stated objectives of public policy. From the late 1960s, policy documents reveal an increasing concern with the development of formal partnerships between different agencies as well as between professional groupings.

In this chapter, we will look at some of the factors that have given rise to the current prominence of interprofessional working. We will discuss common terminology and examine some of the related government policies and professional issues. In addition we will consider some aspects of the position of service users in relation to interprofessional working.

Health and social care in the United Kingdom

Before World War II, there was no national consistency in the standards or organisation of health and social care in the United Kingdom (UK) as services were provided by a mixture of charities, local civic bodies and independent professionals who charged for their services. The Labour government of the 1940s passed key legislation for education, and for the provision of social care for children, older people, people with disabilities and homeless people, as well as establishing the National Health Service (NHS). Until the advent of Thatcherism in the 1980s the post-war consensus meant that health and social services were centrally financed, with differing degrees of local autonomy, while control of service delivery rested largely in the hands of the relevant professions (Allsop 1995, Gladstone 1995). This period was characterised by a relatively cohesive organisation of service delivery at a uniprofessional level, with varying and unpredictable degrees of interprofessional working. Each profession developed in its own way, with little shared tradition of interprofessional collaboration. Users were passive recipients of services, although acknowledgement that there should be channels through which they could have a voice was implicit in the establishment of the Community Health Councils in 1974 (Allsop 1995). Local government controlled social care services, so while the local democratic process had some impact on policy this rarely translated into changes in service delivery.

The economic, social and political changes of the Thatcher era resulted in a major re-organisation of all public services. The market emphasis on the consumer reinforced a developing civic awareness among the general public and led to demands for coherence, accountability and transparency from service providers. At the same time, the Conservative government of the day emphasised particularly tight controls over public expenditure. These conditions paved the way for the restructuring of public services in alignment with models for market-driven organisations, with an emphasis on cost-effectiveness and choice for the consumer. A major development of this era was the creation of the internal market, which resulted in some agencies and professions being assigned to a purchaser role, while others were designated as providers. So, for example, purchaser general practitioners (GPs) were permitted to buy acute services for their patients from provider NHS Trusts that ran the local hospital(s). Initiatives such as GP fundholding shifted financial control to local levels, with NHS Trusts operating as independent companies responsible for their own finances, free to sub-contract services and determine issues such as employment conditions for their staff independently. Similarly, some social services departments set up internal markets while others moved, willingly or not, into purchasing some of their care provision from other agencies (Allsop 1995, Gladstone 1995).

One important consequence of these changes has been the shift of control of service delivery away from health and social care professionals (who had not previously been required to take account of the wider financial implications of service provision) to management bodies and managers. Management's main responsibility became to provide cost-effective services in line with government policy objectives. Another consequence of these changes has been the increased fragmentation in the organisation of service delivery (Allsop 1995, Payne 2000). The negative consequences which can result from a system which has neither cohesive structures for service delivery nor effective interprofessional collaboration have been well-documented; see, for example, Dalley (1993) and the Audit Commission (2000). Increasingly, the solution to these problems has focused on the need for integration of services, an essential feature of which is collaborative working. Interprofessional working has also been thought to be cost-effective in streamlining delivery systems and avoiding duplication (Paul and Peterson 2001). A counter argument suggests that financial constraints can militate against the implementation and maintenance of interprofessional collaboration (Freeth 2001).

The introduction of the private sector to provide services that have histori-cally been the responsibility of the public sector (statutory and voluntary) has further transformed the public services landscape. For example, the private finance initiative (PFI), introduced in the early 1990s, has now become em-bedded in communities across the UK. Through the PFI, a system has been implemented whereby the private sector has become jointly responsible with the public sector for the management and delivery of services in health care, education and the prison system, as well as owning buildings and equipment central to service delivery (Allen 2001). This initiative has removed control even further away from the hands of professionals.

Running in parallel with these managerial and economic changes was the growing recognition that service users have rights to information and to involvement in the planning and prioritisation of services. In 1991, the gov-ernment established the Citizen's Charter Unit to document and disseminate the rights of consumers (that is, the public) as they relate to various fields of public sector activity, and 33 Citizen's Charters had been published by 1993. One of these was the Patient's Charter (DoH 1992), which set standards for providers to meet for certain aspects of health care delivery. This charter ostensibly gives the public control and choice about the care they receive, although the extent to which these factors translate into reality in practice is questionable (Allsop 1995, Øvretveit 1997).

Whatever the gaps between rhetoric and reality, and whatever the differences between political parties and governments, the legacy of the changes in health and social care in the UK over the last two decades is an emphasis on cost-effective integrated services that meet the needs of, and actively involve, service users.

What is interprofessional working?

Interprofessional working requires that personnel from different pro-fessions and agencies work together. There has been extended debate about terminology in this field. Readers will find, among others, the terms multiprofessional, interprofessional, multidisciplinary, interdisciplinary, multiagency and interagency being used to describe what appear to be very similar activities. A broad rule of thumb is that the prefix *multi* tends to indicate the involvement of personnel from different professions, disciplines or agencies, but does not necessarily imply collaboration. The prefix *inter* tends to imply collaboration, particularly in areas such as decision making (Øvretveit 1997, Payne 2000). One way of conceptualising interprofessional work is in terms of the effectiveness of coordination and communication. Social workers, for example, have traditionally emphasised the importance of coordination of services where more than one agency or worker is involved. This occurs in areas such as key aspects of mental health work, community care, and in child protection.

Team is another term which is often used when describing working groups; however, what is meant (and understood) by this word can vary enormously. Teams may be tightly-knit units, composed of individuals who regularly work together; or they may be loosely-woven entities which emerge in an *ad hoc* manner to meet specific demands. A team may just be a convenient way of describing a group of staff with a common manager, but with little else that brings them together. Teams may be formally constituted, with a specified structure and objective, or they may arise organically with no formal recognition. They may be consensual, democratic or hierarchical in nature, or all of these by turn, depending on circumstances. The members of a team may collaborate with one another in practice, or they may act alone on behalf of the team. Teams may draw their members from a single professional group, or from several. These are only some of the variations that can be found, in many different permutations, in team structure and process (Øvretveit 1997, Payne 2000).

In this book, we take interprofessional working to mean collaborative practice: that is, the process whereby members of different professions and/or agencies work together to provide integrated health and/or social care for the benefit of service users. This definition is consistent with that of Wood and Gray who write 'Collaboration occurs when a group of autonomous stakeholders of a problem domain engage in an interactive process, using shared rules, norms, and structures, to act or decide on issues relating to that domain' (1991: 146). The structure and logistics of the systems through which professionals organise their collaborative efforts vary considerably, in part influenced by the history of each profession or service, but are often crucially dictated by government policy and directive. Collaborative practice might take place through a single team of mixed professionals or through different organisations cooperating in planning and providing services. In recent times, the Labour government has invested in new organisational forms that advance collaborative practice to better meet key aspects of their modernisation agenda. Initiatives that aim for social inclusion and/or health improvement include, for example, Sure Start, the Connexions Service, Primary Care Trusts and Local Strategic Partnerships.

Political drivers for interprofessional working

Reference to interprofessional working can be found in the USA in the medical and nursing literature of the 1960s, so the idea of collaborative practice is not new. For example:

> One hospital is reported to have weekly interprofessional ward conferences attended by all members of the clinical team.
>
> (Henderson 1966: 8)

In the UK, reference to interprofessional issues began to appear in the health and social care literature approximately a decade later; see, for example, Black (1977) and Dingwall (1977). The emergence of these ideas did not mean, however, that collaborative practice was necessarily a reality at this time.

Since the late 1970s, health and social care policy in most European countries has been based on meeting the World Health Organisation (WHO) targets for improving health, contained in the Health for All Declaration of Alma-Ata (WHO 1978). During this period the European Union has placed an emphasis on a right of parity for the health and social care of all citizens of member states, thus locating responsibility for the organisation of care with policy makers, answerable to the general public through the democratic process (Thompson and Mathias 1997). In the UK, this has highlighted the tensions between professional autonomy in service delivery on the one hand and the edicts of central governmental control of professional working on the other, illustrated by the introduction of key directives including, for example, the DoH's requirement that health and social care professionals provide evidence based practice.

A chronological examination of UK policies of the last 15 years reveals increasing support for the premise that collaborative practice will improve the quality of service delivery. In 1989, the Conservative government set out principles of collaboration that health and social services authorities were required to follow in order to assume joint financial responsibility for the provision of community care (DoH 1989). A key feature in this document was the idea of effective joint working.

In later documents, there is reference to the concept of a seamless service (DoH 1996a, DoH 1996b) providing care across organisational boundaries. The need for teamworking between different professions was emphasised, as was the promotion of partnerships across the interfaces of primary care in the community, secondary care in specialised institutions, health authorities and social services (NHSE 1996). Similarly, in the field of mental health, the DoH stipulated that health authorities and other appropriate agencies should collaborate in the provision of comprehensive care to target service users (DoH 1998a).

The advent of new Labour saw an emphasis on the need for joined-up thinking across the public sector. In 1998 the government set out its plan to establish Health Action Zones (DoH 1998b) in which all professionals involved in contributing to the health (in the broadest sense) of the local population should come together to plan and deliver services. In the same year, local government and social services White Papers were published, promoting partnership as a key concept in planning and delivering services (DETR 1998, DoH 1998c).

Some policy documents targeted specific professions. Making a Difference (DoH 1999) stated explicitly that nurses, midwives and health visitors were expected to engage in interprofessional practices. This stance was reinforced in a document published in 2000, in which arrangements for workforce planning were criticised for not being:

> Holistic in their approach, looking across primary, secondary and tertiary care or across staff groups.
>
> (DoH 2000: 19)

Currently, the idea of working across traditional boundaries remains central to the policies in a report addressing health inequalities in society (DoH 2003). It is interesting to note that the policy documents have remained similar in both substance and language on the issue of collaborative practice over the period reviewed, despite the transition from a Conservative to a Labour government in 1997, a change which might have been expected to bring alterations in policy direction.

There are a range of explanations for this long-term consensus but the reality of complex long-term social problems has brought universal acknowledgement that agencies and professions need to cooperate if service delivery is not to be fragmented.

> Organisational and professional partiality and territoriality, with their inherent tendencies towards restrictive practices, alongside organisational, philosophical and cultural differences, have long been a detriment to the service user and have contributed to policy failure.
>
> (Miller 2004: 132)

The growth of managerialism is also inextricably linked to the interprofessional agenda. Thatcherism promoted the cult of the manager in part as a way of bringing private sector practices into the public sector. It held the promise of tackling waste and improving performance. Increasing the power of managers was seen as a way of tackling the inefficiencies of professional workers and trade unions and would help put the consumer at the centre of service provision.

Professional drivers for interprofessional working

A central aspect of interprofessional working concerns the relative power of different professional groups. Until fairly late in the 20th century, some (predominantly male) occupational groups were identified as professions. Professions were thought to include those pursuing a particular occupation by completion of a recognised course of education, typically at least to graduate level. Furthermore, they operated autonomously in their sphere of practice, were self-regulating and free from bureaucratic or managerial control (Bilton *et al.* 1996). By contrast, other (predominantly female) occupational groups were considered to be semi-professions, with training rather than education, regulation by members of other occupational groups and with working practices overseen by other professionals or by managers and bureaucrats. In the health and social care arena, only medical practitioners were seen to belong to a profession; members of other occupational groups, for example, allied health professionals, nurses, social workers, and midwives were all considered to belong to semi-professions. The medical profession was accordingly the dominant professional group in health and social care for most of the last one hundred years (Witz 1992).

It has been argued that among the principles of effective interprofessional collaboration are power sharing and non-hierarchical structures (Henneman *et al.* 1995). Some authors have suggested the drive toward collaborative practice has provided members of the semi-professions with an opportunity to raise the status of their own occupational group, and to increase their share of occupational power (Kesby 2002). If interprofessional working is seen as a method of redistributing power, it seems the medical profession has most to lose. Interprofessional relationships are often complex, and allow investigation from a variety of perspectives: for example, the feminist tradition insists that gender relations are key to understanding interaction between professions and semi-professions (Witz 1992). Some of the problems of implementing interprofessional working among professionals whose priorities for advancing their own profession are not necessarily complementary will be discussed in the next chapter.

The effect of interprofessional working on service delivery

There is a general consensus among health and social care professionals that integrated care, with its emphasis on effective collaborative practice, can improve services for users. There is evidence that a failure of collaboration can have tragic consequences (DoH 1994a, Kennedy 2001, Laming 2003) and the breakdown in communication between professionals is a common theme of child protection inquiries. The lack of collaborative practice between agencies and professionals is seen as being responsible for individual tragedies as well as for the failure to tackle general social problems such as social exclusion, homelessness, and crime and disorder.

Despite the widespread assumption that successful interprofessional working will prevent such tragedies and poor practice, the evidence is still to be amassed. There is little research investigating the effectiveness of collaborative practice in terms of outcomes for service users. However, where such research has been undertaken, it offers some reason for optimism, as illustrated by the three examples below.

Bultema *et al.* (1996) report on the implementation of an interprofessional clinical pathway in a psychiatry unit in the USA specialising in the care of older people. This initiative produced a significant decrease in the average length of stay in the unit. Dawson and Bartlett (1996) discussed the process of improving discharge planning in an interprofessional team operating in a UK regional neurological rehabilitation unit. They found that enhanced clarity of role responsibility and prevention of duplication of information resulted in an improvement in both the amount and quality of discharge reports. As a consequence there was more appropriate and timely provision of aftercare in the community. Akhavain *et al.* (1999) describe how two psychiatric teams collaborated in inpatient and outpatient settings in the USA. Improved communication and co-ordination of care enabled more resources to be devoted to increasing and enhancing therapeutic facilities for the service users.

It is worth noting that these three initiatives occurred in dedicated health care settings, involving closely-knit teams of professionals who routinely worked alongside each other. The process of evaluating the outcomes of collaborative practice is more difficult in areas of service provision that require coordination between personnel from different organisations and agencies, who interact infrequently. The concept of interprofessional working is imprecise, and different interpretations have led many researchers to concentrate on issues more easily accessible to evaluation.

The lack of research in this area, in contrast to the plethora of general literature concerning interprofessional issues, underlines how difficult it is to prove that collaborative practice improves service delivery. The nature of research requires that all variables affecting a process under investigation are considered. There are many variables in the delivery of public services and the way in which they interact is complex. Relevant contributing factors include: the amount and quality of social support, the composition of the interprofessional group, the way in which members of the group work together, the physical environment, and the nature of interventions. For this reason isolation of effective interprofessional working as a definitive factor affecting the outcomes of service delivery is challenging at best. However, there remains a logic in concluding that collaborative practice does generally improve the provision of services. Evidence to support this claim is beginning to appear and suggests that service users and professionals are often more satisfied where there is effective and relevant interprofessional collaboration (Akhavain *et al.* 1999, Gerrish 1999).

Whether interprofessional working is always required remains a matter of debate. Despite the current rhetoric, it would be naive to consider interprofessional working as a panacea. It is possible that collaborative practice might encourage an abdication of personal responsibility. There are occasions when a specific professional perspective is appropriate for providing optimum service delivery. Where interprofessional processes and considerations are prioritised these occasions may pass unrecognised, with the potential for detrimental effects on individual service users. Over time, this could result in a dilution of professional knowledge and skills. However, these potential negatives might result from poor interprofessional practice rather than be an unforeseen consequence of good practice. In both health care and social care one commonly expressed fear is of interprofessional working producing the less well paid generic worker, lacking essential specialist skills (Gerrish 1999). Of course, these fears may be the result of professionals trying to protect their own professional status as well as reflecting genuine concerns about a deskilled workforce.

Overall we conclude that collaborative practice appears to hold out the promise of a positive impact on service delivery; however, the manner of implementation remains a crucial issue.

Service user involvement in interprofessional working

The current social and political climate demands that service users are involved in the planning and prioritisation of service delivery. Government rhetoric promotes the principles of choice and control for users within a seamless service. Increasingly, the concept of interprofessional working is understood to include all stakeholders, whether lay or professional, particularly in the fields of mental health and social care. The Social Care Institute of Excellence (www.scie.org.uk) explicitly draws service users into the social care knowledge base and the service user perspective is being emphasised in all courses leading to qualification for health and social care practice. Other policy documents that explicitly promote this idea include Working in Partnership (DoH 1994b) which focuses on improving care for service users with mental health problems, and Our Healthier Nation (DoH 1998b) in which it is proposed that:

> Health Action Zones will bring together a partnership of health organisations, including primary care, with Local Authorities, community groups, the voluntary sector and local businesses.
>
> (DoH 1998b: 43)

However, the structures through which partnerships are to be established are often not clear at the local level. Initiatives such as Citizen's Charters, while making services more responsive to users, have not provided service users with the involvement in planning or prioritising service delivery many were led to expect (Stewart 1995). In reality, extending collaborative practice to include service users has produced little change, although there are some areas where it has been successfully implemented. Davis (2002), for example, outlined how maternity care provision in North Birmingham is being influenced by service user representation.

Exceptions notwithstanding, it appears service users remain junior members in these partnerships. In many areas service providers' obligations have been interpreted only as requirement to provide channels through which users can comment on the services provided, with no obligation for providers to respond substantively to users' comments (Blakemore 2003). It appears that the integration of health and social care services with the full participation of service users remains an unrealised vision.

Conclusion

Changes in the UK health and welfare context in the final two decades of the 20th century, most notably the establishment of the internal market, resulted in the fragmentation of the delivery of health and social care services, with detrimental effects for some service users. A perceived solution to this problem was the development of integrated services, which requires members of different professions and agencies to work together for the benefit of service users. This emphasis on collaborative practice was further driven by the need for services to be cost-effective, as it was assumed that, by preventing duplication of provision, integrated care would require fewer resources.

Successive governments have positioned collaborative practice as a cornerstone of effective integrated service delivery. Professional responses to this development have varied, influenced by issues of power and differing professional agendas. Increasingly, it is assumed that collaborative practice must involve not only professionals but also service users, so that the latter are actively involved in the planning and prioritisation of services. However, in most areas, participation by service users remains limited.

References

Akhavain P., Amaral D., Murphy M., Uehlinger K. and Cardone M. (1999) Collaborative practice: a nursing perspective of the psychiatric interdisciplinary treatment team. *Holistic Nursing Practice* **13**(2): 1–11.

Allen G. (2001) *The Private Finance Initiative (PFI). Research Paper 01/117.* London: House of Commons Library.

Allsop J. (1995) Health: from seamless service to patchwork quilt. In Gladstone D. (ed.) *British Social Welfare: Past, Present and Future.* London: UCL Press, pp. 98–123.

Audit Commission (2000) *The Way to go Home: Rehabilitation and Remedial Services for Older People.* London: The Stationery Office.

Bilton T., Bennett K., Jones P., Skinner D., Stanworth M. and Webster A. (1996) *Introduction to Sociology* (3rd edn). Basingstoke: Macmillan Press Ltd.

Black P. (1977) The child at risk – interprofessional co-operation. *Nursing Mirror and Midwives Journal* **144**(15): 61–4.

Blakemore K. (2003) *Social Policy: An Introduction.* Buckingham: Open University Press.

Bultema J., Mailliard L., Getzfrid M., Lerner R. and Colone M. (1996) Geriatric patients with depression: improving outcomes using a multidisciplinary clinical pathway model. *Journal of Nursing Administration* **26**: 31–6.

Dalley G. (1993) Professional ideology or organisational tribalism? The health service-social work divide. In Walmsley J., Reynolds J., Shakespeare P. and Woolfe R. (eds) *Health, Welfare and Practice. Reflections on Roles and Relationships.* Buckingham: Open University Press, pp. 32–9.

Davis J. (2002) *Finding funding and support.* Antenatal Education – but not as you know it! Paper presented at the 1st Annual Preparing for Parenthood Conference, Birmingham Women's Health Care NHS Trust and The National Childbirth Trust, Birmingham.

Dawson J. and Bartlett E. (1996) Change within interdisciplinary teamwork: one unit's experience. *British Journal of Therapy and Rehabilitation* **3**: 219–22.

DETR (Department of the Environment, Transport and the Regions) (1998) *Modernising Local Government: In Touch with the People.* London: The Stationery Office.

Dingwall R. (1977) *The Social Organisation of Health Visiting Training.* London: Croom Helm.

DoH (Department of Health) (1989) *Caring for People: Community Care in the Next Decade and Beyond.* London: HMSO.

DoH (1992) *The Patient's Charter.* London: Department of Health.

DoH (1994a) *The Report of the Inquiry into the Care and Treatment of Christopher Clunis.* London: HMSO.

DoH (1994b) *Working in Partnership: A Collaborative Approach to Care. Report of the Mental Health Nursing Review Team.* London: HMSO.

DoH (1996a) *The National Health Service: A Service with Ambitions.* London: The Stationery Office.

DoH (1996b) *Primary Care: Delivering the Future.* London: The Stationery Office.

DoH (1998a) *Modernising Mental Health Services: Safe, Sound and Supportive.* London: Department of Health.

DoH (1998b) *Our Healthier Nation – A Contract for Health. A Consultation Paper.* London: The Stationery Office.

DoH (1998c) *Modernising Social Services: Promoting Independence, Improving Protection, Raising Standards.* London: The Stationery Office.

DoH (1999) *Making a Difference: Strengthening the Nursing, Midwifery and Health Visiting Contribution to Health and Healthcare.* London: Department of Health.

DoH (2000) *A Health Service of All the Talents: Developing the NHS Workforce. Consultation Document on the Review of Workforce Planning.* London: Department of Health.

DoH (2003) *Tackling Health Inequalities: A Programme for Action.* London: Department of Health.

Freeth D. (2001) Sustaining interprofessional collaboration. *Journal of Interprofessional Care* **15**: 37–46.

Gerrish K. (1999) Teamwork in primary care: an evaluation of the contribution of integrated nursing teams. *Health and Social Care in the Community* **7**: 367–75.

Gladstone D. (1995) Individual welfare: locating care in the mixed economy. Introducing the personal social services. In Gladstone D. (ed.) *British Social Welfare: Past, Present and Future.* London: UCL Press, pp. 161–70.

Henderson V. (1966) *The Nature of Nursing a Definition and its Implications for Practice, Research, and Education.* New York: Macmillan.

Henneman E.A., Lee J.L. and Cohen J.I. (1995) A concept analysis of collaboration. *Journal of Advanced Nursing* **21**: 103–9.

Kennedy I. (2001) *Learning from Bristol: The Report of the Public Inquiry into Children's Heart Surgery at the Bristol Royal Infirmary 1984–1995.* London: The Stationery Office.

Kesby S. (2002) Nursing care and collaborative practice. *Journal of Clinical Nursing* **11**: 357–66.

Laming, Lord (2003) *Inquiry into the Death of Victoria Climbié.* London: The Stationery Office.

Miller C. (2004) *Producing Welfare: A Modern Agenda.* Basingstoke: Palgrave.

NHS Executive (1996) *Primary Care: The Future.* London: NHS Management Executive.

Øvretveit J. (1997) How to describe interprofessional working. In Øvretveit J., Mathias P. and Thompson T. (eds) *Interprofessional Working for Health and Social Care.* Basingstoke: Macmillan, pp. 9–33.

Paul S. and Peterson Q. (2001) Interprofessional collaboration: issues for practice and research. *Occupational Therapy in Health Care* **15**(3/4): 1–12.

Payne M. (2000) *Teamwork in Multiprofessional Care.* Basingstoke: Macmillan Press.

Stewart J. (1995) Accountability and empowerment in welfare services. In Gladstone D. (ed.) *British Social Welfare: Past, Present and Future.* London: UCL Press, pp. 289–302.

Thompson T. and Mathias P. (1997) The World Health Organisation and European Union: occupational, vocational and health initiatives and their implications for cooperation amongst the professions. In Øvretveit J., Mathias P. and Thompson T. (eds) *Interprofessional Working for Health and Social Care.* Basingstoke: Macmillan, pp. 201–25.

WHO (1978) *Primary health care. Report of the International Conference on Primary Health Care, Alma-Ata, USSR, 6–12 September 1978. (Health for All Series No. 1).* Geneva: WHO.

Wood D.J. and Gray B. (1991) Towards a comprehensive theory of collaboration. *Journal of Applied Behavioral Science* **27**: 139–62.

Witz A. (1992) *Professions and Patriarchy.* London: Routledge.

The Processes Required for Effective Interprofessional Working

Gillian Barrett and Celia Keeping

Interprofessional working involves complex interactions between two or more members of different professional disciplines. It is a collaborative venture (McCray 2002) in which those involved share the common purpose of developing mutually negotiated goals achieved through agreed plans and monitored and evaluated according to agreed procedures. This requires pooling of knowledge and expertise (Cook *et al.* 2001) to facilitate joint decision making based upon shared professional viewpoints (Russell and Hymans 1999, Stapleton 1998).

Although the current health and social care policy agenda is advocating interprofessional and interagency working, policy directives alone appear insufficient to ensure the desired outcome. Each individual requires a set of knowledge, skills and attitudes to enable them to engage in collaborative working relationships, as well as support from relevant personnel within their employing organisation. This chapter explores some of the factors that are likely to enable and encourage different professions to work collaboratively, in addition to considering some of the difficulties that might inhibit interprofessional working. Some suggestions to support professionals in their interprofessional endeavours are then outlined.

Knowledge of professional roles

In order to provide a comprehensive approach to care a thorough holistic assessment of client needs is required. This necessitates a vision extending beyond the remit of a single profession or agency (Hornby and Atkins 2000) and a perception that encompasses the scope of all professionals who might contribute to meeting the needs of particular service users. Both Hornby and Atkins (2000) and Irvine *et al.* (2002) highlight ignorance of both the existence and function of other professions and agencies as a common factor limiting interprofessional collaboration. Therefore, even when a comprehensive assessment is undertaken, unless individual practitioners are well-informed regarding the role, performance (Bliss *et al.* 2000) and professional boundaries of other professions, they may fail to engage with those who could make a valuable contribution to the interprofessional team.

An expectation that individual practitioners be well-informed regarding professional roles and boundaries presupposes that these aspects of professional work are clearly defined, whereas in reality, this may not always the case. Bliss *et al.* (2000), for example, found that district nurses working in palliative care were unable to agree on the parameters of their own role and Booth and Hewison (2002) report role overlap between occupational therapy and physiotherapy in the context of an inpatient stroke rehabilitation unit. Further, advances in professional practice and new developments in health and social care provision mean that traditional roles are being transformed and new or extended roles are being developed, many of which involve cross-professional and cross-agency working (Masterson 2002). It may take some time for those involved in such developments to define their new roles and delineate their boundaries. Lack of clarity and confusion regarding the perimeters of professional roles may be a factor in limiting the utilisation of relevant professionals within interprofessional initiatives (Bliss *et al.* 2000).

Willing participation

Willing participation (Henneman *et al.* 1995) and a high level of motivation (Molyneux 2001) have been cited as central to effective interprofessional collaboration. Participation in collaborative initiatives is influenced by the beliefs held by those involved (Loxley 1997). For example, an individual's commitment to interprofessional working is likely to be linked to a viewpoint that values the ideologies of user-centred services and holistic care (Freeth 2001) and a recognition that 'no one discipline can help people reach their full potential and optimal level of well-being' (Russell and Hymans 1999: 255).

Motivation is associated with a sense of achievement (Franken 1994), therefore, the expectations of those involved in interprofessional initiatives should be realistic. Irvine *et al.* claim that 'unrealistically high expectations ... often leads to judgements of failure' (2002: 207) within an interprofessional context. Although successful interprofessional experiences are likely to increase an individual's willingness to participate (Loxley 1997), a number of difficulties and failures have been documented (Kennedy 2001, Laming 2003). An unsatisfactory experience of interprofessional working and uneven distribution of benefit from the endeavour may adversely affect motivation to sustain collaborative efforts (Freeth 2001).

Confidence

Confidence and competence are crucial to interprofessional working. Molyneux (2001) found that professionals who were confident in their own role were able to work flexibly across professional boundaries without feeling jealous or threatened. Laidler (1991) uses the term *professional adulthood* to describe those who feel sufficiently confident to share knowledge and relinquish exclusive claims to professional territory in order to engage in cross-boundary working; a feature of interprofessional working.

Confidence is closely linked with the concept of individual and professional identity (Loxley 1997). Individual identity comes from a basic physical, emotional, and relational blueprint laid down in early life and is influenced by the groups or roles associated with as an individual matures. Identity is closely linked to self-image and consequently self-esteem (Hornby and Atkins 2000). People gain a strong sense of identity from their work roles, becoming psychologically attached to a particular professional group through the process of professional identity and dependent on its continued stable existence for their own sense of inner well-being.

Professional identity is shaped during pre-qualifying education through a process of socialisation and develops throughout one's career from interaction with, and feedback from, mentors and others (Hudson 2002). A positive professional identity is linked with professional competence and a clear understanding of role and role security (Hornby and Atkins 2000). Role overlap and the blurring of professional boundaries, which may arise through interprofessional working, can result in feelings of anxiety and role insecurity (Booth and Hewison 2002). This in turn can diminish professional confidence (Loxley 1997).

When considering the relationship between competence and collaboration, Stapleton claims that 'collaborative practice is probably not the best model for the inexperienced or less skilled clinically' (1998: 15). The complexities of health and social care, however, are such that service users' needs are unlikely to be met by professionals working in isolation. Consequently mechanisms are required to enable inexperienced professionals and student practitioners to learn how to work within an interprofessional context. Education providers therefore have a responsibility to deliver a professional curriculum that enables practitioners to become competent within their own professional role and sufficiently confident to work interprofessionally.

A combination of personal and professional confidence enables individuals to assert their own perspective and challenge the viewpoints of others (Stapleton 1998). Even if an individual has a positive professional identity, negative or weak individual identity arising from social divisions associated with, for example, class, gender or ethnicity may adversely affect their confidence and thus their ability to be assertive in an interprofessional context. In addition, self-worth is linked with perceptions of power and, although interprofessional collaborative relationships should be non-hierarchal (Stapleton 1998, Henneman *et al.* 1995), low self-worth may alter the power relationships within the group and result in some individuals feeling oppressed.

Open and honest communication

Joint decision making based upon shared professional perspectives requires those involved to engage in open and honest communication (Stapleton 1998). Communication competence contributes to effective interprofessional working and enables those involved to articulate their own perspectives, listen to the views of others and negotiate outcomes. Open and honest communication is, however, dependent upon internal feelings associated with an individual's level of confidence. It requires an *I'm OK – You're OK* (Thomas and Harris 1969) stance whereby individuals relate to one another as adults where honesty is combined with respect and a concern to maintain the dignity of all involved.

Active listening is an important means of facilitating participation. It requires that individuals not only listen attentively to the messages conveyed by others, but also, demonstrate this through the use of verbal and nonverbal feedback (Dickson *et al.* 1989). This involves setting aside stereotypes, preconceived notions and judgements in order to hear what the speaker is saying (Hornby and Atkins 2000). It requires the listener to 'focus on the speaker' (Payne 2000: 160), to maintain eye contact and to recognise silence as valuable time for the speaker to engage in reflection and thought clarification (*ibid*). Paraphrasing and summarising can be used to demonstrate understanding and open questions can be used to express interest and encourage further exploration of relevant issues.

Payne identifies the need for criticism, combining specific detail, constructive suggestions and encouragement. He points out that critical feedback should take place at a time when the recipient 'can be receptive' (2000: 159) and identifies this as being close to the time of the particular situation but 'not in the heat of the moment' (*ibid*).

Trust and mutual respect

Trust, is an 'essential attribute of collaboration' (Stapleton 1998: 12), and depends upon each participant being able to rely upon the 'support, honesty and integrity' (*ibid*) of one another. Cook *et al.* (2001) found that professionals highlighted trust as an important factor in facilitating open discussion and successful role negotiation, both important features of interprofessional working.

Where trust is lacking, participants may react defensively in an attempt to reduce uncomfortable feelings associated with insecurity (Hornby and Atkins 2000). When an individual encounters difficult emotions or a threatening situation they construct defences against their negative feelings. Some defences are healthy if the individual or group is to operate effectively and fulfil tasks on a day-to-day basis, but some defensive behaviours can have a negative impact. For example, within the context of interprofessional working, defensive behaviour might involve devoting time and energy to the justification of limitations, mistakes or failures rather than enabling learning from experience and the generation of alternative solutions.

Trust develops through repeated positive interprofessional experiences and develops gradually over a period of time (Stapleton 1998). It is therefore helpful for professionals engaged in collaborative working to give one another time for trust to develop and to devote time and energy in demonstrating support for one another.

An atmosphere of mutual support is required to enable individuals to feel sufficiently confident and safe to express their opinions without fear of ridicule or reprisal (Stapleton 1998). This is likely to be engendered when each participant feels valued and when relationships are built on mutual respect. Active listening, together with the explicit acknowledgement of each profession's unique contribution and distinct body of knowledge conveys an acceptance of different perspectives. Recognition that different perspectives can lead to innovation and creativity (Stapleton 1998) is likely to be influential in enabling participants to value and respect one another.

Power

Shared power based upon non-hierarchical relationships has been identified as central to effective interprofessional collaboration (Stapleton 1998, Henneman *et al.* 1995). Although this would appear to be a logical distribution of power, Boulding (1990) claims that the larger the number of persons involved in a joint enterprise the more difficult it becomes to maintain equality in terms of power relations and consequently hierarchies develop.

The ideal of shared power could result in everyone assuming that someone other than themselves is responsible for following through agreed decisions. This could result in omissions to the detriment of the service user. For example, Allen *et al.* (2002), reported a delay in home adaptations and failure to liaise effectively with other service providers when multiprofessional teams had no obvious lead professional. To avoid such problems the collaborative team could utilise interprofessional action plans, documenting specific areas of responsibility, review dates and procedures.

Struggles for power are rooted in professional tradition and social difference. Payne identifies power as 'people's capacity to ... get what they want' (2000: 141) exerted through coercion or legitimised through the authority of the profession or organisation. Traditional hierarchies tend to locate power with the medical profession, particularly within a health care environment. If power is to be shared or distributed on a basis of the knowledge and expertise of all professionals involved in particular interprofessional initiatives, medical practitioners will need to relinquish traditionally held dominance. This may not be easy, for example, Cook *et al.* (2001), found general practitioners felt threatened by a redistribution of power and had problems letting go of their traditionally held power base.

This could be compounded by perceptions of a number of the occupational groups in health and social care being regarded as semi-professions on a basis of lacking a unique scientific knowledge base (Bassett 1995, Green 1991

Hugman 1991, Roberts 1994). If some professions see themselves as less powerful than others this could weaken their legitimacy in terms of claiming an equal share of power or in asserting their authority when their professional competence is paramount in meeting the needs of service users.

Professions have fought to strengthen their power through restricted entry, sanctioned through controls associated with qualification and registration. Friedson (1970) identifies autonomy as a defining characteristic of a profession and the concept of clinical freedom has been used to enable some to hold onto power (Loxley 1997). Claims to professional status based upon superior knowledge, autonomy and self-management (Davies 1996) can result in a reluctance to share power based upon a view that only members of the same profession are in a position to influence decision making, actions and outcomes.

Unequal power distribution can be oppressive (Payne 2000) and can limit participation for some group members. As honest and open communication and the sharing of professional perspectives are key attributes of interprofessional working, power differentials must be acknowledged, recognised and resolved. A mechanism for recognising the location of power has been identified by Loxley (1997) who poses the set of questions identified in Table 2.1 to which we have supplied examples.

Table 2.1 Questions to facilitate the location of power within the context of collaborative working

Question	Example
Who defines the problem?	Does everyone make a contribution to problem identification or is this the province of one professional group?
Whose terms are used?	Is everyone involved able to communicate through the use of mutually agreed and commonly understood terms or does one particular professional language predominate?
Who controls the domain or territory?	Is control always mutually negotiated, does it vary in accordance with which professional's knowledge and expertise best fits the particular needs of the service user at a given point in time, or does control sit predominantly with one professional group?
Who decides upon what resources are needed and how they are allocated?	Are resource issues mutually agreed, determined in accordance with varying professional contributions or dictated by one professional group?
Who holds whom accountable?	Is it assumed that one professional group will have overall accountability or is everyone's accountability recognised?
Who prescribes the activity of others?	Is there joint agreement regarding the activities of those involved or does one professional group prescribe activities?
Who can influence policy makers?	Does one professional group have a stronger influence than others in lobbying policy makers?

=========================== **ACTIVITY** ===========================

Think of an interprofessional initiative with which you have been involved. Using the questions identified by Loxley reflect upon the location of power within your chosen initiative.

Conflict

Loxley refers to conflict as being 'interwoven with interprofessional collaboration' (1997: 1) and attributes this to a combination of social and professional difference. Social difference can relate to age, gender, ethnicity, family situation, pay and status differentials. Professional difference can relate to values, priorities, approaches to care and expectations in terms of authority, leadership and what constitutes a successful outcome (Irvine *et al.* 2002). Additional sources of conflict relate to competition for resources (Loxley 1997), invasion of roles and unequal contribution from those involved (Payne 2000). Although conflict is often viewed negatively, it can give rise to positive outcomes. Channeled appropriately it can act as a stimulus for change through the exploration of difference and innovative decision making (Drinka and Clark 2000).

Conflict evokes an emotional response, which is expressed through a range of verbal and nonverbal behaviours, for example, blaming or excluding others, silence, glaring, or slouched positioning (Drinka and Clark 2000). Such responses can be unproductive and Payne recommends those involved should 'avoid reacting emotionally and ... try explicitly to react rationally' (2000: 151). Emotional responses, however, may be unconscious and are not easily subject to an individual's control. Eisenhardt *et al.* (1997) suggest a response that focuses on the issues rather than personalities and recommend negotiated decision making based upon the identification of a range of options.

Dealing with conflict and power differentials is demanding and the process of trying to reach shared decisions is likely to involve a degree of discomfort. In order to protect themselves from such discomfort those involved might collude in what Loxley refers to as a 'myth of togetherness' (1997: 43) where participants see the core elements of interprofessional working as congenial relationships thus avoiding the need to address factors relating to conflict such as differing perspectives and priorities. An emphasis on congenial relationships may result in the abuse of power with stronger members using prescriptive power and coercion to control weaker members thus dominating the decision making process.

Because dealing with conflict can be difficult, avoidance techniques are sometimes used as a protection mechanism. This does not, however, resolve the underlying issues and can result in dysfunctional interprofessional relationships in addition to constraining creativity and impairing efficiency (Drinka and Clark 2000). Preventive techniques in the form of ground rules may be useful. Some examples of ground rules that can be used to prevent or help in the management of conflict can be found below.

- One person talks at a time, while the others listen and don't interrupt

- Commit to establishing a climate of questioning and open discussion

- Everyone has the obligation to give each other honest feedback

- Everyone has an obligation to disagree if they feel they can improve on an intervention

- Recognise that there may be several valid approaches to a situation

- Disagree at the cognitive level versus the affective level

- Create solutions that benefit as many parties as possible
  (from Drinka and Clark 2000: 160)

ACTIVITY

Can you think of any additional ground rules that could help to prevent or manage conflict?

Support and commitment at a senior level

Although interprofessional initiatives may originate from the enthusiasm of front line workers, gain grass roots support and be viewed positively, there may be occasions when new practices are imposed by management or through policy directives. Collaborative working requires changes in, for example, role, task, team structures, geographical location, management and even employer (Cook *et al.* 2001, Molyneux 2001). If imposed, such changes may be perceived as threats (Hudson 2002) and can raise conscious or unconscious anxieties regarding loss of professional identity, which may adversely affect an individual's sense of control.

Unless introduced in a supportive way, change can result in role insecurity and damage to self-confidence (Hornby and Atkins 2000). This in turn can trigger resistance (Hornby and Atkins 2000), resulting in conscious or unconscious defences, such as the withholding of information or the projection of bad feelings onto other professionals. In order to minimise defensive responses, Hornby and Atkins (2000) suggest facilitating an environment in which reactions to change are openly discussed.

Commitment to interprofessional working is required at a senior level as collaborative endeavours can be expensive in terms of time and resources (Fieldgrass 1992). It is important for professionals to be afforded sufficient discretion to enable them to contribute effectively to decision making within the interprofessional team, confident in the knowledge that management will support decisions and authorise the required resources (Hornby and Atkins 2000). For some managers this might be difficult if they fear losing control over staff for whom they are responsible (Hornby and Atkins 2000) or if they have concerns regarding resource implications. Constraining professionals, however, can either marginalise frontline workers from the interprofessional decision making process or can hinder progress, through time lost in consulting with managers before committing to negotiated decisions.

Professional culture

Individuals are attracted to particular professions for complex reasons, some of them beyond conscious recognition. Each professional group has its own culture which encompasses a particular set of beliefs, values and norms. Bion (1961) noted that different groups use particular psychological mechanisms or *basic assumptions* in their operation, each mobilising different emotions, values and ideas in relation to their central task. Building on this idea, Stokes (1994) writes about the way in which professional groups construct their understanding of the nature of presenting problems, possible solutions and the relationship between professionals and clients. One professional group, for example, may hold the belief that the underlying causes of client problems are external to them and lie in structural inequalities. They may, therefore, consider that the most appropriate action to take is to support clients in their fight against social injustices (Stokes 1994). Another professional group may hold the belief that presenting problems are internal to the client and judge one-to-one therapeutic counseling to be the best response. These differing beliefs can result in clashes, with assessment of need and determination of appropriate action being formulated from very different perspectives (Will and Baird 1984, Woodhouse and Pengelly 1991). As stated previously, difference is not necessarily negative. If different beliefs and perspectives are shared through open and honest communication, professionals may be enabled to view problems from new perspectives and this may benefit themselves and the client, however, unless openly acknowledged such differences can be a source of tension and conflict (Irvine *et al.* 2002).

Divided loyalties can be a problem for professionals engaged in interprofessional working, with those involved continuing to remain members of their original professional group. Miller and Rice (1967) found that each group membership carries a greater or lesser degree of emotional significance leading to loyalty and commitment to the group's aims. As the task of the interprofessional group takes on increasing significance members gradually invest more in this group and their loyalties can shift from their original profession-specific group. Excessive commitment to either group membership at the expense of the other, however, can compromise task performance and lead to problems in intergroup relationships. As Zagier Roberts points out:

> Members with loyalty to different home-groups are likely to be competitive, and the collaborative group may fragment into fighting factions.
>
> (1994: 192)

Each professional group has its own specific language and professional jargon, abbreviations and acronyms can hold different meanings within different professional contexts. EBL, for example, can be interpreted as 'estimated blood loss' to a midwife and 'enquiry based learning' to a lecturer. Professionals who engage in collaborative working should be aware of the potential for misunderstanding when jargon, abbreviations and acronyms are used and endeavour to define clearly professional terms or use common language.

Uncertainty

For professionals to work together effectively, clarity is required regarding the parameters of their role in relation to the role of others (Obholzer 1994). Where there is confusion and uncertainty regarding role or role overlap, the interprofessional group would benefit from open discussion and negotiation in order to develop formal or informal interprofessional working protocols. This would enable everyone to have a common understanding of the role, responsibilities and boundaries of each of the professionals involved in a particular collaborative initiative.

The successful negotiation of role and boundaries requires that individuals work flexibly within the context of their work (Cook *et al.* 2001). If negotiation does not take place or agreement is not reached, uncertainty can result in role insecurity (Hornby and Atkins 2000) and conflicting views may inhibit collaborative working. Sometimes, however, particularly when developing new interprofessional ventures, uncertainty, blurring of boundaries and role overlap may have to be tolerated until the team have had time to collectively identify the most appropriate working practices. This is supported by Bateman *et al.* (2003), who in studying a new interprofessional primary care initiative, stated:

> There could be no detailed clarity about particular duties at the outset within an innovatory approach to service provision whose exact nature was still to be defined.
>
> (2003: 144)

Envy

Envy within institutions can be a very destructive force, with authority figures in particular attracting destructive attacks (Obholzer 1994). Within interprofessional working, where traditional hierarchies are often replaced with a mode of operation characterised by a more equal distribution of power where lines of authority are often unclear, conflicts based on envy and rivalry can become focused on sub-groups rather than on traditional authority figures. Stokes (1994) observed many of the difficulties between different professional groups to be like sibling rivalry, characterised by competition for resources and power.

Feelings of envy can also be triggered by perceived differences in the nature and quality of workload or the distribution of resources. Such disparities, both actual and imagined, can lead to hostile splits within and between professionals. As Halton points out, envy acts as a 'spanner-in-the-works' (1994: 15) leading either to a withholding of information or actual sabotage.

Defences against anxiety

Working within a health and social care context can subject those involved to a number of stressful situations which can give rise to high levels of anxiety. In order to protect themselves, individuals may develop defence mechanisms based on projection, which can impede interprofessional working. Jacques (1953) proposed that members of organisations experience common individual emotions in the course of their work. For example, members of the nursing profession, when caring for a terminally ill person, may experience fear associated with having to confront their own mortality. In order to deal with this, difficult feelings are *split* off from the individual's conscious awareness and *projected* onto some other person or group (Moylan 1994). For instance, nurses may project anger onto social workers who may then be seen as *difficult*. This projection not only enables the nurses to experience some relief from their anxieties but also enables them to identify with one another and thus strengthen their sense of group membership. Through the projection of bad feelings onto other people the individual feels some relief as they have now temporarily located the source of their discomfort outside of themselves. Members of other professions are prime targets for such negative projections, and this prepares the ground for a culture of blame to develop.

The strength of such projections can impede communication and effective collaboration. As Hornby and Atkins point out:

> The operation of defences disturbs collaborative practice, but to disturb defences threatens security. This is a formidable block to bringing about change and development in collaborative practice.
>
> (2000: 132)

Such unhelpful projections need to be withdrawn if professionals are to work collaboratively, however, this entails a disturbance of psychological equilibrium and may be resisted as it means that, once again, the individual must confront and deal with the anxiety they were attempting to avoid. Organisations committed to interprofessional working may therefore find it useful to provide support mechanisms that enable individuals to recognise such psychological defence mechanisms and assist them to find alternative ways of dealing with underlying anxieties.

Strategies to support effective interprofessional working

From the above a number of approaches can be identified as useful in preventing or overcoming some of the difficulties associated with interprofessional working. These are considered below.

Reflection and supervision

A combination of self-reflection and supervision can enable individuals to recognise their strengths and limitations in relation to the knowledge, skills and attitudes required for effective interprofessional working. This mechanism can also be useful in facilitating the recognition of maladaptive defence mechanisms in addition to enabling those involved to identify alternative constructive strategies as a means of coping with threat and uncertainty.

Evaluation

Evaluation can be built into interprofessional working as an integral component of joint working. All involved can engage in group reflection in order to
analyse the nature and impact of the interprofessional working relationships.
This could include an analysis of the processes involved in decision making,
role-clarification, negotiation of professional boundaries, work and resource
allocation. Group reflection also provides an opportunity for the analysis
of power distribution and the strategies used to manage conflict. Group
strengths and weaknesses can be identified as a basis for maintaining what
works well and negotiating change as and when required.

Education and training

Freeth identifies education and training as 'pivotal to providing the conditions
and skills required for sustained collaboration' (2001: 40). Bliss *et al.* (2000)
recommend interprofessional education as a means of enabling professionals to
gain an understanding of one another's roles. Interprofessional education
could also facilitate learning relating to the ideology of holistic care, recognition of psychological defence mechanisms and conflict management strategies.

Reinforcement of professional identity

Because interprofessional working can involve changes to roles and boundaries, which in turn can erode professional confidence, mechanisms to reinforce a positive professional identity may be useful. Booth and Hewison in a
study of role overlap between occupational therapy and physiotherapy found
that the 'retention of an element of professional uniqueness was necessary to
maintain professional confidence' (2002: 39). Reinforcement of allegiance
to one's own professional group through attendance at profession-specific
meetings may also help to sustain a positive professional identity.

Managerial support

Managerial support can be demonstrated by expressing interest in interprofessional working, acknowledging associated difficulties and investing in time for
team building to enable relationships to develop at the commencement of an
interprofessional initiative and when new staff replace established members.
Clear guidance relating to the parameters within which professionals can
negotiate regarding role and resource commitment helps to facilitate devolved
responsibility for decision making. Managers also make an important contribution to interprofessional working by selecting appropriate staff, that is, those
who have the required authority, experience, enthusiasm, knowledge and skills
for effective interprofessional working.

Realistic expectations

Expectations relating to individual and joint outcomes must be realistic otherwise idealised personal or joint goals can result in disappointment and perceptions of failure. Hornby and Atkins (2000) refer to the concept of the *good
enough* practitioner as helpful in enabling people to accept that they and
others do not necessarily have to achieve perfection. Professional standards do,

of course, need to be maintained but participants may have to accept that what is realistically achievable may fall below the level of excellence.

It can be seen from the above that interprofessional working is not necessarily an easy option, however, the problems highlighted in this chapter are not insurmountable. Interprofessional education has been asserted as one approach to enhancing collaboration (Horder 1993, Barr 1995), however, all professionals involved in health and social care will be involved in interprofessional working at some time and it may not be possible for everyone to access such educational opportunities. Individuals, groups and organisations will therefore benefit from being aware of the processes required for effective interprofessional working, the associated difficulties and strategies which can be utilised to support and enable those involved to optimise their performance in contributing to the interprofessional endeavour.

References

Allen D., Lyne P. and Griffiths L. (2002) Studying complex caring interfaces: key issues arising from a study of multi-agency rehabilitative care for people who have suffered a stroke. *Journal of Clinical Nursing* 11: 297–305.

Barr H. (1995) *Evaluating Interprofessional Education, Bulletin 10.* London: CAIPE.

Bassett S.E. (1995) Physiotherapy ... what is it? *New Zealand Journal of Physiotherapy* 8: 7–10.

Bateman H., Bailey P. and McLellan H. (2003) Of rocks and safe channels: learning to navigate as an interprofessional team. *Journal of Interprofessional Care* 17: 141–50.

Bion W. (1961) *Experiences in Groups.* London: Tavistock Publications Ltd.

Bliss J., Cowley S. and While A. (2000) Interprofessional working in palliative care in the community: a review of the literature. *Journal of Interprofessional Care* 14: 281–90.

Booth J. and Hewison A. (2002) Role overlap between occupational therapy and physiotherapy during in-patient stroke rehabilitation: an exploratory study. *Journal of Interprofessional Care* 16: 31–40.

Boulding K. (1990) *The Three Faces of Power.* London: Sage.

Cook G., Gerrish K. and Clarke C. (2001) Decision-making in teams: issues arising from two UK evaluations. *Journal of Interprofessional Care* 15: 141–51.

Davies C. (1996) A new vision of professionalism. *Nursing Times* 92(46): 54–6.

Dickson D.A., O'Hargie N.C. and Morrow N.C. (1989) *Communication Training for Health Professionals: An Instructor's Handbook.* London: Chapman and Hall.

Drinka T.J.K. and Clark P.G. (2000) *Health Care Teamwork: Interdisciplinary Practice and Teaching.* Westport: Auburn House.

Eisenhardt K.M., Kahwajy J.L. and Bourgeois L.J. (1997) How management teams can have a good fight. *Harvard Business Review* 75(4): 77–85.

Franken R.E. (1994) *Human Motivation.* Pacific Grove, California: Brooks/Cole Publishing Co.

Fieldgrass J. (1992) *Partnerships in Health Promotion, Collaboration Between the Statutory and Voluntary Sectors.* London: Health Education Authority.

Freeth D. (2001) Sustaining interprofessional collaboration. *Journal of Interprofessional Care* 15: 37–46.

Freidson E. (1970) *Profession of Medicine: A Study of the Sociology of Applied Knowledge.* New York: Harper and Row.

Green S. (1991) Shaking our foundations, part 2: into the future. *British Journal of Occupational Therapy* 54: 53–6.

Halton W. (1994) Some unconscious aspects of organizational life: contributions from psychoanalysis. In Obholzer A. and Zagier Roberts V. (eds) *The Unconscious at Work.* London: Routledge, pp. 11–9.

Henneman E.A., Lee J.L. and Cohen J.I. (1995) Collaboration: a concept analysis. *Journal of Advanced Nursing* **21**: 103–9.

Horder J. (1993) Present and future issues for interprofessional education. *Journal of Interprofessional Care* 7(1): 71.

Hornby S. and Atkins J. (2000) *Collaborative Care: Interprofessional, Interagency and Interpersonal* (2nd edn). Oxford: Blackwell Science.

Hudson B. (2002) Interprofessionality in health and social care: the Achilles' heel of partnerships? *Journal of Interprofessional Care* **16**: 7–17.

Hugman R. (1991) *Power in Caring Professions*. Basingstoke: Macmillan.

Irvine R., Kerridge I., McPhee J. and Freeman S. (2002) Interprofessionalism and ethics: consensus or clash of cultures? *Journal of Interprofessional Care* **16**: 199–210.

Jacques E. (1953) On the dynamics of social structure, human relations. Republished 1955 as Social systems as a defence against persecutory and depressive anxiety. In Klein M., Heimann P. and Money-Kyrle R.E. (eds) *New Directions in Psychoanalysis*. London: Tavistock Publications Ltd, pp. 478–98.

Kennedy I. (2001) *Learning from Bristol: The Report of the Public Inquiry into Children's Heart Surgery at the Bristol Royal Infirmary 1984–1995*. London: The Stationery Office.

Laidler P. (1991) Adults, and how to become one. *Therapy Weekly* 17(35): 4.

Laming Lord (2003) *Inquiry into the Death of Victoria Climbié*. London: The Stationery Office.

Loxley A. (1997) *Collaboration in Health and Welfare: Working with Difference*. London: Jessica Kingsley Publishers.

Masterson A. (2002) Cross-boundary working: a macro-political analysis of the impact on professional roles. *Journal of Clinical Nursing* **11**: 331–9.

McCray J. (2002) Nursing practice in an interprofessional context. In Hogston R. and Simpson P.M. (eds) *Foundations of Nursing Practice: Making the Difference* (2nd edn). Basingstoke: Palgrave Macmillan, pp. 449–69.

Miller E. and Rice A. (1967) *Systems of Organisation: The Control of Task and Sentient Boundaries*. London: Tavistock Publications Ltd.

Molyneux J. (2001) Interprofessional teamworking: what makes teams work well? *Journal of Interprofessional Care* **15**: 29–35.

Moylan D. (1994) The dangers of contagion: projective identification processes in institutions. In Obholzer A. and Zagier Roberts V. (eds) *The Unconscious at Work*. Routledge, London, pp. 51–9.

Obholzer A. (1994) Authority, power and leadership: contributions from group relations training. In Obholzer A. and Zagier Roberts V. (eds) *The Unconscious at Work*. London: Routledge, pp. 39–51.

Payne M. (2000) *Teamwork in Multiprofessional Care*. Basingstoke: Macmillan Press Ltd.

Roberts C. (1994) Theoretical models of physiotherapy. *Physiotherapy* **80**: 361–6.

Russell K.M. and Hymans D. (1999) Interprofessional education for undergraduate students. *Public Health Nursing* **16**: 254–62.

Stapleton S.R. (1998) Team-building: making collaborative practice work. *Journal of Nurse-Midwifery* **43**: 12–8.

Stokes J. (1994) Institutional chaos and personal stress. In Obholzer A. and Zagier Roberts V. (eds) *The Unconscious at Work*. London: Routledge, pp. 121–9.

Thomas A. and Harris M.D. (1969) *I'm OK – You're OK*. London: Arrow Books.

Will D. and Baird D. (1984) An integrated approach to dysfunction in interprofessional systems. *Journal of Family Therapy* **6**: 275–90.

Woodhouse D. and Pengelly P. (1991) *Anxiety and the Dynamics of Collaboration*. Aberdeen University Press: The Tavistock Institute of Marital Studies.

Zagier Roberts V. (1994) Conflict and collaboration: managing intergroup relations. In Obholzer A. and Zagier Roberts V. (eds) *The Unconscious at Work*. London: Routledge, pp. 39–51.

Professional Perspectives

Education

Jane Tarr

Introduction

This chapter provides an overview of educational provision for children and young people outlining opportunities for collaborative practice between staff in schools, local education authorities, and other public service agencies. Inclusive education involves learners who require additional support to enhance their learning capacity. If coherent provision is to be achieved communication processes between professionals and agencies must be effective. The case study of a child with profound hearing loss is used to illustrate the importance of effective communication skills within and between public welfare agencies.

Education services

The education service in England and Wales provides compulsory education for all children between the ages of five and 16. Parents are required by law to send their child to school unless they have special dispensation to provide education at home. Compulsory education usually lasts for seven years in primary school and five years in secondary school although some counties have middle schools providing education for nine to 13-year-olds. Educational provision for children younger than five is sometimes available but this will depend upon resources available in different regions. Post-compulsory education can be accessed either in school or in colleges of further education. Parents have some choice about which school their child attends but this will depend upon availability of places and location of the child's home in relation to the school's catchment area.

Schools and teachers have responsibility for the learning of children within a common curriculum framework laid down by the government as shown in Table 3.1 below.

If a child or young person has a difficulty in learning greater than most learners in his or her school, the teachers may choose to recognise the child as having special educational needs. Teachers will then devise differentiated teaching and learning approaches to meet the child's educational needs. If a broad range of children's services is required a statement of special educational needs, intended to clarify the nature of the additional support to be provided, will be compiled which serves to protect the child by ensuring appropriate support (DfES 2001). As education becomes inclusive increasing numbers of teachers and children need additional support. This requires teachers to work collaboratively in order to best meet the educational needs of the children in their classrooms.

Table 3.1 Curriculum provision between 3–16+ years in England

Age	Name	Compulsory Content	Document
3–5	Foundation Stage	Personal, social and emotional development Communication, language and literacy Mathematical development Knowledge and understanding of the world Physical development Creative development	QCA 2000
5–7	National Curriculum Key Stage 1	English, mathematics, science, design technology, information technology, geography, history, music, art, physical education, religious education	DfEE 1999a
7–11	National Curriculum Key Stage 2	English, mathematics, science, design technology, information technology, geography, history, music, art, physical education, religious education	DfEE 1999a
11–14	National Curriculum Key Stage 3	English, mathematics, science, design technology, information technology, modern foreign language, geography, history, music, art and design, physical education, religious education	DfEE 1999b
14–16	National Curriculum Key Stage 4	English, mathematics, science, information technology, physical education, citizenship, religious education, sex education, careers education and work related learning	QCA 2003
16+	Post-compulsory education, Further Education	More choice available for learners : BTECs, HNDs, National Vocational Qualifications (NVQs), Advanced (A) levels	

School context

Children in primary schools spend most of their time with one class teacher each year. Transition into secondary school at age 11 is challenging as learners meet many different teachers, each responsible for a specific curriculum area. The operation of a school involves teachers and headteacher, administrative staff, school meals supervisory assistants, cleaners and caretakers, all of whom interact with pupils. Recently there has been an increase in additional adults in the classroom who may be trained *nursery nurses* for early years children (3–7 years) but are often unqualified *teaching assistants* and *learning support assistants*. Generally speaking, teaching assistants support the teacher while learning support assistants support the learner. The Connexions initiative (DfEE 2000a) means that every young person aged 13–19 may be allocated a *personal adviser* to support them in the transition from education to employment [editors' note: for information on the Connexions service see Chapter 14]. *Learning mentors* support pupils with their learning across the context of home and school. This range of adults helps to promote quality learning opportunities and experiences. In many cases additional support is targeted towards those children for whom learning is difficult and who may be identified as having special educational needs. The need for effective liaison and communication between additional adults and teacher and between different teachers is crucial if interventions in children's learning are to be effective. It is now recognised that time must be available to allow for this communication.

The regional context

Local education authorities (LEAs) support educational provision in schools by employing administrators, education resource managers, advisory staff, curriculum support teachers, children's officers, education welfare officers, educational psychologists, behaviour support teachers/assistants, special needs teachers/assistants, ethnic minority achievement teachers, early years and childcare educationalists, hospital teachers and community education officers, and tutors. LEA services have traditionally been provided free to schools but as funding is now devolved, schools must buy back the services they require (DfEE 2000b). This has placed pressure on local authorities to provide value for money and has altered the nature of the relationship between local authority personnel and schools. It will often be children and young people identified as having special educational needs that require additional support from external professionals. A brief summary of the roles of these personnel is provided.

Educational psychologists are usually experienced teachers with an additional qualification in educational psychology who work within a team to support schools, families and children. Their role is to assist teachers to devise strategies and activities for individual children, groups of children, classes or the whole school. Such work may include specific individual assessments, presentations, the introduction of a behaviour support programme, leading discussions on teaching and learning approaches, and the allocation of additional monies to employ, for example, learning support assistants or counsellors (DfEE 2000b).

The educational psychologist will often oversee the compilation of statements of education need for individual children (DfES 2001).

The *education welfare officer* works closely with families in the community to ensure the child is able to access educational provision. They work with schools to develop systems and structures to ensure all children and young people feel confident to attend school regularly. Liaison with social services may be required as community care workers and social workers often share similar goals for a child and family.

The *special needs support service* (SNSS) may consist of advisors, teachers and assistants with an area of expertise in the teaching and learning of pupils with special needs. The SNSS *advisor* will support schools in developing systems, policies and teaching approaches to enhance the capacity of the school to include pupils with special educational needs. They will also be involved in the compilation of statements of educational need and the allocation of resources. Teachers and assistants visit schools to advise and work alongside teachers to enhance the capacity of children to learn. The *behaviour support team* operates in a similar way to address issues of pupils' behaviour.

District children's officers have specific responsibility for pupils at risk of exclusion from school, they oversee input from social services and education to ensure the child is maintained in an appropriate educational context.

The *ethnic minority service* comprises a team of teachers and assistants who support schools in providing for pupils for whom English is an additional language. They seek to enhance understanding of different cultural mores, build respect for children's mother tongues and develop pupils' capacity to speak, read and write in English.

Most local authorities continue to maintain *curriculum advisors* for literacy, numeracy and information technology. Specific education initiatives usually have an advisor to support new developments such as the National Numeracy Strategy.

Early years

The Sure Start initiative (DfEE 2000c) encourages social, education and health services to work collaboratively in support of families with children under compulsory school age. When nursery provision is not suitable because of a child's particular needs, a family may be able to access the Portage service. Portage is an educational programme delivered in the child's home by a tutor working alongside parents providing educational activities to promote the overall development of the young child. The breadth of provision for children in the early years depends upon the local authority and the needs and wishes of the family. It is often difficult for families to know what is available from public welfare agencies and local voluntary bodies. The merger of education and social services for early years provision has encouraged sharing of knowledge and information between professionals and with families.

Compulsory schooling

Transition into compulsory education is a traumatic time for many families as the child moves from the small scale nursery, or home context into the highly social world of school. Family centres encourage working partnerships between professionals from different welfare agencies and the nature of their relationship with families enables them to offer personal support at the start of compulsory schooling. Early years personnel may support parents in contacting and visiting schools to aid the transition for children and their families.

The *class teacher* is charged with providing education for every child within whole class and in small group settings and will draw upon parental knowledge, together with any reports and information from health or social services that might inform her of specific provision, to organise classroom teaching. Interagency cooperation is crucial at this transition point as education becomes a major provider for children and families.

The Special Educational Needs Code of Practice (DfES 2001) provides guidance for parents, educationalists and other professionals in processes within the education system to support children who find learning difficult.

The class teacher draws upon the expertise or networking capacity of the special education needs coordinator for support in differentiating activities and teaching strategies for individual children's needs. The class teacher may devise an individual education plan to include specific targets for the child, teaching strategies to be used, any additional provision, and effective systems for review and monitoring of progress. In some cases an additional adult may work with a child for a specified amount of time each week. If the needs of the child cannot be met within the resources of the school then the school will look for support from School Action Plus (DfES 2001: 55) where external specialists are consulted to support the teacher and school in understanding and working with the child. This official recognition of external agencies' involvement could include, for example, consultation with the educational psychologist or the special needs support team, the speech and language therapist or physiotherapist within the health service, and the social worker or the community care worker within social services.

The move to an inclusive education system results in more children with learning difficulties receiving education within mainstream schools and requires teachers to work with other professionals. The following case study highlights the need for enhanced communication between parents, professionals, public agencies and non-governmental organisations to ensure the best interests of the child are realised, considered and acted upon. All names have been changed to ensure anonymity.

This case study was chosen from several studies forming a larger research project seeking to identify good practice in communication between parents and professionals (Tarr 2003).

CASE STUDY

Sofie, an 11-year-old white girl, was born with bilateral centro-neuro hearing loss. She is an only child, living with her mother and stepfather and now attends a special school for the hearing impaired where the mode of instruction is British Sign Language. Her mother discovered through trial and error that signing was valuable for her child and after a long battle with her then oralist local authority, moved house to find a school where signing is the medium of instruction and deaf culture is accepted. The family has extensive interaction with the health service particularly with the paediatrician, the ear nose and throat consultant, and the general practitioner. Communication within the education service has included – mainstream schoolteachers, peripatetic teachers of the deaf, learning support assistant, special needs support teacher, educational psychologist and special educational needs advisors. Sofie has attended three educational settings: a mainstream school with additional support; a specialised unit attached to a mainstream school; and, most recently, a special school for the hearing impaired. The family receives disability carer's allowance but does not have a social worker. They have received support from council housing departments who on three occasions have housed them near to their chosen school. Sofie's mother belongs to the National Deaf Children's Society, is secretary for the local deaf association which runs a centre for the deaf. She is also a school meals supervisor and an active parent governor at her daughter's school.

Following analysis of 12 interviews with parents, the following six aspects of communication were identified as beneficial for professionals working within and across agencies of public service:

a) active listening skills

b) conversational competence

c) different modes of communication

d) sharing of knowledge and information

e) building effective professional relationships

f) building, using and maintaining professional networks.

(Tarr 2003: 210)

Each of these aspects of communication will be addressed.

a) Active listening skills

Sofie's mother held a different viewpoint from the peripatetic teachers for the deaf. Her local authority suggested an oralist approach which seeks to amplify any residual hearing a child may possess with hearing aids, encourages the child to lip read and employs strategies to encourage communication, which may include the use of British Sign Language. Sofie could only communicate through sign language, as her profound hearing loss was not made better by the use of hearing aids. Sofie's mother investigated all aspects of the deaf debate and experimented with different approaches. If the professionals involved had operated what Rogers (1980) calls an *open listening* approach, requiring an attitude of respect, empathy and genuineness, then they could have benefited from her knowledge and been able to provide more appropriately targeted support for the family.

CASE STUDY continued

In the words of Sofie's mother, 'When Sofie was eight months we went for the statutory hearing tests, the spoon in a cup and rattle; she happened to move her arm so she passed that, I totally and strongly disagreed. I decided to seek a second opinion and went to the University where they did a test with electrodes, they said she had a severe hearing loss. We went back to the hospital again because it turned out that the professionals doing the machinery had not done it well, only to be told that she was definitely profoundly deaf with bilateral central-neuro hearing loss. So all of a sudden I had all these wonderful professionals with years of experience coming into my home and my life telling me what to do. I had two peripatetic teachers for the deaf who told me that if Sofie signed and went into sign language, which wasn't really necessary these days because hearing aids are marvellous, she would never read, never write and go to a boarding school at five.'

Active listening skills can enable professionals to demonstrate they can 'respect the validity of differing perspectives and seek constructive ways of reconciling different viewpoints' (DfES 2001: 17). This case illustrates the importance of listening to the client and acknowledging different viewpoints. Similar skills are required from professionals working in different disciplines who may hold different viewpoints. Practitioners may develop an approach that involves reflective listening enabling the speaker and listener to make connections in order to problem-solve together. Skrtic suggests professionals need to engage in a 'process that requires them to adapt, adjust and revise their conventional theories and practices relative to those of their colleagues' (1991: 171). This level of personal and professional reflection is a major factor in active listening, developed by Schön (1987) as *reflection-in-action*, a crucial component in his concept of the reflective practitioner. It is essential to develop self-confidence and flexibility in order to actively listen to others, to recognise potential conflict and the contested nature of different viewpoints, and to attempt incorporation of divergent thinking in the process of devising innovative responses to challenging situations.

An holistic approach to Sofie's profound hearing impairment that involves a capacity to actively listen, would recognise the knowledge and views of her mother and other practitioners in the field. This has the potential to enable different approaches to be explored in the best interest of the child.

QUESTIONS

■ What are the implications of actively listening to your client's viewpoints?

■ Reflect upon the perspective of another professional within your area of public service, what might you learn from listening to their perspective?

■ Give an example of where conflicting viewpoints may occur in your area of professional practice?

CASE STUDY continued

'The ear nose and throat consultant at the hospital asked me how it was going and I told him I had started signing and he told me it wasn't a proper language. I asked him if he signed and he ignored me so I shouted again and he said, "I do not need to because I can hear" my response was to say "Aren't you lucky" picked up my kid and walked out and never spoke another word to him.' (Sofie's mother)

'I am angry because if the professionals in the field of deafness had explained that they did not accept the place of signing I would have moved when she was a toddler to somewhere appropriate. I knew little about how counties thought differently about deaf community.' (Sofie's mother)

'They keep mothers or parents in total ignorance of what is available for the child, what can be done, what cannot be done. Eventually we learned that county policy was not to consider using a signed approach until the child was six or seven years old. So Sofie was refused access to communication. If that had happened to a hearing child for six years, can you imagine what social services would do to you but you have a deaf child and they support it.' (Sofie's stepfather)

b) Conversational competence

Both Sofie's mother and stepfather provide illustrations of difficulties faced by professionals required to initiate and conduct conversations where conflict and contest is possible. To explain to Sofie's parents the reasons for the type of provision available in the county required a high level of conversational competence involving both linguistic skill and sensitivity to language use of others. Clients appreciate a professional's ability to 'participate in conversation situations and to debate or persuade' (Svensson 1990: 53). Few professionals within public services have the motivation or time to engage in such conversation, though the capacity to chat and converse, persuade and convince is a valuable quality for professionals in building good interprofessional understanding (*ibid*). There will always be conflicting viewpoints as people hold different vested interests. Such a rich dynamic can lead to creative solutions if people are able to achieve a balance between the 'interplay of conflict and submission, acceptance and resistance, contestation and negotiation' (Vincent 1997: 276).

Conflicting approaches to the development of communication for the hearing impaired in this case study had a detrimental impact upon the family. Had the ear nose and throat consultant engaged with the different viewpoints, explained his views about signing, and listened to the views of the mother as one would in a conversation, then communication might have been enhanced. Such an approach recognises equal standing between participants although this can be hard to achieve where disciplinary knowledge is so highly prized. In this context sensitive linguistic skill can ensure that complex disciplinary specific language is minimised to encourage a well-informed exchange of perspectives. Sofie's mother had many conversations with professionals through case conferences, consultations, and formal meetings. She is adamant that the most useful occurred in situations where informal exchange of ideas and perspectives took place. Such exchanges are possible through social interaction within organisations such as the National Deaf Children's Society. Informal exchange also took place between parent and learning support assistant, a family friend who visited the home regularly. A realisation that the context has an impact upon the outcome of conversations may result in more suitable venues for interaction. A family centre for those with young children is an ideal opportunity for clients and professionals to interact informally but also for professionals from different agencies to begin to share their expertise through informal conversations.

=== QUESTIONS ===

- Reflect upon your professional conversations and consider areas where misconceptions can arise for the lay person.

- Identify some informal contexts where conversation between different professionals might take place.

- What strategies might you employ to engage with controversial issues and manage conflict?

c) Different modes of communication

Modes of communication employed by professionals range from the written word and the telephone to face-to-face interaction during formal or informal meetings. Each mode has advantages and disadvantages and individual professionals tend to favour a particular mode. Some health practitioners use the written word, some social service workers use the telephone, and some teachers prefer face-to-face interaction. Each different form of communication enables the expression of information in different ways. Collaborative interprofessional practice may require a range of communicative strategies. The multiple understandings that abound in interprofessional collaboration may lead institutions to create what Young (2000) describes as *inclusive political communication systems* through a variety of modes of communication. Leaflets and brochures are frequently used to provide information about professional services but the language of such texts can be inaccessible for some. In order to gain additional financial support or resources the necessary documentation that has to be completed, together with the meetings that have to take place, may deter some parents.

CASE STUDY continued

In order to ensure Sofie received additional resources a statement of her special educational needs was compiled. This was a multidisciplinary assessment involving professionals from health service, education and Sofie's parents. The outcome listed the nature of the additional support to be allocated. The contribution from the mother made mention of sign language and was not taken seriously but on her insistence was included in the statement and read *mother says* at all the points where she described her daughter's signing ability and level of sign understanding.

Sofie's mother said, 'So I rang up to ask. I kept ringing, I did not care what else was going on. Tell her I am in a meeting you could hear it all. I kept ringing, I did not care if I was a nuisance, at the end of the day my focus is my child. I cannot worry about what else they are dealing with.'

Sofie received full-time support from Sally, the learning support assistant who had met her mother at sign language classes. Sofie's mother explains that 'Sally was good, the support of £500 came our way, so we hired a video recorder and we did the Oxford Reading Tree. So we used to go round her house and we videoed in sign all these books, sometimes the shortened versions so we could give her access in her language, to help her to learn English grammar. It was working, she read well.'

Communication procedures are often embedded in institutional forms and taken for granted within professional groups. The statement of educational needs to which parents are asked to contribute is written in formal language. Sofie's mother's contribution was not taken seriously. She used the telephone insistently when trying to gain a place for Sofie in a new school. Her determination to provide for her child led her to create books for Sofie in sign language. Together with the learning support assistant they made signed videos of Sofie's reading books.

Reflection upon the different modes of communication that people are able to use, leads to the recognition that there are stereotypical expectations of people in our society in relation to their understanding of different *languages*. The nature of language is 'embedded in the shapes and characters of our abiding social institutional forms' (Vass 1991: 223) and cannot easily be redistributed without considerable change and development. Professionals may need to consider enhancing their modes of communication in order to ensure understanding across different disciplines.

QUESTIONS

- List the range of ways in which you communicate with clients.

- Consider the most successful modes of communication in your professional work.

- How might you enhance communication systems between different professionals?

CASE STUDY continued

Sofie's mother has always maintained strong connections with the deaf community stating that 'Our social life is either with the deaf or nothing.' When they moved across the country she joined the deaf centre, the deaf youth club, became a parent governor at her child's school and stands on the policy committee for the school's family centre for deaf children. As she says 'I stuck my nose in everywhere, picked up every bit of paper going to know what is the difference between total communication, bilingualism and a signing unit.'

Following the limited resource allocation gained through multidisciplinary assess-ment to create the statement of special educational needs, Sofie's mother gained advice from the National Deaf Children's Society (NDCS) and she managed to achieve full-time signing support for her child during school time. She realised that the debate was complex but that she needed to be insistent if her child was going to get the best provision.

d) Sharing knowledge and information

Parents are often committed to increasing their knowledge and understanding and may know far more about their child than a professional with responsibility for many children. Professional recognition of this insight is frequently limited as illustrated in the case study. Interactions within the deaf community provided the family with considerable knowledge and, in this case, voluntary bodies have been supportive in ensuring knowledge is shared with Sofie's parents. This sug-gests professionals need to cultivate relationships with voluntary bodies in order to gain further insight into a wider range of perspectives.

The capacity to share knowledge and information across different profes-sions and agencies depends upon individuals meeting each other and having time to talk and interact. An example in this case study is the speech and lan-guage therapist working in the school supporting pupils but also sharing knowledge with teachers. Building partnerships through joint planning of pro-vision for vulnerable children is a developing practice (Roaf 2002). Profess-ionals involved in such partnerships can share their knowledge, particularly at the start of the process (Wilson and Charlton 1997).

Successful sharing of knowledge and information between professions and agencies requires the ability to communicate complex knowledge in simple terms. The avoidance of jargon and disciplinary-specific language can aid under-standing. Sharing of knowledge can lead to joint problem solving, challenging assumptions and ideologies, and result in innovative outcomes. The negotiating model of partnership is to be encouraged between professionals, where shared knowledge is developed into shared perspectives. Dale defines such partnership as:

A working relationship where the partners use negotiation and joint decision making to resolve differences of opinion and disagreement, in order to reach some kind of shared perspective or jointly agreed decision on issues of mutual concern.

(1996: 14)

Every professional engaged in sharing knowledge and information must be alert and sensitive to protecting client confidentiality. Professionals working in child protection continually face ethical concerns of confidentiality between agencies (Scott 1997). If parents are kept informed this can alleviate some of the difficulty. Sofie' mother realised when Sofie started school that information had not been shared between health and education. Consequently the teachers were inadequately prepared to support her in mainstream school.

The Special Educational Needs Code of Practice (DfES 2001) promotes the creation of parent partnership schemes within, but independent of, each local authority. Such partnerships are emerging across the country operating in different ways but all aim to support families with children with special educational needs. Sofie's mother was not happy with the statement of educational need, which awarded part-time support from a signing support assistant. As she put it 'I said I thought she had to attend school full time? They said she does. I said she couldn't with only 17.5 hours support she will only be there for 17.5 hours so when do I bring her in and when do I take her home?' With help from the NDCS, *mother says* was removed from the document and full time signing support was awarded.

Sofie and her family moved twice to ensure a place in a school. On both occasions several voluntary bodies helped them in accessing support from housing departments. Had the health and education services shared information with housing departments the family may have been better supported. The creation of systemic procedures for interprofessional sharing of knowledge and information developed through projects that are joint funded and joint planned can lead to what Roaf (2002) has called *joined up action*.

=========== **QUESTIONS** ===========

■ What knowledge/information can parents access in deciding which school to send their child?

■ What further knowledge might be shared between health and education services at the start of compulsory schooling?

■ How might you explain your knowledge of a particular child's needs to a professional working in another discipline?

e) Building effective professional relationships
Building professional relationships with clients and with other professionals requires resources and time. The example below outlines how relationships between school and family can break down, and despite the number of people involved, the situation remained unresolved. To build interprofessional relationships based upon mutual respect and cooperation requires considerable

structural change. Professionals brought together for case conferences seek the best solution for the child but are not always able to discuss issues openly in the absence of trusting professional relationships. The relations are such that everyone feels powerless to act and often only limited solutions to the child's difficulties are found (Todd and Higgins 1998).

CASE STUDY continued

Sofie's mother explains, 'When Sofie was seven years old her mainstream school decided that they could no longer cope with her in school. The annual review became an important conference. We had the bloke from special educational needs department there, her class teacher, all these other people and me sat there. It is unusual for me, in front of professionals but before the meeting ended I left in tears. They were quite concerned after that. It is a shame that you have to break down before they realise that this is a big issue.'

There can be mistrust between professions and 'replacing structural competition with cooperation requires collective action and collective action requires education and organisation' (Kohn 1986: 195). The government is attempting to support different public welfare agencies in working together by encouraging them to bid for project monies. The Children's Fund, Sure Start, and Educational Action Zones are all examples of projects which require multiagency involvement. Skrtic (1991) offers the example of how experts from different fields worked together for the successful Apollo Space Project. Sensitive management, clear organisation and well-defined goals enabled a diverse group of experts to work together. Skrtic is convinced that 'collaboration and mutual adjustment' can lead to the creation of new knowledge and skills as people are expected to 'adjust and revise their conventional theories and practices relative to those of their colleagues' and teams' progress on the tasks in hand' (Skrtic 1991: 171).

QUESTIONS

■ With whom do you have an effective professional relationship? Outline how such a relationship was developed.

■ With which professionals might you build relationships and why?

■ Give examples of multiagency projects taking place in your area of professional practice.

f) Building, using and maintaining professional networks
Sofie's mother spent considerable time building a network of support for herself and her child. She demonstrated this when she visited her local university to gain a second opinion on her child's hearing impairment. Her determination to build, use and maintain a working network of support across public welfare provision, voluntary organisations, friends and family enabled her to

achieve full signed educational provision for her child at a school within walking distance of their home. Following a violent incident for which the police were called, Sofie's mother left her husband and was placed in crisis accommodation near the deaf unit. She then moved again to a different county into local authority housing with a garden backing onto a fully signing school. The network of support surrounding this child and her mother has grown from her determination, her openness and her honesty.

Professionals also benefit from building support networks. Capra reinforces the value of a network in claiming that 'the more complex its pattern of inter-connections, the more resilient it will be' (1997: 295). The nature of teaching work does not always encourage teachers to build networks so they may benefit from joining interschool networks or consortiums, attending courses, joining working groups, using websites or attending meetings to build net-works. The school itself can be used as a venue for groups and activities, which can serve to broaden experiences for the school community.

=========== **QUESTIONS** ===========

■ What are your current networks of personal and professional support?

■ How might you develop this network further, what networks could you join?

■ How might such a breadth of contacts enhance your professional area of work?

CASE STUDY continued

The teachers at Sofie's mainstream school could no longer meet the needs of a child who was profoundly deaf. The trained expert teachers worked in one special-ist unit for deaf children situated very far away from the family home. At the case conference the mother broke down, as she did not wish her child to board at school. She eventually gained the support of the council housing department and by engaging social services together with the police she was rehoused in a place from where her child could attend the deaf unit.

Conclusion

This chapter has outlined the education services for a child with a profound hearing impairment illustrating the challenges faced by the family in oversee-ing professional provision. The family encountered a range of educational pro-fessionals, health practitioners, voluntary workers, and officials working within social services.

Support for the family could have been more cohesive and effective if the professionals involved had developed effective strategies of communication. This chapter proposes the following key areas as essential for the development of collaborative practice:

- active listening skills between client/professional and interprofessional colleagues,

- conversational competence,

- the capacity to use different modes of communication,

- a commitment to sharing knowledge with others involved,

- an ability to build effective professional relationships, and

- the capacity to build, use, and maintain broad professional networks.

Some professionals already use these skills in their work with clients but these same skills are necessary for collaborative working with other professionals.

References

Capra F. (1997) *The Web of Life: A New Synthesis of Mind and Matter.* London: Flamingo.

Dale N. (1996) *Working with Families of Children with Special Needs.* London: Routledge.

DfEE (Department for Education and Employment) (1999a) *The National Curriculum Handbook for Primary Teachers in England Key Stages 1 and 2.* London: The Stationery Office.

DfEE (1999b) *The National Curriculum Handbook for Secondary Teachers in England Key Stages 3 and 4.* London: The Stationery Office.

DfEE (2000a) *Connexions: the Best Start in Life for Every Young Person.* Nottingham: DfEE Publications.

DfEE (2000b) *Educational Psychology Services (England): Current Role, Good Practice and Future Directions – The Research Report.* Nottingham: DfEE Publications.

DfEE (2000c) *Sure Start: Making a Difference for Children and Families.* Nottingham: DfEE Publications.

DfES (Department for Education and Skills) (2001) *Special Educational Needs Code of Practice.* London: HMSO.

Kohn A. (1986) *No Contest: The Case Against Competition.* New York: Houghton Mifflin.

QCA (Qualifications and Curriculum Authority) (2000) *Curriculum Guidance for the Foundation Stage: Early Years.* London: QCA.

QCA (2003) *Changes to the Key Stage 4 Curriculum: Guidance for Implementation from September 2004.* London: QCA.

Roaf C. (2002) *Co-ordinating Services for Included Children: Joined up Action.* Buckingham: Open University Press.

Rogers C. (1980) *A Way of Being.* Boston: Houghton Mifflin.

Schön D.A. (1987) *Educating the Reflective Practitioner: Towards a New Design for Teaching and Learning in the Professions.* San Franciso: Jossey-Bass Publishers.

Scott D. (1997) Inter-agency conflict: an ethnographic study. *Child and Family Social Work* 2: 73–80.

Skrtic T.M. (1991) The special education paradox: equity is the way to excellence. *Harvard Educational Review* **61**: 148–206.

Svensson L.G. (1990) Knowledge as a professional resource: case studies of architects and psychologists at work. In Torstendahl R. and Burrage M. (eds) *The Formation of Professions.* London: Sage Publications, pp. 51–70.

Tarr J. (2003) *The Personal Qualities and Attributes of Professionals Working with Parents of Children with Special Educational Needs.* Unpublished doctoral thesis. Bristol: University of the West of England.

Todd E.S. and Higgins S. (1998) Powerlessness in professional and parent relationships. *British Journal of Sociology of Education* **19**: 227–36.

Vass G. (1991) Marginal dialogues, social positions and inequity in rhetorical resources. In Mettens R. and Vass G. (eds) *Sharing Mathematics Cultures*. Lewes: Falmer Press, pp. 214–31.

Vincent C. (1997) Community and collectivism: the role of parents' organisations in the education system. *British Journal of Sociology of Education* **18**: 271–3.

Wilson A. and Charlton K. (1997) *Making Partnerships Work*. London: Joseph Rowntree.

Young I.M. (2000) *Inclusion and Democracy*. Oxford: Oxford University Press.

CHAPTER 4

Housing

Nancy Carlton and Judith Ritchie

Introduction

The relationship between health and housing has been the subject of research and commentary since Victorian times. During the 19th century developments in, among other things, improved sanitation, disposal of human waste, better housing construction and the reduction in overcrowding served to ameliorate housing conditions contributing to acute infectious diseases. Today it is the chronic non-infectious conditions that represent the primary cause of health problems, and the relationships between housing, health and socio-economic status are diverse and increasingly complex (Dunn 2000).

The findings of research illustrate the links between poor housing conditions and poor health (Leather *et al.* 1994, Burridge and Ormandy 1993, Smith 1989). Accommodation with cold, damp, mouldy conditions, over-crowding or poor repair is shown to have a negative impact on health (Ineichen 1993, Lowry 1991). Studies of the relationship between housing and mental health (Kearns and Smith 1993, Smith *et al.* 1993) illustrate that housing stressors are associated with psychological distress and contribute to mental health problems. Research by Oldman and Beresford (2000) suggests that poor and unsuitable housing has an adverse effect on the physical and mental health of disabled children and their families. Heywood's study (2001) shows that housing adaptations for disabled people successfully keep people out of hospital, reduce strain on carers, and promote social inclusion.

In a longitudinal study examining the links between housing deprivation and physical and mental health using the National Child Development Study (NCDS), the authors conclude that :

> Multiple housing deprivations led to a 25 per cent (on average) greater risk of disability or severe ill health across the life course of the cohort members in the NCDS. Poor housing and health exhibit a dose-response relationship: greater housing deprivation at a point in time will lead to greater probability of ill health, and a sustained experience of housing deprivation over time will increase the probability of ill health.
>
> (Marsh *et al.* 2000: 425)

Most people today own their homes. In 2002 only 30.1 per cent of the population lived in rented accommodation in the United Kingdom. Of those, 9.7 per cent lived in accommodation rented by private landlords or employers, 13.8 per cent lived in housing owned by local authorities, and the remaining 6.6 per cent occupied housing provided by housing associations (ODPM 2003). The diversity of housing provision makes it confusing and difficult for those trying to help people to either access accommodation appropriate to their health and/or social needs or improve/adapt their current accommodation to better meet their needs. Accommodation provided by housing associations (referred to hereafter as *registered social landlords*) or by local authorities is referred to as *social housing*. The social housing sector is generally used to house people who are defined as being *in housing need*, whether that need arises from health or other reasons. However, because of the general shortage of housing in some parts of the country, private rented accommodation is increasingly being used for people in housing need.

There is no single housing profession as such. Housing workers might provide housing advice or manage housing owned by a social landlord; they might work with homeless people specifically or might provide support for people needing assistance with living independently. Refuges for victims of domestic violence are often provided by registered social landlords (RSLs). Some RSLs specialise in providing housing for people with particular physical or mental health problems or for disabled or elderly people; others provide more generic accommodation, known as *general needs* housing. Consequently, a health or social care professional trying to help someone access appropriate accommodation may need to work with one or more agencies involved in the provision of social housing or housing services. Health, social care and housing professionals also work together either in relation to service provision for individuals or in planning and devising strategies to meet the needs of the community as a whole.

In this chapter consideration is given to some of the difficulties people with health or mobility problems might face in finding housing accommodation appropriate to their needs. In suggesting ways in which such difficulties might be addressed the range of housing providers and the diversity of housing services is illustrated. The roles of different kinds of landlords will be described together with consideration of some potential housing solutions for:

- people who are homeless or who need to change their accommodation,

- people whose mobility problems necessitate changes or adaptations to their accommodation,

- people whose accommodation is in such poor condition that it is adversely affecting their health, and

- people requiring support to remain in their current accommodation and achieve independent living.

The means of assisting people in these situations will vary, depending on whether they are homeless, living in their own homes or in rented accommodation. If they are living in rented accommodation, the options will also depend upon whether they are living in the private rented or social housing sector.

Using case studies, the chapter will illustrate some of the ways in which housing, and health and social care professionals work together in successful partnerships for the benefit of individuals with housing needs.

Providers of housing and housing-related services

Social landlords (local authorities or RSLs) are not-for-profit organisations charged with providing accommodation for those who are deprived or in housing need, and supporting people in maintaining their tenancies. Private landlords operate for profit and are less regulated; there is no expectation, legal or otherwise, that private landlords should play a support role for their tenants. The main providers of housing and housing services are briefly described below.

Local authorities

The importance of council housing in numerical terms has diminished since the 1980s. Many council houses have been sold to tenants under the Right to Buy legislation, and other legislative, economic and policy pressures have ensured a steady stream of wholesale or part-transfers of housing stock from local authorities to RSLs. The local authority is now required to take a strategic role rather than act merely as a landlord, and has responsibility for all aspects of housing in its area. In addition, the local authority must produce a number of strategies in collaboration with other statutory and voluntary agencies. These strategies are outlined below.

a) Housing strategy
Each local authority must produce a *housing strategy* to cover all aspects of housing in its area. It must include an analysis of all housing markets and an

assessment of the housing needs of all sections of the community. In addition, local authorities are required to monitor the work of RSLs, and ensure effective and efficient use of resources. The Housing Strategy is a useful source of information with regard to local housing priorities, setting out current and anticipated housing needs and indicating where resources are to be targeted.

b) Homelessness strategy

Brought in by the Homelessness Act 2002, the *homelessness strategy* is the document in which an authority sets out plans for combating and preventing homelessness. The homelessness strategy identifies current and future likely levels of homelessness together with services available to homeless people. Within this strategy authorities must identify resources available both directly and through other local agencies to help prevent homelessness, secure accommodation for those without a home, and provide appropriate support for those who are or have been homeless or are threatened with homelessness.

Local authorities retain ultimate responsibility for administering homelessness legislation, whether or not they have retained their housing stock. This involves not only developing a housing strategy but also offering advice to anyone who is homeless or threatened with homelessness and making decisions about who is accepted as statutorily homeless. Housing professionals and health and social care professionals can effectively work together to ensure not only that appropriate decisions are made for homeless individuals, but also that resources are used effectively and efficiently.

c) Supporting people strategy

The *supporting people strategy* is a wide and varied programme providing housing-related support services to the more vulnerable members of society (Griffiths 2000, www.spkweb.org.uk/). Initiated in 2003, the programme is designed to improve partnership working between local authorities, health services, the probation service, voluntary sector organisations, RSLs, support agencies and service users in the provision of housing-related support to vulnerable groups. There are 150 Administering Authorities established to manage programmes locally and to formulate a strategy for their area, assessing the current and future needs for low-level housing support. This is an important strategy for all those involved in the care and support of people who come within the supporting people remit as it sets out the spending priorities for the forthcoming five years. Supporting people client groups include:

■ people who have been homeless or sleeping rough,

■ ex-offenders and people at risk of offending and imprisonment,

■ people with a physical or sensory disability,

■ people at risk of domestic violence,

■ people with alcohol and drug problems,

- teenage parents,

- elderly people,

- young people at risk,

- people with HIV and AIDS,

- people with learning difficulties,

- travellers, and

- homeless families with support needs.

Registered social landlords

The term *registered social landlord* is used to describe organisations providing housing on a not-for-profit basis. This includes most housing associations, charitable trusts, local housing companies, and recently formed stock transfer associations. Their aim is to provide low-cost housing either for rent, or for some form of low-cost home ownership. They are usually governed by a board of trustees or a management committee. Most are funded partly through public money allocated by the Housing Corporation and partly from loans from banks or building societies. This mix of public and private money has made RSLs the government's vehicle of choice for building new housing stock since the 1980s. Many housing associations offer general needs housing whereas others are specialised and only offer housing for a particular client group, for example, for older people, for those with learning difficulties, or for those with mental health needs.

Private sector landlords

Local authorities often use private rented sector housing to address the issue of homelessness, hence working with the private sector is an important part of the strategic role of the local authority. However, much of the private sector remains unregulated, although there are growing calls for this to change in order to offer protection to those vulnerable people housed, sometimes unsatisfactorily, in private rented properties. Where people are housed in accommodation defined as a house in multiple occupation (HMO) under a contract between the local authority and a private landlord the property will have been visited and vetted for its suitability both for the standard of facilities and for fire prevention. An HMO is a dwelling originally built as accommodation for a single family unit but now being used to house more than one household or a number of individuals. Some local authorities use HMOs to house young people or homeless families. However, finding private sector rented accommodation to meet the health needs of a particular individual is difficult and the potential for making adaptations will depend on the willingness of the landlord to permit such work. Research by Carlton *et al.* (2003a) into the living conditions of older people in the private rented sector identified problems that give serious cause for concern for the health and well-being of some vulnerable people who live in private accommodation.

Voluntary organisations

Voluntary autonomous not-for-profit organisations managed by an unpaid board or committee make an important contribution to the supported housing sector. Many voluntary organisations were set up to help house those with a particular need, for example, the single homeless, young people, or those with mental health issues. Voluntary organisations often work in collaboration with RSLs to provide support for RSL tenants, and because of changes in funding, some are being incorporated into RSLs. Funding for voluntary organisations comes from various sources, but most will access at least some funds from the supporting people budget.

Interagency working

Means *et al.* (1997) note that health and social care professionals may need to work together with housing staff in order to meet the needs of individuals or households in the following circumstances:

- during the process of housing allocation for people who want to move into social housing or people who are already living in social housing and want to transfer to another property within that sector,

- enabling individuals or households to *stay put* within their own homes through installation of adaptations or repairs/improvements to the property, and

- assessing individuals for care and support packages when they have health and housing needs.

Access to social housing

Access to social housing usually requires an assessment of the applicant's housing need taking into account such factors as the age, mental and physical health and vulnerability of the applicant and/or members of the applicant's household. Other factors considered are whether the applicant is homeless, whether the household includes dependent children or someone who is pregnant, as well as the condition of the household's current accommodation. People are then placed on a waiting list or housing register. In some areas there is a separate list for each housing organisation; other areas operate a Common or Joint Housing Register where applicants complete only one form to apply for housing from any local social housing provider. Priority for housing is usually determined by a points system based upon the factors listed above. Where applications are made on health grounds, a reference is required from a health professional stating that the current housing is having a detrimental effect on the health of the applicant or on the health of a member of their household.

There is a belief that allocation according to housing need has led to a concentration of deprived households on unpopular estates, thus contributing to social exclusion and neighbourhood decline (Brown *et al.* 2000). In response the government has promoted a policy of choice, following the recommendation in the Housing Green Paper (DETR 2000) for radical change in the way people are allocated social housing.

A number of local authorities have piloted Choice-Based Lettings Systems (ODPM 2004) where social housing applicants are assessed for housing need in less precise categories such as the broad bandings of: those in urgent need; those with a housing need; and those with no immediate housing need. Details of available properties are then advertised with information about who would be eligible to apply. The major change is that applicants need to actively apply for a property, rather than wait to be allocated accommodation. This may prove a significant barrier for those less able to organise themselves for whatever reason. Authorities are charged with trying to ensure that the vulnerable are not disadvantaged by this system, and close interagency collaboration is likely to be required to make sure that people's needs do not go unnoticed.

Local authorities have a statutory duty to advise and assist homeless people and to help some categories of homeless people find accommodation. Only people who are judged to be eligible (which depends on their citizenship/immigration status), unintentionally homeless and in priority need will be offered rehousing, although others are entitled to information and assistance. The Housing Act 1996 and the Homelessness Act 2002 contain definitions of what it means to be *unintentionally homeless* and *in priority need* but it should be noted that those who are literally roofless make up only a small percentage of the homeless. Health and social care workers may have contact with many people who are homeless in the sense of living in unsuitable housing. They may be in danger from violence or threats of violence, staying with friends temporarily, or being threatened with eviction through no fault of their own, and each of these situations renders a person homeless. However, while a local authority can rehouse those who are homeless but not in priority need if there is sufficient social housing available or if there is somewhere suitable in the private sector, there is no statutory duty for them to do so.

CASE STUDY: JOE

Joe, a white male now in his mid-20s, left home at 17 because of an abusive stepfather. He lived with friends until he found work and could afford to rent a private sector bedsit. Things began to go wrong when he met an older group of young men and was drawn into their heavy drinking lifestyle. For Joe, perhaps because of unresolved issues in his past, this quickly became an alcohol dependency. As a result he lost his job, was evicted from his bedsit, and because as a private sector tenant there was no automatic recourse to housing advice, Joe thought that, as a young single person, there was no one likely to offer him help.

Joe began living on the street. He heard about a *one-stop-shop* run by the local council giving advice to homeless people. The one-stop-shop is an interagency project with representatives from the local authority's homelessness team, social services and the health service working together in the same building in order to provide a single point of assessment for an individual. Unfortunately, Joe, who did not cope well with being *street homeless*, only went to the advice centre when drunk and became abusive when having to wait his turn to be seen. Consequently he was repeatedly turned away.

An individual's needs are often complex, and despite the provision of services such as this multiagency advice centre it may be problematic to connect the individual with the service.

QUESTIONS

■ What do you consider to be Joe's needs at this time?

■ What service providers would need to be involved in meeting his needs?

■ How might Joe best access these services?

> **CASE STUDY continued**
>
> Joe is met by a street outreach worker employed by a voluntary agency acting as part of the council's strategy for combating street homelessness. The outreach worker makes an appointment for Joe to attend a meeting at a day centre for homeless people where his needs can be assessed. Joe misses several appointments, but does eventually attend and has his housing, health and support needs assessed. A social services officer who works with the contact and assessment team also gives him a formal alcohol assessment.
>
> Having made contact with the day centre, Joe begins to use it and accesses the services of the nurses who attend the centre on a twice-weekly basis. A four-way meeting is organised between Joe, the hostel nurse, the outreach worker and the alcohol worker. It is agreed that Joe is ready for a detoxification programme, and a place is found for him in a residential centre with a subsequent referral to a long stay hostel where he would be able to stay for up to three years.

It is important that Joe receives treatment quickly, and this is dependant on the availability of places in a detoxification unit. Following detoxification, Joe will need to be placed in a hostel, and it is at this point that interagency working often breaks down. Hostels are usually run by RSLs or voluntary organisations, and each tends to have its own referral criteria. People can self-refer to some hostels, although they are more likely to be referred by outreach teams or community health workers. One problem for health and social care workers is knowing which hostels are available and the details of their particular referral criteria. The local authority should make such information available, and the Supporting People team should provide information about every form of provision in the local area that provides support for vulnerable people.

Too often, placing an individual in a hostel is seen as a success, and the momentum is lost in tackling issues that need to be addressed if someone like Joe is to move towards independence. Effective interagency working can make the difference between the hostel placement being little more than a temporary shelter and being a time of transformation. Hostel workers alone are unlikely to have the skills to meet all of Joe's needs. For example, Joe still has issues related to his abusive stepfather and access to floating support is essential in helping him towards independent living.

CASE STUDY continued

Being placed in the hostel is very much a starting point for Joe. His needs are assessed by his key worker in the hostel, and a package of support is agreed.

He will be registered with a GP and could be referred to a community mental health team.

Once Joe is ready to move on from the hostel, he will come into contact with the Supporting People team, and should be referred to some form of floating support.

Staying put

Another important interface between housing and health and social care occurs when people find that their home itself has become disabling. This can happen at any time through illness or accident, but is more likely as people grow older. Social services and the occupational therapy service are often the first point of contact, but housing has an important role to play.

If people are in local authority or RSL rented accommodation, it is possible that the landlord has a budget for minor aids and adaptations and may assist with necessary alterations. A transfer into an already adapted home or to a house closer to important amenities may also be possible. Disabled Facilities Grants may be available for alterations or adaptations [editors note: see Chapter 8 for further information on housing adaptations].

An important source of help for all tenures can be a home improvement agency (HIA). Having grown in number and importance since their inception in the 1970s, HIAs do not fund required works, but do enable people to obtain funding either through grants, loans or equity release. They also help plan required works and negotiate with builders as part of the general aim of helping individuals maintain their homes to a decent standard. HIAs have now been incorporated into the supporting people programme. This may have some benefits in raising their profile and ensuring a minimum standard of service delivery but whether the necessary level of funding is maintained under supporting people will depend on the strategic value placed on the service by the local authority.

Care and support packages

The Department of Health's National Service Framework for older people (www.dh.gov.uk/) acknowledges the important role of housing, and various standards, such as Standard 6 (prevention of falls) and Standard 8 (promoting an active and healthy life in old age), are unachievable without addressing issues of housing.

The Health and Social Care Change Agent Team (CAT) was established in January 2002 to reduce the number of delayed transfers of care (or delayed hospital discharges) and associated arrangements. Hospital discharge planning is a priority for all services because of the serious consequences of delayed or inappropriate discharge on both service user and provider. Acknowledging the important role of housing in this process CAT set up a Housing Learning and Improvement Network in November 2002. This continues to provide a useful source of information of best practice in this area of work (www.dh.gov.uk).

CASE STUDY: ROSE

Rose is a white 75-year-old widow recently admitted to hospital for a medical condition. For the past 12 years she has been living in the home of relatives although there is some conflict with her relations. She is ready for discharge, but her family has refused to take her back as they plan to move to a smaller house and will no longer be able to care for her.

Rose is accustomed to undertaking personal and domestic tasks. While living with her relatives she was able to bathe without attendance, did the washing up and often helped with the cooking under the watchful eye of family members. The shopping, cleaning and other domestic activities were done by her relatives.

Sheltered housing, or independent accommodation with warden support, became less popular from the 1980s as a result of increased longevity and better health in old age. This together with people's higher expectations of accommodation has led to an unwillingness to accept the small flats on offer in many sheltered housing schemes. The move into sheltered accommodation often now comes at a time of crisis when people are far frailer than previously with the result that a rather different form of service is required. Sheltered housing now comes with varying levels of support, and some schemes have been created specifically to meet the needs of the frail older person. The role of the warden in such schemes is as coordinator of complex interagency services. In many instances interagency working enables people to stay out of residential care for longer than would otherwise be the case.

QUESTIONS

■ What sort of accommodation do you think would be suitable to meet Rose's needs on discharge from hospital?

■ Whom would you contact to try to assist Rose in finding such accommodation?

■ What assistance might she require from health and social care professionals to find appropriate accommodation?

■ What level of support might she need to live independently?

CASE STUDY continued

Following an application made on her behalf by her relatives and a social worker, Rose was assessed as an urgent medical priority case by the district medical officer, and she moved into a ground floor self-contained one bedroom RSL flat in extra care sheltered accommodation within one month of applying to the local authority.

Rose is delighted with her current accommodation, enjoys its spaciousness and comfort and finds the carers attached to the scheme very supportive and helpful without being overbearing. She has not done any cooking since she moved because she is not sure she would be safe cooking on her own. Meals on wheels delivers a meal to her flat each day, and a friend of the family helps with the washing, cleaning, shopping and collecting the pension.

Rose still lives within walking distance of where she has lived for most of her adult life and has a wide circle of relatives and friends who visit regularly. She has become a close friend with one of the other residents, and they have tea together twice a week as well as attending activities that interest them in the sheltered scheme.

She believes that her health and overall quality of life has improved as she no longer has to deal with difficult personality differences on a daily basis and revels in being able to live independently. Her use of health services comprises regular visits to the practice nurse for blood pressure checks and she says that she has significantly reduced the number of GP appointments since the move. However, her use of other services has increased as she has twice-daily visits from scheme care assistants and meals on wheels service. She arranges and pays for her home help service privately.

Rose is full of praise for how her housing needs were met and has no plans to move again.

Whether or not Rose will be able to remain in her flat will depend on her ongoing capacity to care for herself and the level of frailty the scheme is able to cope with. Interagency working is vital in sheltered accommodation to ensure that people's capacity to cope is carefully monitored, so that they can be moved to a higher care environment when necessary.

Conclusion

Partnership between local authorities and the health and housing services (and other social services) has been fraught with difficulties in the past, and effective interagency working continues to be difficult to achieve. Arblaster *et al.* state that government policies such as the development of competition in public services and customer choice, reducing public expenditure, and user involvement 'are at times contradictory and together they tend to work against the achievement of effective collaboration between housing, health and social care agencies' (1996: xiv). Their work highlights the need for sufficient time and resources to be devoted to working in partnership, for better communication between agencies and service users, and for joint interagency procedures to be developed. Supporting people should help to address these issues.

The supporting people policy initiative was planned and developed over a period of five years. During this time Watson *et al.* (2003) conducted a review of the planning process and found a number of systemic problems that could inhibit effective service provision. For example, the authors found that housing, health, probation, and social services lacked agreed definitions of marginal, hard-to-reach or high-risk groups and had no clear understanding of service options. They also concluded that inherent in the programme 'there is a tension between the need to develop individual needs assessment and defined eligibility criteria on the one hand, and the policy objective of creating wider access to services and building an inclusive approach' (*ibid*: 30). There was considerable scepticism, too, about the financial capacity of supporting people budgets to develop support services to the private sector and, in particular, to potentially large numbers of owner-occupiers. At the time of writing it is too soon to evaluate whether the objectives are being met and whether these systemic problems will be overcome in the longer-term.

One of the most problematic areas for partnership working, and an area where effective partnership is essential, is in meeting the complex needs of some homeless people. Effective interagency working becomes especially difficult to achieve when the organisations involved work within geographical boundaries that are not co-terminus, and when the organisations have different objectives and ways of working with the same client group. A recent study by Carlton *et al.* (2003b) found that agencies involved in delivering services to homeless people across a sub-region did not communicate with each other well and often had competing aims and incompatible protocols for dealing with clients. Problems were compounded by different organisational cultures in each agency and by a lack of understanding of the way other agencies operate.

Both Joe and Rose were appropriately rehoused and received the support they required. This is not always the case and many people fall through the support networks, often with dire consequences. There are a number of works on interagency working that should be helpful for practitioners in this field, in particular those by Means *et al.* (1997), Arblaster *et al.* (1998), and Balloch and Taylor (2001). Although effective partnership working is difficult to achieve it is nevertheless possible given sufficient commitment and resources.

References

Arblaster L., Conway J., Foreman A. and Hawtin M. (1996) *Asking the Impossible? Interagency Working to Address the Housing, Health and Social Care Needs of People in Ordinary Housing.* Bristol: The Policy Press.

Arblaster L., Conway J., Foreman A. and Hawtin M. (1998) *Achieving the Impossible: Interagency Collaboration to Address the Housing, Health and Social Care Needs of People Able to Live in Ordinary Housing.* Bristol: The Policy Press.

Balloch S. and Taylor M. (eds) (2001) *Partnership Working; Policy and Practice.* Bristol: The Policy Press.

Brown T., Hunt R. and Yates N. (2000) *Lettings: A Question of Choice.* Coventry: Chartered Institute of Housing.

Burridge R. and Ormandy D. (eds) (1993) *Unhealthy Housing; Research, Remedies, Reform.* London: E. and F.N. Spon.

Carlton N., Heywood F., Izuhara M., Pannell J., Fear T. and Means R. (2003a) *The Harassment and Abuse of Older People in the Private Rented Sector.* Bristol: The Policy Press.

Carlton N., Ritchie J. and Harriss K. (2003b) *Cross-Boundary Issues in Homelessness Services for People with Multiple Needs.* Unpublished research report for Bristol City Council, Bath and North East Somerset Council, South Gloucestershire Council and North Somerset Council. Bristol: University of the West of England.

DETR (Department of the Environment, Transport and the Regions) (2000) *Quality and Choice: A Decent Home for All. The Housing Green Paper.* London: HMSO.

Dunn J.R. (2000) Housing and health inequalities: review and prospects for research. *Housing Studies* **15**: 341–66.

Griffiths S. (2000) *Supporting People all the Way; An Overview of the Supporting People Programme.* York: Joseph Rowntree Foundation.

Heywood F. (2001) *Money Well Spent: The Effectiveness and Value of Housing Adaptations.* Bristol: The Policy Press.

Ineichen B. (1993) *Homes and Health; How Housing and Health Interact.* London: E. and F.N. Spon.

Kearns R.A. and Smith C.J. (1993) Housing stressors and mental health among marginalised urban populations. *Area* **25**(3): 267–8.

Leather P., Mackintosh S. and Rolfe S. (1994) *Papering Over the Cracks: Housing Conditions and the Nation's Health.* London: National Housing Forum.

Lowry S. (1991) *Housing and Health.* London: British Medical Journal.

Marsh A., Gordon D., Helsop P. and Pantazis C. (2000) Housing deprivation and health: a longitudinal analysis. *Housing Studies* **15**: 411–28.

Means R., Brenton M., Harrison L. and Heywood F. (1997) *Making Partnerships Work in Community Care: A Guide for Practitioners in Housing, Health and Social Services.* Bristol: The Policy Press.

ODPM (Office of the Deputy Prime Minister) (2003) *Housing Statistics 2003.* Norwich: TSO.

ODPM (2004) *Piloting Choice-Based Lettings: An Evaluation.* Housing Research Summary No. 208. London: ODPM.

Oldman C. and Beresford B. (2000) Home, sick home: using the housing experiences of disabled children to suggest a new theoretical framework. *Housing Studies* **15**: 429–42.

Smith S.J. (1989) *Housing and Health: A Review and Research Agenda.* Discussion Paper No. 27. Glasgow: Glasgow University Centre for Housing Research.

Smith S.J., Alexander A. and Hill S. (1993) *Housing Provision for People with Health and Mobility Needs: Guide to Good Practice.* Edinburgh: The University of Edinburgh, Department of Geography.

Watson L., Tarpey M., Alexander K. and Humphreys C. (2003) *Supporting People: Real Change? Planning Housing and Support for Marginal Groups.* York: Joseph Rowntree Foundation.

CHAPTER

Medicine

Lindsay Dow and Nansi Evans

The role of medical practitioners

Most people are familiar with doctors diagnosing and treating people who develop or experience ill health as they will usually have encountered them in either general practice (primary care) or less frequently, in hospital (secondary care). Primary care accounts for 90 per cent of the work of the health service. Consultation with a doctor in adulthood becomes more common with increasing age so that 90 per cent of adults aged 80 years and over see their general practitioner (GP) at least once a year (Scottish Executive 2000). When a patient consults with a doctor about a symptom such as joint pain, the doctor tries to identify possible causes and attempts to relieve the pain. The outcomes from a consultation between a patient and doctor may be further investigations such as an X-ray and a follow up appointment to discuss the results, prescription of a drug or organisation of a non-drug treatment such as physiotherapy. The doctor may discuss other options as well such as a change of lifestyle, for example, taking up exercise or trying to lose weight. Hence a consultation includes time for explanation of the diagnosis, discussion of treatment options and negotiation as to which option would be most appropriate and, depending on the nature of the problem, this may be backed up with written information.

All doctors study for about five years before they qualify. Following their undergraduate years, they spend 12 months as a junior doctor before becoming registered with the General Medical Council. Most doctors will then choose to train for general or hospital practice. Training for general practice requires a minimum of two years hospital experience in different specialities and a year as a GP registrar after which the doctor can work as a GP. Training in a hospital speciality (for example, paediatrics or orthopaedic surgery) requires several years before the doctor would become eligible to apply to be a consultant in that speciality. Major changes are taking place with the legal regulation of the hours that doctors are allowed to work and other care health professionals, such as nurses, are now undertaking what were once the tasks of junior doctors. Training of all junior doctors is being revised so that they have closer supervision and assessment of their performance. The jobs they undertake in training will be tailored more specifically to their chosen future careers (DoH 2003). It is anticipated that these changes will improve the quality of training and help to identify strengths and weaknesses of trainees so the training programmes can better meet their needs. Training will also be geared more towards preparing the doctor for practice and one example is training in areas such as interprofessional teamworking.

GPs are traditionally self-employed, working for the National Health Service (NHS), each providing ongoing care for approximately 1800 patients registered with them. They may work alone, or more commonly in partnerships with other doctors. GPs may work from premises that they share with other members of the Primary Health Care Team including administrative staff, for example, the practice manager and clinical staff such as district nurses, health visitors, midwifes and community psychiatric nurses. In recent years, increasing numbers of GPs are opting to work as salaried employees. From April 2004, the new GP contract allows GPs to hand over night and weekend medical care to others (previously GPs had 24-hour responsibility for their patients). GPs continue to be responsible for general illnesses, chronic disease management, and non-specialist terminal care. However, they have the ability to opt out of certain services such as minor surgery and antenatal care and also have the opportunity to bid to provide more enhanced services, for example, specialised care of the homeless, minor injury services and so on. In addition, GPs are encouraged to attain certain standards based on best available evidence. These include clinical areas such as diabetes and coronary heart disease, as well as patient experiences, for example, the duration of appointments and practice organisation issues (www.bma.org.uk, www.nhsconfed.org).

The responsibilities of medical practitioners

GPs manage the medical treatment of patients who may be acutely ill and expected to recover, terminally ill, or who suffer from a chronic disease. Increasingly, GPs are expected to anticipate disease and aim for prevention by, for example, treating high blood pressure to reduce the risk of stroke. The GP may be the first point of contact for people with a wide range of needs that can be a combination of physical, psychological, social and emotional problems. They are considered gatekeepers to other services, particularly within the NHS, and have a duty to refer patients to secondary care, either as an inpatient to a ward or to a consultant outpatient clinic if more specialist care is needed. Each year, 12 per cent of the patients seen in primary care are referred for secondary care (Coulter 1998). Most GPs have facilities for taking blood and other specimens which are then transported to a hospital pathology laboratory for analysis. GPs may also have direct access to request certain hospital tests for patients to aid diagnosis, examples include chest X-rays or ultrasound scans. Where appropriate the GP can also refer to other professionals, such as physiotherapists or social workers. In some cases the GP would coordinate all aspects of care in the community setting. The referring doctor retains overall medical responsibility for the patient and must be satisfied that other professionals are appropriately qualified and professionally accountable (GMC 2001). More recently, nurses with specialist knowledge and skills in primary and in secondary care are having an increased role as gatekeepers, the most well known example being those involved in NHS Direct (BMA 2002).

The General Medical Council (GMC) publication Good Medical Practice (2001) sets out the duties and responsibilities of doctors. It states that patients are entitled to good standards of practice and care from their doctors. Essential elements include professional competence, good relationships with patients and colleagues and observance of professional and ethical obligations.

The GMC requires doctors to continue to study after qualifying in order to maintain standards. The need for life-long learning is relevant in all areas of health care since new knowledge, techniques and treatments capable of influencing health care delivery continue to emerge. Most doctors take postgraduate exams and attend educational updates to further their studies and careers. The Department of Health (DoH) has introduced appraisal for all NHS doctors which allows for regular feedback on past performance, consideration of continuing progress and the opportunity to identify educational and development needs. Consultants are appraised by two colleagues, using a structured approach drawn up by the DoH. Appraisees are required to develop a portfolio of evidence showing participation in training over the previous year. The outcomes of an appraisal process will form the development plan for the doctor for the forthcoming year and may include, for example, an intention to audit one part of the service they are involved in running. The appraisal process involves a judgement regarding whether the objectives set out in the development plan have been achieved and if not, how this can be addressed. Appraisal summaries will inform the five-year revalidation process where a decision is made as to whether the doctor is able to continue in medical practice.

Working in the NHS requires the commitment of all staff to high quality care. Quality improvement is maintained through clinical governance. Each NHS Trust and Primary Care Trust in the UK has a clinical governance system described by Scally and Donaldson as:

> a system through which NHS organisations are accountable for continually improving the quality of their services and safeguarding high standards of care by creating an environment in which excellence in clinical care will flourish.

(1998: 61)

Processes to improve and maintain high standards in patient care in line with the requirements of the new GP contract are continually being developed. For example, a group of nurses, doctors and administrative staff linked to a general practice could agree to review, with patient representatives, the care they provide to adults who have diabetes. In doing this they would:

■ identify and analyse research publications and national guidelines on standards for best care,

■ obtain feedback from patients who have diabetes regarding their experiences of the service received from staff within the practice,

■ undertake audit and risk management by reviewing the practice records to ensure the correct assessments are being carried out, focusing on the ability to identify and manage patients most at risk of developing complications from the condition, and

■ promote professional development by collecting information and providing opportunities for staff education and training in the field.

This process could be developed further if, for instance, it was carried out across a Primary Care Trust so that a larger number of practices and patients were included. Results from such a large survey could be used to produce a report for access by patients and staff and could include goals for achieving service improvements in the local population.

Interprofessional working

Multidisciplinary teams and interprofessional working are increasingly common as a means of delivering health care (Eva 2002). The doctor remains accountable for providing medical care within the team and for her or his own professional conduct. Effective communication between colleagues and respect for the skills of other professionals is important for interprofessional working.

Doctors have tended to be leaders of such teams because of their training, status and responsibilities. Traditionally doctors were male, while other health care professionals were more likely to be female. Today, doctors are just as likely to be female, the status and training of other health care professionals has been enhanced and multidisciplinary teamworking has become less hierarchical. Whoever leads the team needs to ensure that:

■ all team members understand their personal and collective responsibility for the safety of the patient, and for openly discussing and recording problems that may either relate to problems the patient may be having or the team member may be having in working with him or her,

■ patient care is coordinated and patients know whom to contact if they have concerns or queries,

■ there are regular reviews and audit of standards and performance, and

■ a system for dealing with problems in performance or conduct of team members is in place.

(GMC 2001: 14)

Working with different professionals can be especially challenging if there has been little or no opportunity for collaboration at the undergraduate stage. Each profession has a particular approach to patient care and while some overlap commonly exists in assessment processes, there may be occasions where priorities for treatment in an individual patient clash. For instance, doctors may wish to treat a patient with lung cancer in whom the chance of success is low and where the treatment has significant side effects. The patient may wish to leave the decision for treatment with the doctor. The nurses who care for the patient on a daily basis may feel the level of suffering from side-effects is so great that treatment should not continue. These differences of perspective are important and it should be recognised that nurses often hold patient comfort, dignity, lack of pain and suffering as priority values. These values are also a priority for doctors but are judged against evidence of the cancer responding to intensive treatment. Finding a best solution for the patient means that health care professionals must meet, share their views, justify treatment approaches, involve the patient and if necessary seek an independent opinion. Doctors may spend only short periods with a patient whereas nurses often have prolonged contact. As a result patients might express their concerns regarding treatment to a nurse rather than a doctor. Successful interprofessional working relies upon sharing patient concerns as well as professional perspectives, values and beliefs (Molyneux 2001, Freeman 2000).

Patients sometimes have unrealistic expectations about what can be achieved through medical interventions and it is a doctor's responsibility to maintain a high standard of medical practice and care, and show respect whatever the reason for consultation (Baker *et al.* 2003). Kennedy suggests:

> We have all been willing participants in the creation of the myth [of modern medicine]…because it seems to serve our interests to believe that illness can be vanquished.

(1981: 641)

A particular challenge for GPs is the tendency of people to seek medical solutions to problems that are not purely medical (for example, drug addiction, relationship problems and poor housing). Some have concluded that this is due to the medical profession actively colonising areas that were not previously subject to medical scrutiny (Illich 1990). Others feel that the medical profession is responding to society's demands, and political changes:

> The new government policies no longer focus on health in the familiar sense of treating illness and disease, but encourage a redefinition of health in terms of the ways in which we live our lives.

(Fitzpatrick 2001: 8)

Increasingly medical information has become more easily available through the media and via the Internet. Medical dramas on television and media coverage of advances in technology combine to generate unrealistic expectations as to what medicine can achieve.

With an ageing population, more patients have complex needs that require involvement of specialists from nursing, physiotherapy, occupational therapy, speech and language therapy, dietetics, social work and pharmacy backgrounds. When doctors work collaboratively with other health and social care professionals it is possible to provide a more integrated response to complex problems. Each health and social care professional brings different expertise and therefore working as a team they are likely to be able to provide a more appropriate response than a doctor working alone. Successful interprofessional work requires a high level of communication and willingness to listen and modify opinions. The advantages of working collaboratively when patient problems are complex include:

■ a wider range of expertise is available to inform problem solving,

■ the burden of difficult challenges can be shared,

■ tasks can be divided between those involved, and

■ team members can support and motivate one another.

An understanding of the roles of different professionals and an appreciation of the benefits to patients of interprofessional working is becoming a core curriculum component in the training of health and social care professionals.

Many patients expect consultations with their doctors to be confidential and occasionally ask that certain sensitive details are not recorded or shared with others (for example, sexually transmitted disease). Should additional health care professionals be involved in the patient's care, the doctor would explain to the patient the benefit of sharing relevant information, but cannot normally disclose such information without the patient's consent. This can cause conflict as care of the patient is the doctor's first concern and a doctor is required to work with colleagues to best serve the patient's interest (GMC 2001). It may be that the doctor feels able to withhold sensitive information from other professionals, with no detrimental effect to either patient or colleagues. If a doctor feels there is a conflict of interest, is unable to persuade the patient to allow information to be shared, and is in doubt as to how to proceed, then it is advisable to seek advice from one of the professional bodies, such as the Medical Defence Union or Medical Protection Society, which specialise in issues of law and ethics relating to medical practice. Every NHS doctor must be a member of such an organisation, which also provides medico-legal representation.

Home visits are reserved for patients who are too ill or too frail to attend the surgery. A medical assessment undertaken in a patient's home is often difficult for practical reasons (for example, poor lighting, limited equipment and so on) and is more time consuming than a surgery consultation.

CASE STUDY

Mr Gregory Fitzpatrick is an 84-year-old Caucasian who lives alone in a small rural cottage. He has asthma, and in recent weeks has become increasingly frail, has lost weight and is short of breath and wheezy. For many years he has been prescribed inhalers to use daily to control his asthma but now forgets to use them regularly. During the last week, he is waking up most nights coughing and is wheezing more on exertion. He can no longer walk to the shops half a mile away. This was his main contact with people in the village.

Mr Fitzpatrick has one son living 15 miles away who is becoming increasingly worried about his father's health and calls the GP, Dr Bernice Williams, to see if anything can be done. Bernice decides that Mr Fitzpatrick needs a medical assessment and discusses with the son whether it is possible for his father to attend the surgery.

Bernice visits Gregory at home later that day where she examines him and finds he has a chest infection exacerbating his asthma. Bernice advises admission to the local hospital for blood tests, X-ray and treatment, but Gregory declines and insists on staying at home. Bernice is concerned that he will not be able to remember the extra medication which will be needed to treat his infection and asthma, so with his consent she telephones his son to inform him of these concerns. His son contacts a neighbour who agrees to collect the prescribed antibiotics and steroid tablets for Gregory to take over the next week. Bernice also discusses with Gregory the need for input from other professionals as soon as this can be arranged and once back at the surgery telephones the social worker to request an urgent assessment for home care and other services.

At this stage the immediate priority for Bernice is to treat the acute medical problem. After this other concerns such as control of his chronic asthma and his ability to care for himself at home in the longer-term can be assessed in detail.

Bernice passes on details to the doctor on duty that night in case of deterioration and arranges to review Mr Fitzpatrick the following day at home. Bernice finds that Gregory's condition has improved and he agrees to see her at the surgery later in the week for blood tests. Bernice also requests a chest X-ray at the local hospital. The diagnosis so far has been based on the patient's history and a medical examination. The blood tests and X-ray will provide further information that will confirm the diagnosis, or point towards further problems that may be contributing, for example, anaemia, and other lung or heart disease.

Gregory makes a good recovery from his infection and his test results are normal. He realises that he needs help to look after himself but wants to maintain his independence at home. At review, Bernice is able to discuss various options with him. The social worker has already organised meals on wheels and a weekly visit to a day centre. The social worker also requested a home assessment from the occupational therapist who can provide practical advice and equipment such as bath rails, kitchen equipment and modified seating. Bernice can also organise a physiotherapist to make an assessment of Gregory's mobility. Usually older people like Gregory become less mobile when they are unwell with an acute problem and may need physiotherapy to help them move about again with safety. Recently, the government has invested substantial sums of money into provision of health care in the community so that older people can be treated in their homes and avoid coming to hospital. Bridging the gap between hospital and home is termed *intermediate care* and the occupational therapist and physiotherapist are part of an intermediate care team. Previously, provision of services to treat people in their homes was scanty and geographically variable in both quantity and quality.

QUESTION

▓ Which other professionals might the GP work with in order to meet Gregory's needs and maintain his independence?

While team meetings to review patient progress are well-established in secondary care, communication between different professionals in primary care is usually less well-structured. This is mainly due to greater numbers of patients seen in general practice, and the difficulty of getting all professionals together, as they may be based at a number of sites and have to allocate time for home visits. However, communication and referrals between professionals in primary care are documented in patient records. GPs and practice nurses use the same records and these are increasingly likely to be on a computer database. Other community staff, for example, district nurses and physiotherapists, often use different records and send copies to the GP.

Following discussion with the practice nurse who runs an asthma clinic, the doctor encourages Gregory to attend the following month. Most general practices now have clinics to monitor patients with chronic disease. The nurse will ensure that Gregory is using his inhalers correctly, and if his asthma control is not good, will liaise with Bernice. If Mr Fitzpatrick is having trouble using conventional inhalers, there are devices that can make the process easier for him.

Gregory returned to his normal self, was enjoying his visits to the day centre and walked very slowly each morning to the village shop to get his paper but three months later he became unwell again, had a fall and was found on the floor by his neighbour. Gregory agreed to be admitted to the district general hospital and was taken there by ambulance. Gregory made a steady recovery and was medically fit for discharge a week later. However, he had to stay in hospital for a further week because of shortages of home care staff and drivers for the meals on wheels service. The hospital team met prior to Gregory's discharge where they realised that Gregory could not manage at home without these vital services. Information about Gregory's level of dependence at home and the adaptations he might need had been communicated to the hospital nurses via social services.

The hospital team hold regular meetings where each patient on the ward is discussed. This is an opportunity for people to share different perspectives and plan jointly. Those attending include the consultant, junior doctor, ward manager, staff nurse, physiotherapist, occupational therapist and social worker. Depending on how things are organised, part of the time may be reserved for one or two patients to be discussed in depth and at these times, the patient and where appropriate, their carer, may be invited to join the meeting. Some professionals, for example dieticians, speech and language therapists, may only be involved with a few patients so they may not attend the meeting. By having a written record of their reports or a discussion prior to the meeting another health professional may communicate their views and feedback any decisions made.

The discussions are generally led by the nurses as they tend to have the best overview of the patient, the involvement of the family and any potential problems that need solving. One of the doctors will undertake the record keeping. Many teams are using multiprofessional records as the current system of many different uniprofessional records can be dangerous and inefficient. The absence of information in a patient's record or the oversight of a vital piece of medical information held in another part of the health record not usually seen by a doctor, could have an adverse effect for a patient and presents a very real risk.

QUESTION

■ What concerns might arise regarding the use of shared multiprofessional records?

The potential for the future

Patients have a high level of trust in doctors (Mainous *et al.* 2001) and satisfaction rates remain high (OPSR/MORI 2002). The provision of health care is becoming increasingly complex and in general, patients have better access to information with higher expectations of their doctors. Doctors have to balance their traditional professional autonomy with their involvement in interprofessional teams. This is well-developed in the palliative care setting, where there is a tradition of teamworking in the provision of care to patients with incurable diseases (Woof *et al.* 1999).

There continues to be discussion about the desirability of patient-held records to facilitate communication between professionals and to involve the patient in her or his care (Jones *et al.* 1999). This already happens in maternity care, where community midwives, GPs and hospital staff use the same set of records, usually paper, which the pregnant woman brings with her. Computer records have the potential to improve interprofessional working and to allow better information flow between primary and secondary care (Ward and Innes 2003). However this needs to be balanced with the need for confidentiality, as not all information is relevant to every professional involved with patient care. With modern technology, even with staff working from different bases, it is vital that there is one site for storing related information about a single patient so that everyone can access it and make informed decisions.

The sharing of responsibility is a key element of interprofessional working (Bliss *et al.* 2000, Freeman 2000, Gilbert *et al.* 2000). Traditionally, doctors have responsibility for the overall medical care of patients and may work alone at night and weekends when acute and difficult problems present. The primary aim of interprofessional working is a better outcome for the patient, but there are also the benefits of improved support and shared decision making for the professionals involved in what is often difficult and demanding work.

References

Baker R., Mainous A.G., Pereira Gray D.J. and Love M.M. (2003) Exploration of the relationship between continuity, trust in regular doctors and patient satisfaction with consultations with family doctors. *Scandinavian Journal of Primary Health Care* 21: 27–32.

Bliss J., Cowley S. and While A. (2000) Interprofessional working in palliative care in the community: a review of the literature. *Journal of Interprofessional Care* 14: 281–90.

BMA (British Medical Association) (2002) *The Future Healthcare Workforce: A New Model for NHS Care*. London: BMA.

Coulter A. (1998) Managing demand at the interface between primary and secondary care. *British Medical Journal* 316: 1974–6.

DoH (Department of Health) (2003) *Unfinished Business Proposals for Reform of the SHO Grade*. www.dh.gov.uk accessed August 2004.

Eva K.W. (2002) Teamwork during education: the whole is not always greater than the sum of the parts. *Medical Education* 36: 314–6.

Fitzpatrick M. (2001) *The Tyranny of Health*. London: Routledge.

Freeman M. (2000) *Interprofessional Teamwork*. IP Conference Launch Day 20 September, Parallel Session One, University of the West of England, Bristol.

GMC (General Medical Council) (2001) *Good Medical Practice* (3rd edn). London: GMC Publications.

Gilbert J.H.V., Camp R.D., Cole C.D., Bruce C., Fielding D.W. and Stanton S.J. (2000) Preparing students for interprofessional teamwork in health care. *Journal of Interprofessional Care* 14: 223–35.

Illich I. (1990) *Limits to Medicine Medical Nemesis: The Expropriation of Health*. Harmondsworth: Penguin.

Jones R., McConville J., Mason D., Macpherson L., Naven L. and McEwan J. (1999) Attitudes towards and utility of, an integrated medical-dental patient-held record in primary care. *British Journal of General Practice* 49: 368–73.

Kennedy I. (1981) *The Unmasking of Medicine*. London: Allen and Unwin.

Mainous A.G., Baker R., Love M., Pereira Gray D.J. and Gill J.M. (2001) Continuity of care and trust in one's physician: evidence from primary care in US and UK. *Family Medicine* 33: 22–7.

Molyneux J. (2001) Interprofessional teamworking: what makes teams work well? *Journal of Interprofessional Care* 15: 29–35.

OPSR/MORI (Office of Public Services Research, MORI) (2002) *Monitoring satisfaction trends from 1998–2002*. London: Cabinet Office.

Scally G. and Donaldson L.J. (1998) Looking forward: clinical governance and the drive for quality improvement in the new NHS. *British Medical Journal* 317: 61–5.

Scottish Executive (2000) *Our National Health: A Plan for Action, A Plan for Change*. www.gmc.uk.org accessed October 2003.

Ward L. and Innes M. (2003) Electronic medical summaries in general practice – considering the patient's contribution. *British Journal of General Practice* 53: 293–7.

Woof R., Carter Y. and Faull C. (1999) Palliative care: the team, the services and the need for care. In Faull C., Carter Y. and Woof R. (eds) *Handbook of Palliative Care*. Oxford: Blackwell.

www.bma.org.uk New GMS Contract 2003.

www.nhsconfed.org.

CHAPTER

Midwifery

Sue Davis and Rosemary Greenwood

Introduction

The role of the midwife is complex, diverse and privileged. Midwife means *with woman* (Davies and Wickham 2000) and in the United Kingdom (UK) it is a legal title conferred only on those whose names appear on the Nursing and Midwifery Council (NMC) register of midwives. Midwives, who may be female or male, provide care for women during pregnancy, during childbirth and in the postnatal period; care which extends to other members of the woman's family. This chapter outlines the role of the midwife and illustrates some aspects of interprofessional midwifery practice.

The role and function of the midwife

Reference to the activities of midwives can be found in the accounts of daily life in the ancient Greek world (Tower and Bramall 1986) but the legal status of the midwife in the UK dates back only to the 1902 Midwives Act. To qualify as a midwife it is necessary to undertake an approved educational programme. Direct entry students must complete a three-year programme while a shorter 18-month course is available to those already qualified in adult nursing. Midwives require a detailed knowledge of biological, psychological, social and spiritual aspects of pregnancy and childbirth. Some midwives have developed specialist roles in practice but all midwives act as educator, advisor and provider of information for women and their families in order to help them make informed choices during pregnancy, labour and in the postnatal period. Midwives may also be involved in preconception care and preparation for parenthood. They may be employed within the NHS, the private sector or work independently in a self-employed capacity.

A midwife is defined as:

> a person who, having been regularly admitted to a midwifery educational programme, duly recognised in the country in which it is located, has successfully completed the prescribed course of studies in midwifery and has acquired the requisite qualifications to be registered and/or legally licensed to practice midwifery. She must be able to give the necessary supervision, care and advice to women during pregnancy, labour and the postpartum period, to conduct deliveries on her own responsibility and to care for the newborn and the infant. This care includes preventative measures, the detection of abnormal conditions in mother and child, the procurement of medical assistance and the execution of emergency measures in the absences of medical help. She has an important task in health counselling and education, not only for women, but also within the family and community. The work should involve antenatal education and preparation for parenthood and extends to certain areas of gynaecology, family planning and child care. She may practice in hospital, clinics, health units, domiciliary conditions or in any other service.
>
> (UKCC 1998a: 25)

Midwives practice in a range of settings and are trained to deliver effective care both in situations where pregnancy proceeds without complications and in situations where a pregnancy deviates from the normal.

Most women will experience a normal delivery supported by a midwife, providing effective midwifery practice. Some women will have, or will develop, factors that put their health and the health of the fetus at risk and the midwife plays a vital role in identifying potential risk factors. The ability to recognise deviations from what is understood as a normal pregnancy, and to act in appropriate ways following that recognition, are essential aspects of midwifery practice. Examples of such situations might include the detection of a breech presentation following abdominal palpation at 37 weeks gestation or the identification of abnormally high blood pressure in the pregnant woman.

A woman's experience of each pregnancy is unique and midwives use their professional judgement to ensure that each woman receives the midwifery care she requires. The midwife takes cognisance of the physical, social, spiritual and psychological needs of the woman as well as observing and assessing maternal and fetal health. Assessment involves, for example, determining pre-existing illness or risk factors, such as a family history of genetic disorders, or being involved in the monitoring of accepted normal parameters for fetal growth and development through abdominal palpation or ultrasonography. Assessment of the woman's needs includes providing an opportunity for her to express her individual priorities and wishes in relation to pregnancy and childbirth, and to make sure that care is tailored to meet those needs without compromising the well-being of the fetus.

Midwives remain alert to the possibility that a woman may be subject to physical and/or psychological abuse from her partner. In such an instance the midwife may become a confidante working collaboratively with the woman and with other professionals in the attempt to ensure the safety of both mother and unborn child.

Effective communication skills are essential if midwives are to assess, plan, implement and evaluate care appropriate to both the needs and wishes of the woman. The 1976 Congenital Disabilities Act makes it a legal requirement that all records of care provided by a midwife be kept for at least 25 years and the responsibility to keep accurate records is one of the Midwives Rules set by the statutory body responsible for regulating midwifery practice (UKCC 1998a).

Although autonomous practitioners, midwives must work collaboratively with other professionals. At different times midwives will work with, amongst others, health visitors, social workers, physiotherapists, occupational therapists, general practitioners, obstetricians, paediatricians and neonatal nurses. Midwives will generally work with either doctors or other midwives in meeting the health care needs of a woman experiencing a normal pregnancy and delivery. The midwife is never usually in a position to relinquish care of a mother and baby except to another midwife or registered medical practitioner when the individual case demands it. For example, where there is an emergency or where there is a deviation from a normal pregnancy or labour, a midwife is obliged under the Midwives Rules (UKCC 1998b) to seek the assistance of a doctor or other qualified health care professional with the expertise to provide the necessary care.

A government all-party report (DoH 1993a) emphasised the need for an increase in midwifery-led care, continuity in the midwifery carer, and improved choice for women. The report also indicated a need for more community midwifery care in response to calls for a return to a less medicalised maternity service and in response to a move towards a principle of woman-centred care. Henley-Einion (2003) suggests that while the aims may not have been achieved, the report did highlight the often limited choices available to women in different care settings.

Midwives work in different settings and the Midwifery Rules permit midwives to work as independent private practitioners (NMC 2004). Women may choose a midwife employed by a hospital trust, a midwife employed by a primary health care trust, an independent midwife, or an obstetrician to assist at the birth. This choice is facilitated by the different patterns of midwifery care on offer. It should be noted that the list below is neither definitive nor exhaustive and not all patterns will be available to all women as local arrangements of midwifery services differ. The main patterns of midwifery care are outlined below.

- Domiciliary in and out (DOMINO) delivery involves a community midwife or a team of community midwives providing midwifery care throughout a woman's pregnancy, delivery and in the initial postnatal period. A member of the community midwifery team or the individual midwife will provide antenatal care in the woman's home or in a community clinic, accompany the woman and her partner into hospital to deliver the baby and continue the care when mother and baby return home (usually after six hours or following an overnight stay). This is considered midwifery-led care as identified in the Changing Childbirth recommendations (DoH 1993b).

■ Consultant care encompasses collaboration between midwives and obstetricians in the provision of care during the antenatal, delivery and immediate postnatal periods. This pattern of care is often used when the woman has a risk factor (such as diabetes) identified during her pregnancy. In this instance an obstetric consultant is identified as the lead professional.

■ Shared care is collaborative care provided by the midwife and the general practitioner during the antenatal, the birth and the postnatal period.

■ Independent care involves a midwife providing care for the mother throughout pregnancy, labour and in the postnatal period at home or in a birth centre.

All midwives, whether employed or independent, remain professionally accountable to a supervisor of midwives. The role of a supervisor of midwives developed as a result of the 1902 Midwifery Act, which required the appointment of inspectors to monitor practice as a means of maintaining standards and preventing poor quality midwifery care. These inspectors were not midwives but were more likely to be environmental health officers. Subsequent midwifery acts established systems for the licensing of midwives and the Central Midwives Board came into being in 1936 remaining until 1972 when the United Kingdom Central Council for Nurses, Midwives and Health Visitors took over the statutory responsibilities for midwifery practice (Kirham 1995). In 1936 an amendment to the 1902 Midwifery Act enabled the Central Midwives Board to set the rules by which midwives trained and worked. These rules required that supervisors were either medical practitioners (obstetricians) or experienced domiciliary midwives, although they had no role in hospitals until 1942 as most midwives at this time worked in the community health setting. It should be remembered that home births were the norm until the inception of the NHS in 1948 when free access to doctors became available at the point of need. By 1977 all supervisors of midwives were required to be practising midwives thus ending the influence of obstetricians on midwives practice. In 1993 a stipulation was introduced to the Midwives Rules that midwives should undertake a prescribed programme of preparation to be a supervisor. To be considered to take on the role of supervisor midwives must have a minimum of three years midwifery experience, one year of which must have been within the previous two years. To become a supervisor of midwives one can either nominate oneself or be nominated by a peer. A three-month distance learning preparatory course must be completed, preferably before starting as a supervisor of midwives, but in any case within one year of appointment, and this is followed by the requirement to complete 15 hours of study every three years. This helps midwives maintain competence as part of the aims of protecting the public and supporting midwives in practice. Following the National Health Service Reform and Health Care

Professionals Act (DoH 2002) the responsibility for standards of care now lies with the Nursing and Midwifery Council (NMC) which established local supervising authorities to provide support for supervisors of midwives. The NMC supports the concept of midwives working in partnership with women to respect the wishes, and meet the needs, of individual women and their families as part of a comprehensive midwifery service.

The White Paper entitled Saving Lives: Our Healthier Nation (DoH 1999) highlights the need for partnership working between individuals and organisations and the fictitious case study that follows outlines some aspects of the interprofessional working of midwives.

CASE STUDY: CHLOE

Chloe is a 15-year-old black girl living at home with her parents and sister. She attends the local comprehensive school and has an active sexual relationship with her boyfriend. Because she had not had a period for three months Chloe used a pregnancy testing kit obtained from a pharmacy to see if she was pregnant. The result of the test was positive and Chloe calculated that she was about 14 weeks pregnant.

QUESTION

■ What professionals might Chloe consult for support and advice?

Even though young women are more likely to tell their parents of their pregnancy than they are to consult a health care professional, they are often apprehensive and consequently delay informing parents (Birch 1989). Allen *et al.* (1998) suggest 75 per cent of patients under the age of 16, and 50 per cent of those between 16–19 feared their GP could not, or would not, preserve confidentiality regarding requests for contraceptive services. Many pregnancies in this age group are concealed (Allen 2003) and concerns regarding confidentiality may be a factor in explaining why a proportion of teenage pregnancies get to 20 weeks, or more, before a health professional is consulted.

Chloe could obtain support and advice from a number of different professionals including, a school nurse, a midwife, a health visitor, a general practitioner (GP), or she could confide in support workers in a voluntary organisation such as the Pregnancy Advisory Service. When she does meet with a midwife it is essential that Chloe be assured of the confidential nature of the relationship between midwife and pregnant woman.

CASE STUDY continued

Chloe informs her mother of the pregnancy and together they consult their GP who, after an initial assessment refers Chloe to Rosanna, the community midwife.

The first antenatal contact a woman has with a midwife is known as a booking visit, an historical term from the time when it was customary to book the place of confinement. Chloe's booking visit may take place in her home or in a local health centre. Chloe may wish to be accompanied by her mother, another family member, or a friend. The aim of the visit is to enable Rosanna (the midwife) to start to develop a relationship with Chloe and her family (DoH 1993a). Rosanna will begin to assess Chloe's physical health, and her psychological and social needs, and will use the opportunity to talk to Chloe about lifestyle issues that could affect the pregnancy. Issues such as smoking, drug and alcohol use, and diet can all have an impact on pregnancy and Rosanna will use this time to encourage Chloe to think about changes she might want to make to her lifestyle (Crafter 1997). Should she decide to make lifestyle changes Rosanna will be able to work with Chloe and use her knowledge of local services to enable Chloe to make the identified changes become a reality. Rosanna will also ask Chloe about her past medical history. This will help her in identifying actual or potential risk factors relevant to Chloe's pregnancy. Rosanna will record Chloe's blood pressure to establish a baseline for future comparison. This will assist in the process of monitoring the pregnancy and aid the early detection of changes that might be indicative of potential problems associated with the pregnancy. Chloe's weight and height may be recorded and blood will be taken to screen for anaemia, rubella immunity, Hepatitis B, HIV and syphilis. Urine will be tested for glucose, protein, blood and a pH level.

The booking visit also provides an opportunity for Rosanna to talk to Chloe about antenatal screening for abnormalities (NHS 2003). Antenatal screening can only occur with the consent of the woman. Although Chloe is not yet 16 (that is, younger than the legal age for giving consent) she can give consent for screening tests if she is sufficiently competent to understand what is involved and what the implications might be. Rosanna, using the Fraser guidelines, determines such competence. The Fraser guidelines were produced as a result of the historic ruling of Lord Fraser in the case of Gillick vs West Norfolk and Wisbech Area Health Authority (1985), and are often referred to as Gillick competence. Lord Fraser's ruling effectively allows professional discretion in determining the competence or otherwise of a person younger than 16 to make a decision related to their health care. Nevertheless, there is an assumption that health care professionals will try to convince Chloe to inform her parents, and will only proceed with screening tests without her parents' knowledge if Chloe refuses to tell them, or if she refuses to allow a health care professional to tell her parents. The results of screening tests for Down's Syndrome and HIV may lead to other, more difficult decisions which may have an adverse effect on Chloe's physical or psychological health.

If Chloe is undecided about continuing with her pregnancy the booking visit may provide an opportunity for Chloe to talk to Rosanna about her options. Using her counselling role, Rosanna may be able to help Chloe make a decision or she may believe it is best for Chloe to receive further information and counselling with a specialist screening counsellor.

CASE STUDY continued

As part of the booking visit a pregnancy care plan is discussed with Chloe and she is referred to the obstetric team for consultation at a local maternity hospital of her choice. This will influence the pattern of care Chloe receives and, because of her age, it is quite likely to be shared between the obstetric consultant and Rosanna.

Rosanna helps Chloe to construct a personalised birth plan that will enable her to feel she has control over the delivery of her baby. The birth plan is a record of Chloe's choices and decisions about how she wishes childbirth to proceed and will include statements about pain relief, positions to be adopted in labour and interventions such as an episiotomy. Such decisions are based upon discussion between Rosanna and Chloe regarding her options in relation to childbirth. Rosanna is able to draw on her knowledge and expertise to assist Chloe by explaining the advantages and disadvantages of different options. The birth plan will also note who Chloe wishes to support her during labour. This might be, amongst others, her partner, her mother or a friend, or she may wish to have all 3 present. The birth plan forms a component of Chloe's client-held records and this means the professionals who attend her delivery will have access to a record of her expressed wishes.

Rosanna has regular contact with Chloe in order to monitor the progress of the pregnancy and to assess the health of both Chloe and fetus. The patterns of visits are negotiated with Chloe (National Collaborating Centre for Women's and Children's Health 2003) and depend upon a number of factors including Chloe's needs and the general progress of the pregnancy. The higher the level of risk the greater the frequency of visits from Rosanna. Because of her young age, Rosanna identifies Chloe as a vulnerable teenager and notifies social services. Chloe is allocated a named social worker, Anna, who assesses her needs and, amongst other things, gives financial advice to the family. Rosanna and Anna work collaboratively to support Chloe throughout her pregnancy and after the birth.

As part of collaborative working the midwife has a responsibility to liase with, and inform the local health visitor of Chloe's pregnancy as the health visitor may wish to make a home visit when Chloe is 34 weeks pregnant as a means to ensuring that, when the midwife's professional contact with Chloe comes to an end, the health visitor will be in a position to continue support for Chloe. Under normal circumstances the woman and her baby will be discharged from midwifery care between ten and 28 days after birth but in some cases the midwife will continue to be involved and work in partnership with the health visitor. Jennie (the health visitor) has a responsibility to monitor the progress and well-being of infants from 14 days until five years.

Although premature labour is more common in women of Chloe's age than in older women (SEU 1999), Chloe's pregnancy continued to full term.

CASE STUDY continued

Chloe has a normal delivery in hospital attended by Rosanna. Chloe decided to breast feed her baby and although she was accomplishing this well initially, once discharged home she experiences some difficulty and decides to formula feed her baby.

Chloe has developed a close relationship with Rosanna and needs the opportunity to build a good working relationship with Jennie, her health visitor. Rosanna and Jennie discuss how they can work together to support Chloe. They decide to visit Chloe together in order to assess her needs, discuss options and agree an action plan with Chloe. In order to facilitate a smooth transition from one professional to another, it is agreed that Rosanna and Jennie will visit on alternate days. Rosanna and Jennie communicate with one another to ensure that they are consistent in the advice they give to Chloe. In addition to offering practical help with feeding, both the midwife and health visitor are able to give information and advice on general health issues for Chloe and her family, and specific information on child health. Liaison with Anna, Chloe's social worker would also continue to ensure support is available for the family.

The Social Exclusion Unit (SEU) Report on teenage pregnancy (1999) highlighted the need for health professionals to work with young mothers under the age of 16 to enable them to return to school. Chloe, like all other 15-year-old girls, is required by law to complete her full-time education [editors' note: for more information on education see Chapter 3] and the midwife is ideally placed to work with the health visitor to assist Chloe to begin to plan for a return to school. The local education authority (LEA) has an obligation to ensure that educational provision does not exclude Chloe. Financial assistance is available for Chloe to help with child-care costs involved with a return to school and LEAs provide an educational support service through a wider community education service either at home or within school. Some LEAs have developed teenage pregnancy units with childcare provision to enable teenagers to continue their education. The number of units has been increased as a result of the Sure Start programme and each will normally have Connexions personal adviser, social work, health visitor, youth work and midwifery services attached. Midwives might offer, for example, parent education sessions to teenagers within the units. While such units offer facilities attractive to some pregnant teenagers and teenage mothers, others find the units isolate them from their peers. Those who decide to return to their original school may have difficulty in adjusting.

The midwife's role encompasses all aspects of pregnancy and childbirth and, whereas it is possible for a midwife to work in isolation, women's expectations and the continued existence of vulnerable groups makes it imperative that midwives develop their potential to work interprofessionally with a range of professionals who might provide support to pregnant women and new mothers. The case of Chloe provides an example whereby midwives can work collaboratively to support a young girl through pregnancy into motherhood.

References

Allen I., Dowling S.B. and Rolfe J. (1998) *Teenage Mothers Decisions and Outcomes*. London: Policy Studies Institute.

Allen E.J. (2003) Aims and associations of reducing teenage pregnancy. *British Journal of Midwifery* 11: 366–9.

Birch D. (1989) School girl mothers. In Studd J. (ed.) *Progress in Obstetrics and Gynaecology: Vol 7*. Edinburgh: Churchchill Livingstone, pp. 75–90.

Crafter H. (1997) *Health Promotion in Midwifery*. London: Arnold.

Davies L. and Wickham S. (2000) The concept of 'Care' in midwifery practice. *Midwifery Matters* 85: 8–9.

DoH (Department of Health) (1993a) *Changing Childbirth. The Report of the Expert Maternity Group*. London: HMSO.

DoH (1993b) *Changing Childbirth. Part 2 Survey of Good Communication Practice in Maternity Services*. London: HMSO.

DoH (1999) *Saving Lives: Our Healthier Nation*. London: The Stationery Office.

DoH (2002) *National Health Service Reform and Health Care Professionals Act*. London: The Stationery Office.

Gillick vs West Norfolk and Wisbech Area Health Authority (1985). All E R402.

Henley-Einion A. (2003) The medicalisation of childbirth. In Squire C. (ed.) *The Social Context of Birth*. Oxford: Radcliffe Medical Press, pp. 173–85.

Kirham M. (1995) The history of midwifery supervision. In Kirham M. (ed.) *Super-Vision Recommendations of the Consensus Conference of Midwifery Supervision*. London: Books for Midwives, pp. 1–14.

National Collaborating Centre for Women's and Children's Health (2003) *Antenatal Care – Routine Care for the Healthy Pregnant Woman – Clinical Guidelines*. London: RCOG (Royal College of Obstetricians and Gynecologists) Press.

NHS (National Health Service) (2003) *Antenatal Care Routine Care for the Health of Pregnant Women*. Clinical guideline 6. National Institute for Clinical Excellence.

Nursing and Midwifery Council (NMC) (2004) Midwives rules and standards: Standards 05-04. London: NMC.

SEU (Social Exclusion Unit) (1999) *Teenage Pregnancy: A Report*. London: HMSO.

Tower and Bramall (1986) *Midwives in History and Society*. Beckenham: Croom Helm.

UKCC (United Kingdom Central Council) (1998a) *Midwives Rules and Code of Practice*. London: UKCC.

UKCC (1998b) *Nurses, Midwives and Health Visitors (Midwives Amendment) Rules*. London: HMSO.

CHAPTER

Nursing

Derek Sellman, Matthew Godsell and Mervyn Townley

Introduction

In the United Kingdom (UK) the title registered nurse can be used only by someone whose name is currently on the national register of nurses held by the Nursing and Midwifery Council (NMC). There are four traditionally recognised disciplines within nursing: adult nursing, children's nursing, learning disabilities nursing, and mental health nursing. Each of the four nursing disciplines claims a particular specialist area of practice and at present each has its own separate section of the NMC register.

Students of nursing undertake a three-year full-time (or equivalent) course of study in preparation for registration and subsequent practice as a nurse. The three-year course comprises 2300 hours of practice and 2300 hours of theory. The first year of the course is known as a common foundation programme (CFP) where students of all four nursing disciplines pursue a common curriculum. Successful completion of the NMC-specified competencies for the CFP enables a student to begin a discipline-specific programme. The student who successfully completes the three-year course will obtain an academic as well as a professional qualification. While nursing courses are undertaken within higher education institutions most nurses study for a diploma although there is some degree level provision. Following qualification a nurse can register with the NMC and it is a professional requirement that nurses continue to develop their knowledge and skills; a requirement that is part of continuing professional development linked to registration to practice which must be renewed every three years.

At the point of registration a nurse becomes accountable for her or his own practice. The nature of this professional accountability has been a debate of some significance since at least the 1980s and reflects what some consider to be an emerging sophistication in nurses' perceptions of themselves as autonomous and professional care givers. Nurses have struggled to define both the nature of nursing and what it is to be a nurse and as a consequence there are a number of competing theoretical positions within the literature. Thus while many believe nursing to be a matter of common knowledge it remains the case that the supposed common knowledge has continued to defy articulation. This is to say that while everybody thinks they know what nurses do nobody has yet been able to capture nursing in a formal universally acceptable definition.

This is partly because there is so much variation in what nurses do in providing care that spans the full range between the emotional and the social as well as the physical. In addition to the four different disciplines of nursing there are numerous nursing roles including: research nurses, school nurses, community nurses, consultant nurses, nurse teachers, public health nurses, nurse managers, infection control nurses, chemotherapy nurses, and so on. What each of these types of nurses actually do can be so different that it is difficult to encapsulate a single idea of the nurse.

A commonly expressed view is that doctors cure while nurses care. While caring is often considered to be a central concept of nursing the idea that nursing is caring is as simplistic as the idea that doctoring is curing. Nevertheless a number of nurse scholars have attempted to develop an account of *nursing as caring* and while this is superficially attractive it becomes problematic because the concept of caring appears to be as difficult to articulate as the concept of nursing.

One commonly cited definition of nursing is as follows:

> The unique function of the nurse is to assist the individual, sick or well, in the performance of those activities contributing to health or its recovery (or to a peaceful death) that he would perform unaided if he had the necessary strength, will or knowledge. And to do this in such a way as to help him gain independence as rapidly as possible.
>
> (Henderson 1966: 15)

A more recent definition is that nursing is:

> The use of clinical judgement in the provision of care to enable people to improve, maintain, or recover health, to cope with health problems, and to achieve the best possible quality of life, whatever their disease or disability, until death.
>
> (RCN 2003: 3)

These two definitions span a period of nearly 40 years and the fact that efforts continue to be expended on the attempt to define nursing indicates the complexity of the task. It is not the purpose of this chapter to attempt a definition of nursing nor to provide a definitive account of what nurses do. Rather the aim is to provide a snapshot of some professional nursing activity using two scenarios, both of which incorporate some elements of interprofessional working.

Whilst it is true that nursing is a universal activity performed by trained and untrained individuals in both voluntary and paid capacities, this chapter is concerned with the work of professional nurses working in the UK at the beginning of the 21st century. It should be recognised that the work of nurses is not exclusive to registered nurses; many others provide nursing care within and outside of the formal organisation of care delivery. In hospital and community settings nursing may be given by health care assistants (albeit under the supervision of registered nurses) who may have undertaken some training and education. But a great deal of nursing care is provided on a voluntary basis by friends, family, and others in the community. The importance of the role of these carers and the significance of their contribution to health and social care should not be underestimated.

In addition, the boundaries that separate the four disciplines of nursing are not always easy to distinguish. Patients, after all, do not necessarily fit neatly into one of the four categories. Both adults and children may have learning disabilities and/or suffer mental health difficulties as well as a requirement for nursing care for physical illnesses or the promotion of positive health.

It should be pointed out that amongst nurses there is a healthy debate about the proper term that should be used to describe those who are in receipt of professional nursing. Nurses who work in acute areas of practice, particularly within hospital settings, tend to use the term patient, those working with people with learning disabilities tend to consider service user to be the appropriate term, clients is the term often employed by mental health nurses, and children appears to be the preferred term of children's nurses. It is sometimes claimed that the term patient indicates a passive role, while some say the term client suggests a partnership; others claim service user is more egalitarian. In the nursing literature it is not unusual to see the phrase patient or client, or patient/client. Such language can be cumbersome and confusing. For this reason patient, client, and service user will be used as interchangeable terms throughout this chapter implying nothing more than a word to represent someone receiving nursing care.

To outline some of the complexities of nursing the chapter is in two sections. In section one the case of a man with moderate learning disabilities who has suffered a heart attack offers an insight into the roles of both adult and learning disabilities nurses. Section two outlines the child and adolescent mental health services (CAMHS) using the case of Theresa to illustrate some aspects of the work of both children's and mental health nurses.

Section 1: Adult and learning disabilities nursing

CASE STUDY 1: FRANK BURTON

Frank Burton has been transferred from a coronary care unit following an acute myocardial infarction (heart attack). He is a 45-year-old white male with moderate learning disabilities. Frank appears to understand the content of most ordinary conversations but cannot comprehend much of the information he has been given about his heart condition. His ability to articulate thoughts, feelings, and ideas is limited. He has had some difficulty adjusting to being in hospital although he clearly enjoys aspects of the ward routine including the company of the other men and watching television. When the food trolley arrives Frank wants to try all items from the menu and gets upset when told the meals have been ordered for other people. On occasions he appears to be suspicious of the staff and has been reluctant to let some of the doctors and nurses carry out routine procedures.

Since his father's death two years ago, his mother has been his sole carer. Frank has had minimal contact with the health and social care services. He has not required support with any of the basic activities of daily living. He is continent, ambulant, and can wash and dress himself – although his mother does all of the washing and cooking at home. She admits they have got into a routine that has encouraged Frank to rely on her instead of learning to do things for himself. While her husband was alive he had insisted Frank should live at home but Mrs Burton is not happy with things as they are. She has asked the nursing staff if there is anything they can do to help.

Nursing care for Frank

Care and treatment for people who suffer a heart attack is well-established (NICE 2001). Throughout his stay in hospital Frank's nursing care will be based on a protocol for cardiac rehabilitation adapted to his own particular needs. While in the coronary care unit an assessment of Frank's nursing requirements led to the formulation of a nursing care plan. This care plan will be reviewed in the light of Frank's changing needs now that he has been transferred to the medical ward but the main features of his nursing care will continue to revolve around the protocol. It is particularly important for the nurses to monitor Frank's haemodynamic status by recording his blood pressure and pulse, and by observing the electrical activity of his heart (he may continue to be attached to a cardiac monitor and will have a 12-lead electrocardiogram (ECG) recorded regularly). These observations provide an indication of his cardiac recovery and help to determine the most appropriate stage of his rehabilitation. The nurses will also aim to ensure Frank remains pain free and can breath easily so that he can undertake the recommended amount of physical activity. Typically, patients remain in bed for the first 24 hours following a heart attack and then slowly build up their levels of activity so that after four or five days of uncomplicated recovery they will be able to walk around the ward. Since his admission Frank has found it difficult to remember what he is allowed to do and the nurses have often had to remind him not to do too much.

A further essential feature of cardiac rehabilitation is the need to help people recognise how to avoid further cardiac problems. Part of the nursing care plan is to help Frank understand what has happened to him and the benefits associated with adopting a healthy lifestyle and diet.

David, Frank's primary ward nurse, has explained these aspects of the protocol to Ishani, a student nurse who is in the second week of her allocation to the ward. Ishani has recently had a series of lectures about the role of the nurse in health promotion and knows that if she is going to be effective in promoting a healthy lifestyle she needs to be able to provide accurate information to Frank in a form that he will understand. She notes the nursing record shows Frank has difficulty understanding and remembering new information. David has already told her that on this ward they use a standard approach to health promotion that involves providing written information and then checking patients understand which lifestyle changes will reduce the likelihood of further heart attacks. Ishani recognises this standard approach will need to be adapted to take account of Frank's learning disabilities and discusses her ideas with David.

The nursing team recognises the need to work with Frank and his mother to develop an individual care plan that will create opportunities for establishing long-term strategies designed both to promote Frank's recovery and to reduce the risk of further heart attacks. Cardiac rehabilitation starts on admission, proceeds throughout a hospital stay and continues after transfer to the community. A successful plan will require contributions from a number of different health and social care professionals working collaboratively during his rehabilitation. Suggestions for improving Frank's care include making information about heart attacks and risk factors easier for him to understand, encouraging him to do more things for himself (including looking after his own personal hygiene needs), and creating links with other professionals who can provide ongoing support for him in the community. Ishani thinks that it should be possible to ask the speech and language therapist to undertake a communication assessment that would help in devising effective communication strategies.

QUESTIONS

- Which professionals would the nurse need to work collaboratively with in order to meet Frank's needs?

- Which professionals are likely to be involved in Frank's care when he has been discharged?

- Will all Frank's care be delivered by professionals?

- What are *informal carers* and how might they contribute to Frank's care?

- Will everyone understand an *individual care plan* or *person centred planning*?

- Do professionals share the same models and concepts for example, holism, activities of living?

■ Is communication the most important issue?

■ If Frank has not been able to contribute to the discussion so far how will the team find out about his views?

■ Who would be the best person to represent him and why?

■ How would you ensure effective communication with Frank?

■ How would you ensure effective communication with other groups of professionals and carers?

Ishani believes that effective communication is vital if Frank is to be able to understand both what has happened to him and why a healthy lifestyle would help him to reduce the risk of further heart attacks. Although Frank does not always respond to questions he does respond to facial expressions, gestures, paralanguage, the tone of other peoples' voices and touch. The nursing team believes that concentration on nonverbal as well as verbal techniques will encourage Frank to trust them and increase the likelihood that he will work with them in implementing the plan for his recovery. Some team members believe it pointless to describe everyday aspects of communication as part of a strategy designated as an individual care plan. Other members of the team think it appropriate to specify the detail of the communication strategies to be used to improve their relationship with Frank. The team recognises the importance of including Mrs Burton in the decision making process wherever possible. They are aware that she is the person who knows him best, that she is capable of explaining some things to him when they cannot, and that she is the most appropriate person to represent his likes and dislikes on those occasions when Frank cannot articulate them for himself. Bollard has stated:

> People with learning disabilities often rely on a carer to explain their health needs.
> Developing relationships with the person who has learning disabilities and the carer
> is likely to be crucial to the successful adoption of a health promotion approach.
>
> (2002: 6)

The ward nursing team works in collaboration with doctors, the cardiac rehabilitation nurse, an occupational therapist, a physiotherapist and a dietician in order to meet Frank's needs. David contacts the primary health care services on behalf of the interprofessional team hoping to find a community learning disability nurse willing to work with the hospital team to develop a plan of care to meet Frank's needs both in hospital and when he returns home. David was informed that people with learning disabilities have been encouraged to use ordinary rather than specialised services wherever possible. The document Valuing People states:

> Because mainstream health services have been slow in developing the capacity
> and skills to meet the needs of people with learning disabilities, some NHS

specialist learning disability services have sought to provide all encompassing services of their own. As a result the wider NHS has failed to consider the needs of people with learning disabilities. This is the most important issue that the NHS needs to address for people with learning disabilities.

(DoH 2001a: 60)

When talking to the primary health care services David found clarifying the resources available for Frank more difficult than anticipated because health practitioners who have infrequent contact with people with learning disabilities knew little about the document Valuing People or the Government's proposals for improving services for people with learning disabilities. Frank had little contact with his general practitioner (GP) prior to his heart attack and it was suggested the GP would need to assume a more significant role when Frank was discharged from hospital. David was advised to visit the Department of Health web site (www.dh.gov.uk/Home) and look at some of the information on health action plans and health facilitation.

A health action plan for people with learning disabilities is designed to provide details of 'the need for health interventions, oral health and dental care, fitness and mobility, continence, vision, hearing, nutrition and emotional needs as well as details of any medication taken, side effects, and records of any screening tests' (DoH 2001a: 64). The plan should be reviewed at different stages in a person's life. Guidance from the Department of Health suggests that it will be good practice to offer a review of a plan when there have been changes in an individual's health status (for example, as a result of inpatient treatment), or when planning a transition for those living with older family carers. A health facilitator (who may be any health or social care worker) will work with GPs and others in the primary care team to identify patients with learning disabilities. They will also need to make collaborative links with colleagues from social services and education as appropriate. The task of the health facilitator is to ensure that people with learning disabilities get access to the health care they need from primary and secondary NHS services (DoH 2001a).

Jukes believes that health facilitators 'need to demonstrate strong leadership qualities and management of change qualities across the boundaries of health and social care' (2002: 694). Valuing People notes that community learning disability nurses are 'well placed' (DoH 2001a: 63) to fulfil the role of health facilitators. Similarly the document Nothing About Us Without Us calls for 'the role and value of community nurses to be built upon' (DoH 2001b: 20). Additional guidance produced by the Department of Health encourages service users to believe other practitioners will be prepared to respond to their needs:

- Talk to your doctor, nurse or another health worker. Ask them to help you start making a Health Action Plan (DoH 2001c: 4).

- Make an appointment to see a health worker you know and trust. This might be a doctor, nurse, or someone else who helps you with your health (DoH 2001c: 5).

David is pleased he has found this information but is feeling frustrated because it tells him what might happen or should happen but it does not provide clear guidance about what to do if Frank does not have a health action plan or a named health facilitator. All of the information he has gathered points to the significance of the contribution from the health facilitator but David suspects that this role has been constructed to address deficiencies in current services. None of it tells him what to do next. It seems as if everyone is waiting or expecting changes to occur but it is difficult to see who is responsible for making things happen. When he began he had hoped to be able to find somebody that could work with the team to improve Frank's care while he is in hospital, and provide ongoing support and guidance through rehabilitation and discharge.

QUESTIONS

■ Identify some of the factors that might explain why Frank had little contact with his GP or other health workers before his heart attack.

■ Why are some groups more likely to be marginalised or excluded from health care than others and what are the consequences of exclusion?

■ How do professional and regulatory bodies monitor the currency of practitioners' knowledge and skills?

■ Do you think all of the practitioners involved in Frank's care will have received some education or training on meeting the needs of people with learning disabilities?

■ Do all of the practitioners need to have input on learning disabilities or is specialised knowledge unnecessary because the care and treatment that Frank requires is no different from the care and treatment that any other person would require?

■ What should David do next?

Section 2: Child and adolescent mental health services

This section provides an outline of the role of nurses who work in the child and adolescent mental health services (CAMHS). Throughout the UK CAMHS is organised in different ways as a result of both local service development and reorganisation attempts to offer a coherent service in any given region. The Health Advisory Service Report (HAS 1995) describes CAMHS as a four-tiered system of care (see Figure 7.1).

At tier one (which is considered as part of the primary care services) a range of nurses may be involved in the promotion of mental health for children. Most of the work at this stage is likely to be health promotion or simple strategies that do not require specialist training in children's mental health. By way of an example, school nurses may be involved in sex education, advice and guidance about aspects of bullying, recognition of specific mental health problems, and teaching stress reduction strategies to children.

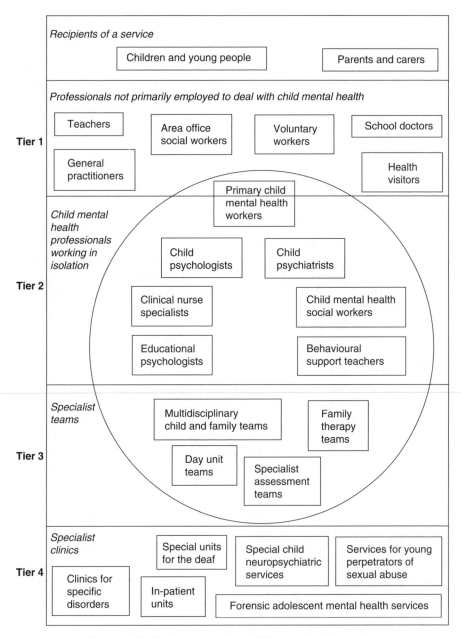

Recipients of a service

Children and young people

Parents and carers

Professionals not primarily employed to deal with child mental health

Tier 1

Teachers

Area office social workers

Voluntary workers

School doctors

General practitioners

Health visitors

Child mental health professionals working in isolation

Primary child mental health workers

Tier 2

Child psychologists

Child psychiatrists

Clinical nurse specialists

Child mental health social workers

Educational psychologists

Behavioural support teachers

Specialist teams

Multidisciplinary child and family teams

Family therapy teams

Tier 3

Day unit teams

Specialist assessment teams

Specialist clinics

Special units for the deaf

Special child neuropsychiatric services

Services for young perpetrators of sexual abuse

Tier 4

Clinics for specific disorders

In-patient units

Forensic adolescent mental health services

Figure 7.1 The four-tier model of child mental health provision.
Source: Spender et al. (2001) *Child Mental Health in Primary Care.*
Oxford: Radcliffe Medical Press.

There is evidence of considerable mental health problems and disorders in children and young people. Spender *et al.* (2001) suggest 2–5 per cent of children seen in primary care settings have mental health problems as their main complaint, and the Audit Commission (1999) suggests one in five children/adolescents suffer from some form of mental health problem. This means there are significant numbers of children and young people who will come to the attention of different professionals working in tier one services. When more specialised help is required referrals can be made to one or more of the other three tiers of CAMHS. The introduction of the proposed Primary Mental Health Care Worker (PMHCW) can be seen as a response to the recognition of a need to bridge the gap between the services at tiers one and two (the PMHCW might be any one of a number of professionals but is often a nurse).

Those working in tier two services include professionals who are trained specifically in assessment and management of children and young people with mental health problems. Professionals in tier two services work alongside other CAMHS professionals to undertake formal assessment of clients and work with other, non-CAMHS, professionals to offer advice and to suggest appropriate therapeutic interventions.

Tier three and four services are normally considered to provide specialist services for children and adolescents with mental health problems and disorders. Tier three involves professional teams working collaboratively to provide services and tier four provides highly specialised services in the form of intensive packages of care including: inpatient facilities, eating disorder teams, and secure units usually on regional, rather than local, basis. Nurses who are part of CAMHS specialist teams will have completed some form of post-registration education in children and young persons' mental health. It is the specialist services provided in tiers three and four that will be the focus of the remainder of this section.

The specialist services of tiers three and four are organised in different ways and located in different settings in different parts of the UK. In some areas tier three community teams are based on the same site as tier four inpatient units and, in some cases, close working relationships have developed between the two. In others areas there may be as many as five or six services based in different parts of a trust, all with small teams of different professionals with inpatient and day patient services organised as separately managed units. Some of the professionals in these small teams will liaise with professionals of the same background in the other teams – others may not. This variation in the configuration of CAMHS has been a cause of concern in a number of reports including the Health Advisory Service Report (HAS 1995) and Everybody's Business (NAW 2001). Advice on service configuration features strongly in the National Service Frameworks for Children in both England and Wales.

Although there is concern about some aspects of the variation in service provision there is a recognition of the need for flexibility in order to meet local and national mental health needs of young people. The specialist CAMHS teams may be based in small general hospital sites, children's hospitals, health centres or may be housed in purpose built premises. Most teams will have at least one nurse although there are some teams without nurses. Under the current salary structure there is a belief that nurses represent value for money and consequently form the largest professional group in the specialist services (Joughin *et al.* 1999).

Children and young people who are referred to the specialist services present with a range of difficulties including: eating disorders; mood disorders; severe anxiety; hyperactivity; and various behavioural problems. Although any illness in a child is likely to create anxiety for parents this is particularly marked with issues that relate to mental health. There remains stigma and ignorance around mental health problems and disorders (MHF 1999) and this can make it especially difficult for children, young people, and their parents. For nurses and other professionals one of the most challenging aspects to the work arising from this is to engage children, young people, and their families with the range of therapeutic activities on offer. Parents can feel that they have failed in their parenting role in some way and this has been known to result in conflict with CAMHS professionals. One of the most important roles that nurses may find themselves required to fulfil is to help parents develop strategies to deal with the complex problems and needs of their children. This may mean running specific parent training programmes such as the *Webster-Stratton* training programme (Webster-Stratton and Hammond 1997) or the *Three P's* programme (Sanders *et al.* 2003).

As well as specific therapeutic skills for different situations there are a number of recurring themes that nurses working in CAMHS need to recognise as important. There have been some well-documented cases, including the Climbié Report (Laming 2003) highlighting the need for effective child protection measures to be in place across agencies [editors' note: more details on the case of Victoria Climbié can be found in Chapter 10]. Corby (2000) notes that there is a high correlation between child abuse and mental health problems and it is now widely accepted that communication between agencies is essential. Nurses working within CAMHS must therefore develop the skills to recognise abuse, act appropriately using local procedures, and be able to communicate effectively with other professionals.

Children and young people who make use of CAMHS may be of any age between four and 18. In tier four services, day and inpatient treatment units tend to distinguish between, and work separately with, children (usually taken to include 4–11-year-olds) and adolescents (12–18). Other, sessional type, services based in clinics typically work with children and young people across the age range. This requires that nurses, like other professionals, be flexible in the therapeutic approaches used. Parental consent is required for all treatment approaches with young children but if adolescents are competent to give consent, as determined by using the Fraser guidelines (Brazier 2003), there is no formal requirement for parental consent. The issue of consent for treatment raises a related issue of confidentiality. All nurses are bound by the professional code of conduct (NMC 2002) and this means that, in the case of a competent young person, the young person's permission is required before the release of her or his confidential information. This can create difficulties for nurses working with young people who experience problems in their relationship with their parents. Parents often ask for information about what their child is saying or doing in therapy sessions and sometimes become angry and frustrated when told that this is confidential. This is a particularly sensitive area and one in which many nurses become skilled. Of course, there are limits to this confidentiality especially where information is revealed in relation to child protection issues or illegal activities. All CAMHS nurses need to ensure their clients understand that such limitations to the confidential nature of the therapeutic relationship exist.

Issues of interprofessional working in CAMHS

Inpatient units are typically staffed by a nursing team in order to provide cover for the 24-hour period while day units tend to be staffed during normal office hours. There is no nationally agreed formula for the configuration of nursing staff so the skill mix across the UK varies considerably. Indeed the background of CAMHS nurses also varies insofar as there may be any combination of children's, adult, learning disability, and mental health nurses in post, although the majority of nurses working in CAMHS have a mental health qualification. In addition there may be other professionals such as occupational therapists, teachers (who provide statutory education services), play therapists, social workers, psychologists, psychotherapists, and psychiatrists. Many teams remain influenced by the view that the consultant psychiatrist is the natural leader of the multidisciplinary team and consequently has the most power and control in decision making. This hierarchy is challenged in some teams where nurses (or other team members) exert a strong influence. Tensions sometimes arise in the relationships between nurses and other team members (especially medical staff) as a result of these sorts of dynamics. In the inpatient units nurses provide care for the full 24-hour period while other professionals work more traditional sessional hours (usually 09.00–17.00). These working practices need careful management in order to provide young people with the maximum benefit to be gained from the range of skills and approaches of each professional. One of the most important themes to arise in these environments is the need for consistency of approach to care. Effective communication is considered to be essential in the provision of a consistent service to children and young people with mental health problems and disorders.

Similar issues can arise in CAMHS teams based in clinics and/or community settings. Such teams are also made up of a range of different professionals although with fewer nurses. A typical team might comprise of two nurses, a consultant psychiatrist, a psychologist, a social worker, a family therapist and a play therapist. CAMHS teams seem to function best where the professional background of each team member is utilised to meet specific needs of clients and where the traditional hierarchy and power relationships have been eroded. Indeed, current strategies including Everybody's Business (NAW 2001) and the forthcoming National Service Framework for Children (see DoH 2003) support the development of non-hierarchical teams in recommending that CAMHS should aim for clear and effective ways of interprofessional working.

The skills of CAMHS nurses

From all that has been said so far it can be seen that nurses make up a significant part of the professional workforce offering services to children and young people with mental health problems or disorders. Individual nurses often develop specific therapeutic skills and collectively there is a wide range of different skills and knowledge among nurses working in CAMHS. This would typically include: core counselling skills; knowledge of child development; an understanding of parenting skills; and working in teams to assess risk factors and recognise stress and distress in relationships.

Currently there is no requirement for the inclusion of children's mental health issues within the pre-registration education for nurses although some recommendations have been made to incorporate these issues into the curriculum (Townley 2002). Nevertheless, many of the skills learnt as part of pre-registration education for children's or mental health nursing are relevant and readily transferable to the CAMHS environment. In addition, once working in CAMHS nurses often take the opportunity to develop more specialist skills by accessing post-registration education. Such courses are designed to provide nurses with appropriate knowledge and skills and would include *inter alia* courses in family therapy, cognitive behavioural therapy, psychotherapy, group work, as well as more specific courses for working with certain client groups such as those with eating disorders or attention deficit hyperactivity disorder.

From this it should be apparent that CAMHS offers a complex range of services from a number of different professionals with various backgrounds. The way in which these professionals interact can vary enormously depending on where the service is, how the team is configured and, of course, the individual personalities and experiences of each professional. The following case study of a young person referred to a tier three CAMHS team is used to illustrate some of these complexities.

CASE STUDY 2: THERESA

Theresa is a 15-year-old Caucasian girl admitted to a general hospital children's unit following an overdose of paracetamol tablets. She has revealed that she has recently self-harmed by cutting her arms and she has several scars as a result.

This particular children's unit employs a nurse to liaise between the ward and CAMHS; a role similar to that of the primary mental health care worker (PMHCW). As such she is able to offer advice, support, and supervision to the ward nurses who, generally speaking, lack experience of children's mental health problems, and she acts as a link between the two services. It is envisaged that the PMHCW will undertake a similar role by liaising with the primary care services. One of the advantages of a liaison nurse is that she is in a position to make a risk assessment once the routine medical assessment has been completed. There is evidence to suggest that nurses and other health and social care professionals have negative attitudes towards young people who self-harm (Bywaters and Rolfe 2002). The liaison nurse can help to reduce the stigma associated with mental health problems in children and young people and this can be of enormous benefit to both staff and the young people themselves.

The normal process for this particular CAMHS team requires a written referral which is then considered against agreed criteria at the weekly team meeting. Although not an emergency service, in this case and because of the concerns of the liaison nurse, the team agreed to visit Theresa before receiving a written referral. The consultant psychiatrist made the first visit because she is the only member of the team with the authority to prescribe medication. From the information provided the team believed Theresa might be found to be clinically depressed and might need to be prescribed antidepressant drugs. Other team members are neither qualified nor permitted to prescribe medicines although there is some discussion about the possibility of allowing CAMHS nurses to prescribe for certain conditions under particular circumstances. One example would be that CAMHS nurses might be permitted, given the appropriate education, to prescribe medicine to children suffering from attention deficit hyperactivity disorder (ADHD).

CASE STUDY continued

Following the assessment by the consultant psychiatrist it was thought Theresa was not clinically depressed and therefore did not require a course of antidepressant medication. However, it was clear she was experiencing some emotional turmoil in several aspects of her life including in her relationships with her mother and her boyfriend as well as some difficulties in school. Self-harm seemed to be her way of coping.

The team believed they could offer support to Theresa, monitor her mood and provide some therapeutic interventions in relation to her self-harming behaviour. Each of these entail therapeutic approaches that could be provided by several members of the team. Sanura, a nurse, was the one CAMHS team member with specific experience of working with clients such as Theresa and because Sanura had both the expertise and the capacity to take on a new client she became Theresa's key worker.

It is important that the needs and interests of a client are taken into account when choosing the most appropriate professional to engage in therapy with the client. However, this can have the effect of reducing the exposure of other team members to working with certain client groups and, as a result, some team members may miss opportunities to develop particular skills. In some instances the decision about which team member is to be the primary worker for a given client is a pragmatic one. That is, it may need to be whoever is available and has the time to accept another client. There are long waiting lists for CAMHS (Audit Commission 1999) and consequently some team members with particular skills are in such demand that they simply may not have the capacity to meet the needs of clients with urgent needs in the timeframe required.

Sanura discussed with Theresa the most appropriate place for meeting. Options include: in the family home, in the clinic setting, at school, or in a neutral setting such as a local café. In some cases it is helpful to meet the child with her or his parents and in other instances it is appropriate to meet with the whole family. On some occasions there will be a need for two professionals from CAMHS to meet with the family or child. One underlying principle in deciding when and how to meet with a child or young person is that her or his wishes and needs should be taken into account. In this case Sanura and Theresa agreed to meet in the clinic.

During the course of Sanura's counselling work with Theresa it became known she had been hit on the back of the head by her father six months ago. All professionals in CAMHS must undertake training in child protection and all services are required to have child protection procedures in place. Good practice entails exploring what confidentiality means at the beginning of any therapeutic process and Theresa had been informed that if she or any other child was thought to be at risk from harm or had been harmed then this would need to be reported. Following advice from the local authority social services department duty officer, who noted this was not an emergency child protection situation because the reported hitting had occurred several months earlier, Sanura thought a discussion of the issues could wait until the next scheduled weekly team meeting. At the meeting it was felt that the parents should be asked to meet with someone from the team to discuss parenting strategies with a specific remit to ensure that the risk to Theresa of being hit again might be reduced. If one therapist undertakes therapeutic interventions with different individuals from the same family there is always the possibility of a conflict of interest. For this reason the team came to the view that it was important that Sanura should not be involved in the work with the parents as this could affect her therapeutic relationship with Theresa. Following discussion the team recognised that the social worker was the most appropriate team member to work with Theresa's parents because of his experience and expertise in child protection issues. This work involved two sessions during which Theresa's parents were invited to explore parenting strategies and issues related, in particular, to the setting of boundaries of acceptable behaviour for Theresa in order to reduce the likelihood of harm to Theresa.

CASE STUDY continued

Sanura's work with Theresa lasted for a number of months and as a result she learned to manage her feelings in more constructive ways and this reduced her tendency to self-harm. She would talk to friends about her feelings and she recognised the need to remove herself from situations when she began to feel angry. She also learned to talk with her parents which resulted in more realistic expectations on the part of Theresa and her parents. Theresa did not stop self-harming altogether but did recognise the need to take more control of her situation.

Counselling was the most appropriate intervention with Theresa but other therapeutic approaches may be used by CAMHS professionals depending on the individual needs of the client. For some clients family therapy is perceived to be the appropriate form of work. Many nurses, and others, working in CAMHS have experience with working with families as units and some have formal training as family therapists. Although not always possible it is common to do this work with two professionals as this provides two perspectives on family dynamics and enables support and supervision for team members.

Some clients benefit from pharmacological therapy. Young people who suffer from clinical depression can be helped by the use of antidepressant drugs and other examples include: the use of medication where a young person has a psychosis, suffers from ADHD, or has a severe anxiety state. As a general principle psychiatrists will only prescribe drugs for young people where there is evidence for its likely effectiveness. Where medication is prescribed one part of the role of a CAMHS nurse is to help monitor the effectiveness of medication on the young person.

Some young people experience mental health problems as a result of illegal drug use and some CAMHS team members are trained in the use of a substance use screening tool and may well liaise with a local substance use service if it is felt to be of therapeutic value to a particular client. Substance use services have a wealth of experience in dealing with substance users. Part of a CAMHS nurse's role is to be able to both recognise when there is a need to link with other services and to be able to access such other services. This requires knowledge and understanding of appropriate services from which CAMHS clients might benefit.

Conclusion

This chapter has offered an insight into the nature of some aspects of the work of the four disciplines of nursing, together with some examples of interdisciplinary and interprofessional working. Individual nurses work in different settings using different sets of skills but share a common goal of providing a comprehensive service tailored to meeting the nursing needs of each patient. The recognition that a service can only meet all the health and social care needs of patients if nurses work collaboratively with other professionals is beginning to make a real difference to nursing practice.

References

Audit Commission (1999) *Children in Mind. Child and Adolescent Mental Health Services.* London: Audit Commission.

Bollard M. (2002) Health promotion and learning disability. *Nursing Standard* 16(27): 47–55.

Brazier M. (2003) *Medicine Patients and the Law* (3rd edn) Harmondsworth: Penguin.

Bywaters P. and Rolfe A. (2002) *Look Beyond the Scars.* London: NCH.

Corby B. (2000) *Child Abuse. Towards a Knowledge Base* (2nd edn) Buckingham: Oxford University Press.

DoH (Department of Health) (2001a) *Valuing People: A Strategy for People with a Learning Disability in the 21st Century.* London: DoH.

DoH (2001b) *Nothing About Us Without Us.* London: DoH.

DoH (2001c) *Health Action Plans.* London: DoH.

DoH (2003) *Getting the Right Start: National Service Frameworks for Children Emerging Findings.* London: DoH.

Henderson V. (1966) *The Nature of Nursing A Definition and its Implications for Practice, Research, and Education.* New York: Macmillan.

HAS (Health Advisory Service) (1995) *Child and Adolescent Mental Health Services. Together We Stand.* London: HMSO.

Joughin C., Jarrett L. and Maclean-Steel K. (1999) *Focus on Who's Who in Child and Adolescent Mental Health Services.* London: Royal College of Psychiatrists' Research Unit.

Jukes M. (2002) Health facilitation in learning disability: a new specialist role. *British Journal of Nursing* 11(10): 694–8.

Laming, Lord (2003) *Inquiry into the Death of Victoria Climbié.* London: The Stationery Office.

MHF (Mental Health Foundation) (1999) *Bright Futures. Promoting Children and Young Peoples Mental Health.* London: Mental Health Foundation.

NAW (National Assembly for Wales) (2001) *Child and Adolescent Mental Health Services Everybody's Business.* Cardiff: National Assembly for Wales.

NICE (National Institute for Clinical Excellence) (2001) Prophylaxis for patients who have experienced a myocardial infarction: drug treatment, cardiac rehabilitation and dietary manipulation. www.nice.org.uk/article.asp?a=11385 accessed October 2003.

NMC (Nursing and Midwifery Council) (2002) *Professional Code of Conduct.* London: NMC.

RCN (Royal College of Nursing) (2003) Defining nursing. www.rcn.org.uk/downloads/definingnursing/definingnursing-a5.pdf accessed April 2003.

Sanders M.R., Markie-Dadds C. and Turner K.M.T. (2003) *Theoretical, Scientific and Clinical Foundations of the Triple P – Positive Parenting Program: A Population Approach to the Promotion of Parenting Competence.* http://www.triplep.net/files/pdf/Parenting_Research_and_Practice_Monograph_No.1.pdf accessed November 2003.

Spender Q., Salt N., Dawkins J., Kendrick T. and Hill P. (2001) *Child Mental Health in Primary Care.* Oxford: Radcliffe Medical Press.

Townley M. (2002) Mental health needs of children and young people. *Nursing Standard* 16(30): 38–45.

Webster-Stratton C. and Hammond M. (1997) Treating children with early onset conduct problems: A comparison of child and parent training interventions. *Journal of Consulting and Clinical Psychology* 65: 93–109.

CHAPTER

8

Occupational Therapy

Fiona Douglas and Stephen Evans

Introduction

Occupational therapists work in both health and social care environments focusing on the extent to which service users are able to carry out day-to-day activities. For occupational therapists, occupation is defined as everyday, routine and personally meaningful activities. The list of activities that most people do, and take for granted, includes such seemingly simple tasks as putting out the rubbish, cleaning their teeth and washing or ironing clothes. Other things that individuals do which are especially meaningful to them might include, for example, making a meal for family or friends, walking the dog, playing with the children or repairing the car. These lists merely illustrate the point that ordinary activities are important for people and contribute to meaningful patterns of daily life that make us who we are; and these activities are our occupations (Wilcock 1998a, Kramer *et al.* 2003).

The work of occupational therapists involves assisting individuals in the pursuit of their everyday occupations. Usually this assistance is needed when an individual's capacity to pursue their occupations is compromised in some way. This chapter provides a brief review of the genesis of occupational therapy; offers an insight into the work of the occupational therapist; and, using a case study, illustrates the collaborative nature of occupational therapy.

Origins

Occupational therapy is a relatively new profession with origins in the 19th century movement pressing for moral treatment of the insane (Peloquin

1989). In 1917 this approach to mental health care was adopted by the National Society for the Promotion of Occupational Therapy which later became the American Occupational Therapy Association (Christiansen and Baum 1997). The six people credited with founding occupational therapy as a profession are: William Rush Dunton – a psychiatrist; George Edward Barton – an architect; Eleanor Clarke Slagle – an almoner/social worker; Susan Cox Johnson – a teacher of arts and crafts; Susan Tracy – a nurse; and Thomas Bessell Kidner – another architect. They shared a common belief in the merits of occupation as therapy and their different professional backgrounds illustrates the diversity from which occupational therapy originated and which continues to influence current practice.

In Britain elements of occupational therapy were in evidence following the first world war with the rise in demand for rehabilitation services. However, the development of the profession in the United Kingdom (UK) began towards the end of the 1920s with the opening of the first occupational therapy clinic (The Allendall Clinic) in 1929 and the first occupational therapy training school (Dorset House) in 1930, both in Bristol (Wilcock 2002).

The nature of occupation

While the term occupation is often used to describe the type of paid employment people undertake, the wider meaning of occupation includes ordinary everyday activities. We say that someone is occupied (perhaps even preoccupied) when they are engaged with a task and this illustrates our recognition of the wider general meaning of occupation. In the early part of the 20th century, when the profession was founded, this general meaning of the term occupation described any activity that kept a person busy. It was selected by the founders as a term broad enough to encompass all aspects of activity that people would carry out.

Many things influence our occupations, not only what we do but also the way in which we do them. Cultural, family and social aspects of our lives, as well as the physical environment in which we live are perhaps the most obvious influences on our occupations. This means that our occupations are uniquely individual, although influenced by culture, learning, and environments (Zemke and Clark 1996).

The nature of occupational therapy

To become an occupational therapist requires graduate level study and once qualified, an occupational therapist must be registered with the health professions council (HPC) in order to practice anywhere in the UK. There are more than 20 university-based undergraduate pre-registration programmes in the UK each one registered with the World Federation of Occupational Therapists (WFOT). WFOT status ensures comparable standards and means graduates are eligible for state registration in any WFOT affiliated country. In the UK pre-registration programmes for occupational therapy are currently validated jointly by the HPC and the College of Occupational Therapists.

The idea that people are occupational beings, or that people need to be engaged in activities, is fundamental to the concept and the practice of occupational therapy. The assumption is that doing meaningful things is necessary for the well-being of the individual and provides opportunities for both health and personal choices. The work of occupational therapists is therefore an attempt to enable individuals to engage in meaningful occupation. This requires a perspective that recognises each person as a unique individual whose well-being is best served by matching occupation to ability without limiting that person's capacity to meet challenges.

As a result, occupational therapists consider partnership working to be essential (Law *et al.* 2002) and this partnership includes not only *working with* service users, but also with carers as well as with different health and social care professionals. Occupational therapists work in diverse health and social care settings and may work in various interprofessional teams. For example, occupational therapists may work as part of a team with almost any combination of, amongst others, nurses, physiotherapists, homecare workers, equipment service personnel, social workers, speech and language therapists, doctors, clinical psychologists, community care workers, music therapists, teachers, architects, builders, and surveyors.

CASE STUDY

Ahmad comes from a family who describe themselves as of Pakistani origin. He was 23 when first referred to the social services occupational therapy team. Ahmad has cerebral palsy, a condition that, in Ahmad's case, limits his ability to communicate and leaves him dependent on others for all activities of daily living. Ahmad had been able to live at home supported by care workers through a care package overseen by a homecare manager who ensures the appropriate services are delivered. The homecare manager referred Ahmad to the occupational therapy team because there were a number of challenges in assisting Ahmad with instrumental activities of daily living including unresolved manual handling issues. Ahmad had fallen several times while being assisted to mobilise and had, on occasion, been aggressive towards homecare staff. If these challenges continued it was likely the care package would be unsustainable and Ahmad might need to be placed in temporary residential accommodation until the manual handling issues could be resolved.

The homecare staff believed Ahmad's occupational performance in mobility and in other instrumental activities of daily living could be improved by environmental adaptation. Environmental adaptation is one of the core professional skills of occupational therapists.

QUESTIONS

- In what ways might Ahmad communicate?
- Why might Ahmad be aggressive towards staff?

Section 1 of the Chronically Sick and Disabled Persons Act 1970 establishes the right of a person to be made aware of relevant services within the local authority (Dimond 1997). In addition, section 47 of the NHS and Community Care Act 1990 places a duty upon the local authority to carry out an assessment for any individual who would appear to be eligible for its services. Because it seemed possible that the homecare package would be withdrawn the homecare manager believed it appropriate to refer Ahmad to the occupational therapy team.

The priority given to a referral is determined locally, but guided by the government's Fair Access to Care Criteria which facilitates a 'more consistent approach to eligibility and fairer access to care services across the country' (DoH 2002: 1). There are four 'bands of the seriousness of risk to independence or other consequences if needs are not addressed' (*ibid*: 4–5) and referrals are classed as low, moderate, substantial or critical. Ahmad's referral was categorised as critical as it came within the description stating 'vital support systems and relationships cannot or will not be sustained' (*ibid*: 4). Because Ahmad's mental impairment means he is unable to contribute to discussions about his care, Cathryn (the occupational therapist) arranged to visit at a time when she could speak with Ahmad's parents to carry out an assessment. In conversation with Ahmad's parents Cathryn was able to ascertain Ahmad was dependent upon his parents and homecare staff in all activities of daily living. He was able to walk short distances with the help of one carer, but generally was only able to get around when pushed in a wheelchair.

QUESTION

■ What anxieties might Ahmad's situation create for his parents?

A draft Mental Incapacity Bill aims to create a new statutory framework for decision making in relation to those who lack capacity to make decisions about financial and welfare matters (DCA 2003). This Bill will offer assistance where currently there is uncertainty because, as Dimond reminds us 'for adults of 18 and over who lack the ability to make their own decisions there exists a vacuum in law' (1997: 284). In the meantime, occupational therapists, like all other health and social care professionals working with people who lack the capacity to give a valid consent, have a duty to act in the service user's best interests, as recognised in common law (COT 2003). This intensifies the need for occupational therapists and other health and social care professionals to work together in order to ascertain the needs of individuals, and to advise each other of the ability of the individual to give informed consent.

QUESTION

■ What tensions for professionals might this *vacuum* in the law create?

At the time of the occupational therapy assessment, Ahmad lived in a four bedroom house with his parents, grandparents and three siblings. He shared a bedroom on the first floor with his younger brother. There was a single bathroom situated on the same floor used by all members of the family. There was insufficient space for hoisting and mobility equipment in either the bathroom or bedroom so Ahmad and his carers had to carry out instrumental activities of daily living, including transfers, with little in the way of assistive equipment and in cramped conditions. As a result Ahmad had fallen several times and there were concerns about the health and safety of his carers. A stair lift had been installed although this did not operate on the three stairs Ahmad needed to negotiate between his bedroom and the bathroom.

QUESTION

■ What pressures might the situation put on other members of the family?

The predominant philosophy of care for people with learning disabilities during the last two decades has been normalisation (Churchill 1998) as well as the maximisation of development potential for each individual. The practical operation of the philosophy of normalisation frequently involves care professionals implementing a strategy of risk management for each individual client (Dimond 1997, Saunders 1998) in order to identify the potential risks of harm to the service user, and their carers, and to determine a strategy for minimising those risks. In considering the legal context of risk management, Saunders claims that 'one of the most powerful elements of risk management is the necessary and explicit involvement of the multi-professional team in the decision making process' (1998: 251).

Cathryn attempted to explore risk management issues but found Ahmad's parents believed manual handling was not an issue. In fact they tried to insist the carers, both family members and homecare staff, should continue to bear Ahmad's weight when physically assisting him. For cultural reasons they also expected Ahmad be washed with running water whilst seated in the bath; an expectation that ruled out the use of an over-bath shower. The mornings had become particularly stressful and it was while the homecare staff were assisting Ahmed to get up, washed and dressed that he began to display challenging behaviour. The falls had also occurred in the mornings when homecare staff were helping Ahmad to get out of bed.

According to Mandelstam (2001a), under the Health and Safety at Work Act 1974, occupational therapists and the institutions they work for have a professional and legal obligation in relation to the safety of their clients and carers, as well as to their colleagues and themselves. Manual Handling Operations Regulations (MHOR 1992) require a risk assessment to be carried out to avoid manual handling risks as far as is reasonably practicable. The regulations indicate that a risk assessment must be carried out by a competent person (Mandelstam 2001b). Because of the difficulties caused by the limitations of the physical environment and because of the complexity of Ahmad's needs Cathryn recognised the necessity of an expert risk assessment. A joint risk assessment was undertaken by Cathryn and the local authority's health and safety officer including observation of the work of the homecare staff with Ahmad. Following this assessment it was clear the physical environment faced by Ahmad and his carers was one with such high risks as to make the continued safe activity of service user or carers unsustainable in the long-term, necessitating a substantial change of the physical environment. However, carrying out major adaptations to a home is a long and often complicated process and cannot be considered as a short-term solution to an identified critical need.

The need to work interprofessionally is part of the Code of Ethics and Professional Conduct for occupational therapists (COT 2000) and in order to develop an intervention plan to explore the possibility of changing Ahmad's physical home environment, the views of all stakeholders and professionals involved in Ahmad's care needed to be drawn together. Cathryn used the case-work documentation to identify the professionals involved in Ahmad's care and requested a case conference with Ahmad's parents. This meeting included the community physiotherapist, the homecare manager, the social worker, the manager of Ahmad's day centre, the local authority's health and safety officer, the occupational therapist from the community learning disabilities team and the clinical psychologist as well as Ahmad's parents.

=================================== **QUESTIONS** ===================================

- What contribution to Ahmad's needs could be made by each of the professionals invited to the case conference?

- Can you think of any others who could have been invited?

- What information and support do you think Ahmad's parents would need prior to the meeting?

Recent reports of service user groups for people with learning disabilities note that service providers such as social services, health and education still do not work together well (Mendonca 2004). The range and source of services in a local community provided to any one individual can be broad and diverse and, as Lloyd puts it 'health and local authorities and the non-statutory sector can be found providing similar services for people with similar needs in similar buildings and settings' (1998: 73). He goes on to say that the prevailing model of community based social work is found within multidisciplinary teams, such as community learning disability teams, which vary in composition, but can include nurses, psychologists, physiotherapists, social workers and occupational therapists. Dedicated multidisciplinary teams are not always feasible in community service provision due to the fragmentation of services, often arising from funding differences. This necessitates interagency collaboration. 'Multidisciplinary and interdisciplinary work requires that the occupational therapist identify the key operational links that should be established' (Brown 2002: 321).

It should be noted that the occupational therapist working with the community learning disabilities team had different responsibilities and remit to Cathryn, the occupational therapist working from the social services department. However, the involvement of both in the interprofessional decision making process was appropriate as the former had recently worked with Ahmad in using biomechanical approaches to improve postural management and positioning while Cathryn was involved in assessing the potential for environmental adaptation to facilitate occupational performance.

The case conference took place at Ahmad's home and was initially tense as his parents confirmed their expectations of the support that could be provided. The physiotherapist noted that Ahmad's performance in mobility could not be improved any further with rehabilitation alone and might deteriorate. However, it was also a constructive step forward in establishing a performance baseline for Ahmad as previously key professionals from the day centre, physiotherapy and homecare had not discussed Ahmad's level of mobility or performance of activities of daily living as one group with his parents. Also, the clinical psychologist, who had not previously been directly involved with Ahmad agreed to work with him on his challenging behaviour.

In establishing this baseline it was agreed between the interprofessional team and Ahmad's parents that the level of support required could not be delivered within the existing physical environment context. Ahmad's parents accepted the home environment was limiting but would not consider the option of rehousing. They agreed that an architect could be consulted to see if the home could be adapted to better meet Ahmad's present and future needs. That is, whether the barriers to safe mobility and manual handling by carers could be removed or minimised by means of new construction. In the short-term the risks identified by the health and safety officer together with the occupational therapist could not be wholly alleviated. However, the occupational therapist provided some assistive equipment that temporarily facilitated improved moving and handling and the homecare staff were satisfied that the interprofessional team were now working together with the same long-term aims.

Section 2 of the Chronically Sick and Disabled Persons Act 1970 places a responsibility upon the local authority's social services to provide assistance by means of 'any works of adaptation in his home or the provision of any additional facilities designed to secure his greater safety, comfort or convenience' (Dimond 1997: 249). Since the enactment of the Local Government and Housing Act 1989 housing authorities have approved disabled facilities grants that can have a variety of purposes including, facilitation of access to a room used for sleeping and a room with a lavatory, bath, shower and wash hand basin for a disabled person (Dimond 1997).

Section 47(3)(b) of the NHS and Community Care Act 1990 stipulates that the local authority must notify the relevant local housing authority if there is seen to be a need for the provision of any services that fall within the latter's function (Dimond 1997). This raises an obligation upon the social services occupational therapist to contact the housing department on the service user's behalf regarding an application for a disabled facilities grant. Service users are also entitled to approach the relevant housing authority themselves to apply for a disabled facilities grant. In this case the housing authority is advised to contact social services occupational therapists to determine need.

The disabled facilities grant comes under the provisions of Part I of the Housing Grants, Construction and Regeneration Act 1996. This Act and supporting literature suggests practical advice can be obtained from relevant officers in the housing department or a local home improvement agency. For major work it recommends employing a qualified architect or surveyor to plan and oversee the work. These professionals may also introduce builders and other external contractors to carry out the required work (ODPM 2002). Therefore new agencies have been introduced to the process requiring further interagency collaboration.

Ahmad's parents agreed the best solution would involve the construction of a first floor extension with sleeping and bathing facilities specifically designed for Ahmad. Consultation on the plans for the extensions included all the health and social care professionals involved with Ahmad and his family. The architect visited the site to work with Cathryn and homecare staff to consider the advantages of different designs to ensure safe moving and handling. Proposals were referred back to the health and safety officer for his comments and support. The duration of the proposed work was likely to cause Ahmad further challenges to his occupational performance in his home environment. This was partially resolved by the social worker who arranged temporary respite care for Ahmad while new facilities were built. In order to do this the social worker required a schedule with precise timings of the crucial work that affected Ahmad's access to key facilities within his home. Cathryn worked with the architect and the social worker in order to minimise the disruption to Ahmad during the building work. At the appropriate times, Ahmad was able to go for respite care at a residential facility specifically for young adults with severe learning difficulties.

In all, the time from the initial assessment by the social services occupational therapist to the completion of the adaptation work was approximately 18 months. Ahmad now has his own bedroom with en-suite bathing facilities. It has a profiling and height variable bed, a ceiling track hoist, a wet-floor washing area (that meets his cultural needs) and toilet, a mobile shower chair and most importantly, sufficient space for Ahmad and his carers to move around in. Ahmad's parents and clinical psychologist report that he appears happier since moving into his new bedroom and is not displaying challenging behaviour as often.

Conclusion

Ahmad's occupations were enabled by providing an environment allowing him to engage with culturally and socially acceptable meaningful activities. In this case it was the occupational therapist who orchestrated the contributions of other professionals so that by working together Ahmad suffered minimal disruption during the environmental adaptations. With the support of his parents, the focus remained on Ahmad to ensure his ability to carry out day-to-day activities was enhanced. The result was a reduction in the number of episodes of challenging behaviour and he seemed to really begin to enjoy his new surroundings, enhancing his health and well-being.

Wilcock (1998b, 2003) suggests that society needs to be enabled to see people as occupational beings with an innate drive to be engaged in meaningful activities, for it is through such activities that individuals experience well-being and health. She proposes a new direction for occupational therapy in which occupational therapists take a lead in enabling individuals and society to adopt this thinking.

References

Brown G. (2002) Cerebral palsy. In Turner A., Foster M. and Sybil E. (eds) *Occupational Therapy and Physical Dysfunction: Principles, Skills and Practice*. Edinburgh: Churchill Livingstone, pp. 319–39.

Christiansen C.H. and Baum C.M. (eds) (1997) *Occupational Therapy: Enabling Function and Well-being* (2nd edn). New Jersey: Slack.

Churchill J. (1998) The independent sector. In Thompson T. and Mathias P. (eds) *Standards and Learning Disability* (2nd edn). London: Bailliere Tindall, pp. 46–67.

COT (College of Occupational Therapists) (2000) Code of Ethics and Professional Conduct for Occupational Therapists. London: COT.

COT (2003) *Professional Standards for Occupational Therapy Practice*. London: COT.

DCA (Department of Constitutional Affairs) (2003) *Draft Mental Incapacity Bill:Overview of Bill*. www.dca.gov.uk/menincap/overview accessed March 2004.

Dimond B.C. (1997) *Legal Aspects of Occupational Therapy*. Oxford: Blackwell Science.

DoH (2002) *Fair Access to Care Services: Guidance on Eligibility Criteria for Adult Social Care*. www.doh.gov.uk/assetroot/04/01/96/41/04019641.pdf accessed March 2004.

Kramer P., Hinojosa J. and Royeen C.B. (eds) (2003) *Perspectives in Human Occupation: Participation in Life*. Baltimore, Maryland: Lippincott Williams and Wilkins.

Law M., Baum C. and Baptiste S. (2002) *Occupation-Based Practice: Fostering Performance and Participation*. New Jersey: Slack.

Lloyd M. (1998) Local authorities. In Thompson T. and Mathias P. (eds) *Standards and Learning Disability* (2nd edn). London: Bailliere Tindall, pp. 68–80.

Mandelstam M. (2001a) Safe use of disability equipment and manual handling: legal aspects – part 1, disability equipment. *British Journal of Occupational Therapy* **64**: 9–16.

Mandelstam M. (2001b) Safe use of disability equipment and manual handling: legal aspects – part 2, manual handling. *British Journal of Occupational Therapy* **64**: 73–80.

Mendonca P. (2004) *Rights, Independence, Choice and Inclusion*. London: Learning Disabilities Task Force. www.dh.gov.uk/assetRoot/04/07/47/27/04074727.pdf accessed March 2004.

MHOR (Manual Handling Operations Regulations) (1992) *Statutory Instrument 1992 No. 2793*. www.hmso.gov.uk/si/si1992/uksi_19922793_en_1.htm accessed March 2004.

ODPM (Office of the Deputy Prime Minister) (2002) *Disabled Facilities Grants*. ODPM Free Literature, Code 96 HC 202B, London.

Peloquin S. (1989) Moral treatment: contexts considered. *American Journal of Occupational Therapy* **43**: 537–44.

Saunders M. (1998) Risk management. In Thompson T. and Mathias P. (eds) *Standards and Learning Disability* (2nd edn). London: Bailliere Tindall, pp. 248–60.

Wilcock A.A. (1998a) *Occupational Perspective of Health*. New Jersey: Slack.

Wilcock A.A. (1998b) Occupation for health. *British Journal of Occupational Therapy* **61**: 340–5.

Wilcock A.A. (2002) *Occupation for Health: A Journey From Self-health to Prescription, Vol 2*. London: British Association and College of Occupational Therapists.

Wilcock A.A. (2003) Occupational science: the study of humans as occupational beings. In Kramer P., Hinojosa J. and Royeen C.B. (eds) (2003) *Perspectives in Human Occupation: Participation in Life*. Baltimore, Maryland: Lippincott Williams and Wilkins, pp. 156–80.

Zemke R. and Clark F. (1996) *Occupational Science: The Evolving Discipline*. Philadelphia: F.A. Davis.

CHAPTER
9

Physiotherapy

Diane Hawes and Dianne Rees

The roots of the professional body, the Chartered Society of Physiotherapy (CSP), can be traced to 1894, when four nurses established the Society of Trained Masseuses to give credibility to their profession which was under threat from individuals offering other services under the guise of massage. The Society evolved over time; it gained a Royal Charter in 1920, amalgamated with the Institute of Massage and Remedial Gymnastics and in 1944 adopted its current name, the Chartered Society of Physiotherapy. In 1977 the CSP was granted professional autonomy by the Department of Health, which enables physiotherapists to assess and treat patients without requiring a doctor's referral first (CSP 2004).

Physiotherapists who train in the United Kingdom (UK) and who wish to work in the National Health Service (NHS) must undertake a course of study validated jointly by the CSP and the Health Professions Council (HPC) and be registered with the HPC. From July 2003 the titles physiotherapist and physical therapist have become protected in law which means it is not permissible for those without appropriate training to set themselves up in private practice as physiotherapists and treat patients. Before this membership of the CSP was the only guarantee that a physiotherapist was appropriately trained. Patients are now better protected if they opt for private physiotherapy treatment as fraudulent practitioners will be prosecuted (HPC 2004).

Physiotherapists from abroad who wish to work in the NHS must be able to demonstrate to the HPC that their course of physiotherapy study was of an equivalent standard to UK programmes. If this cannot be demonstrated, the applicant will be required to undertake a period of adaptation, involving study with a UK university and/or a period of supervised work in a physiotherapy department, before they can gain HPC registration.

Since 1992 all UK physiotherapy pre-registration courses have been degree programmes and since 2002 an honours degree is required. The length of study varies with the nature of the programme. Many courses last three years, but some higher education institutions offer accelerated programmes, for example, to students already holding an honours degree (or a higher award) in a science related subject. Many are now offering, or are developing, part-time programmes enabling students to spread their studies over a longer period of time.

Physiotherapy is one of a number professions identified as being allied to health. Allied health professions (AHPs) include, amongst others, speech and language therapists, occupational therapists, paramedics, podiatrists, dieticians, orthotists, radiographers and art therapists, but exclude doctors, nurses, midwives and dentists. Dictionary definitions tend to describe physiotherapy as the treatment or prevention of injury or disease using physical means, and list possible interventions such as exercise, massage and heat treatment. What such definitions fail to capture, however, is the breadth and complexity of physiotherapy today. The CSP describes physiotherapy as:

> a health care profession concerned with human function and movement and maximising potential. It uses physical approaches to promote, maintain and restore physical, psychological and social well being, taking account of variations in health status. It is science based, committed to extending, applying, evaluating and reviewing the evidence that underpins and informs its practice and delivery. The exercise of clinical judgment and informed interpretation is at its core.
>
> (2002: 19)

Physiotherapists work in a diverse range of environments, with an ever increasing range of treatment options and patient groups which makes it difficult to describe precisely what it is physiotherapists do. Although physiotherapists have been able to work as autonomous practitioners for more than 25 years, autonomy does not equate with working independently from other health and social care professionals, particularly within the NHS, where the emphasis is on *effective* teamwork in order to promote high standards of patient care.

New career pathways are developing for physiotherapists in the NHS as their skills of assessment, clinical reasoning and treatment become more widely recognised and valued. Meeting the Challenge: A Strategy for the Allied Health Professions (DoH 2000a) details government plans for developing and supporting the AHPs, identifying them as central to the delivery of key priorities of the programme of NHS reforms published in The NHS Plan: A Plan for Investment, A Plan for Reform (DoH 2000b). The development of therapist consultant posts is identified as helping to promote improved quality, service and outcomes for patients, as well as providing new career opportunities, increasing retention of experienced staff and strengthening professional leadership (DoH 2000a). Therapist consultants are experts in a particular field (such as physiotherapy or occupational therapy) and work with senior nursing and medical staff to draw up local care and referral protocols (DoH 2000a). The first UK therapist consultant in physiotherapy was appointed in 2002. In addition to therapist consultants, there is a growing number of expert physiotherapists whose role involves working beyond the recognised scope of physiotherapy practice. These extended scope practitioners might, for example, spend part of their time working alongside doctors in an outpatient clinic, assessing and diagnosing patients and ordering tests, such as X-rays.

Physiotherapists work in a variety of NHS healthcare settings, including hospitals, general practitioner surgeries, rehabilitation units and community settings, such as the patient's own home and special schools. However there are many physiotherapists working outside the NHS including those who are based in industrial and commercial firms as part of occupational health teams providing services for the workforce. Having a physiotherapist on site reduces the need for staff to travel for physiotherapy outpatient treatment, thereby minimising time lost from work. Physiotherapists also work in private practice, as sports physiotherapists, and in various other working environments.

The fortnightly CSP news magazine, Physiotherapy Frontline, illustrates the range and variety of work available to qualified physiotherapists. Although most job advertisements are for NHS or Primary Care Trusts, there are often many for other types of employers. For example, Physiotherapy Frontline has, at one time or another, contained advertisements placed by the English Institute of Sport, Rolls Royce plc, Total Fitness UK Ltd., the Ministry of Defence, Ballet Rambert, Norwich City Football Club, BUPA, and various private clinics and voluntary organisations.

Physiotherapists have traditionally used a wide variety of physical means to treat patients. Manual techniques (such as complex joint mobilisations and soft tissue massage), progressive exercise therapy, ice, and electrotherapy techniques (including ultrasound, thermal energy and interferential therapy), have a range of therapeutic applications. These include pain relief, reduction of muscle spasm and encouraging the healing of tissues. Suitably trained physiotherapists, with highly developed knowledge and skills in their specialist area of practice, can administer injections of drugs, such as steroids for the relief of joint pain. Government plans to increase supplementary prescribing of drugs is likely to be extended to physiotherapists by September 2004 (Blackledge 2003).

Student physiotherapists need to acquire underpinning theoretical knowledge of, amongst other things, anatomy, physiology, human movement, pathology, physical principles and electrotherapy. They are required to learn practical skills such as massage, manual handling techniques, exercise therapy, mobilisation of joints and soft tissues, use of electrotherapy modalities, hydrotherapy techniques, and techniques to improve respiratory function. Other important skills student physiotherapists acquire are those of clinical reasoning and problem solving. As qualified professionals they will be expected to examine and assess patients regularly throughout a programme of treatment and this requires students to become competent to make informed decisions about the most appropriate and effective treatment methods for each individual patient, often in collaboration with other professional groups.

The core areas of clinical training all student physiotherapists must complete in order to qualify are disorders of human movement and function affecting the neuro-muscular, musculo-skeletal, cardio-vascular and respiratory systems. The student must acquire detailed knowledge of a variety of conditions affecting these systems and become adept at employing a range of skills in the examination, assessment and treatment of patients.

By the time they graduate students will have acquired knowledge, understanding and experience of aspects of professional life that are not specific to physiotherapy. Students develop social skills and understanding of effective teamwork, as they interact with physiotherapists working in different areas of practice, with a range of other professionals and with members of the public. They work in teams of physiotherapists for specific areas of practice, areas such as the provision of respiratory care, or the treatment of patients with rheumatological conditions. They also work collaboratively with other health and social care professionals, some of whom may be located together, and students learn that effective interprofessional working and communication are considered essential for high quality patient care. The Core Standards of Physiotherapy Practice (CSP 2000) are a set of specific statements that apply to all physiotherapists, student physiotherapists and physiotherapy assistants. Standard 13 states:

> Physiotherapists communicate effectively with other health professionals and relevant outside agencies to provide an effective and efficient service to the patient.
>
> (CSP 2000: unnumbered)

Undertaking clinical placements in a range of specific areas of patient care, often in different geographical locations, facilitates professional development. As students become more experienced they are expected to become increasingly responsible for their own decision making and treatment outcomes; to show a developing understanding of the roles of other professionals with whom they work; and to demonstrate an awareness of the NHS as an organisation.

After qualification some physiotherapists undertake further training in specialised areas such as ergonomics, sports therapy, drug prescription, and veterinary physiotherapy. Graduates can also further their educational qualifications by enrolling on programmes leading to Masters degree and/or Doctorate. Many physiotherapists are involved in research as part of their work. This may involve collaboration with other professions, not necessarily from healthcare, in the search for better approaches to patient care. One example might involve a physiotherapist working with an engineer to investigate possible improvements in wheelchair design.

It is not the purpose of this chapter to explain the nature of physiotherapy practice in all healthcare settings. Rather, a case study will be used to explore the role of the physiotherapist in one specialised area (neurology) in order to highlight profession-specific interventions and to illustrate some aspects of interprofessional working. It should be noted that physiotherapists working in other specialist areas are likely to develop different physiotherapy skills although effective teamworking skills are a common feature of professional practice.

CASE STUDY

Bill is a white, 55-year-old bus driver. He is married to Marie who works full-time in a bank. Bill is recovering in hospital after suffering a stroke, while gardening, two weeks ago. The stroke was caused by a bleed into the left side of his brain damaging brain tissue surrounding the blood vessel. When Bill was admitted to the hospital's 20-bedded stroke rehabilitation unit (SRU) from the accident and emergency department he remained unconscious for two days. During this time Bill needed a high level of care from the nursing staff as well as from the physiotherapists in order to prevent the potential complications of immobility including the development of a respiratory infection or debicutus ulcers (pressure sores). Two days after his stroke Bill gradually began to regain consciousness. Each side of the brain is responsible for controlling movement of the opposite side of the body, so, for Bill the stroke resulted in paralysis of the right side of his body. At first he was unable to move his right arm or leg at all, had weakness in the trunk muscles on his right side and had a reduction in sensation throughout the right side of his body. Within a few days of regaining consciousness Bill began to recover some movement in his right arm and leg. It became apparent he was having difficulties with speech. He appeared to understand what was said to him but when he tried to respond found difficulty in expressing words and jumbled up his sentences.

After two weeks, Bill continues to have difficulty controlling the movement of his right arm and leg and the weakness in his trunk muscles limits the amount of time he can stay upright before becoming fatigued. The muscles around Bill's shoulder, in his arm and hand remain weak with a degree of flaccidity (the technical term for muscles that lack normal tone). He is beginning to regain some movement in the muscles in his right arm and hand, although the strength has not yet recovered sufficiently to enable him to pick up anything with his right hand, or to use the hand skillfully during activities such as feeding or dressing.

Bill is now able to walk short distances with the help of two people, one on each side, but finds it difficult to control the muscles in his right leg and he is worried that the limb might give way underneath him. In addition to having abnormal motor control of his muscles, Bill is still experiencing some altered sensation (due to reduced information reaching the sensory cortex of the brain) although this seems to be improving slowly. This compounds his movement problems as the impaired sensations of touch and proprioception reduces Bill's awareness of the location, position and movement of his right arm and leg unless he is able to see them.

The provision of coordinated patient care and rehabilitation in the unit is the responsibility of an interprofessional team of occupational therapists, physiotherapists, speech and language therapists, nurses, social workers, a dietician and doctors. The team holds a weekly meeting to review the progress of each patient and to plan ongoing care. Interprofessional care plans and treatment records for each patient have recently been introduced which avoids some of the problems associated with keeping separate profession specific records. This has helped all members of the team remain informed of treatment and care developments as well as providing insight into the involvement of other professionals. Hence this has fostered effective communication between members of the team. The Unit has 24-hour medical and nursing cover every day of the week although other therapy staff, including physiotherapists, tend to work during office hours (Monday to Friday 08.30 to 16.30). Patients on the SRU do not normally receive sessions from physiotherapists during the weekend unless they have serious respiratory problems. Should this need arise a patient will be treated by one of the physiotherapists providing weekend cover for the whole hospital.

Of three physiotherapists working on the SRU, it is Sasha who takes the lead in Bill's physiotherapy. However the physiotherapists work as a team and frequently give each other practical assistance and advice. The physiotherapists are provided with valuable support from a physiotherapy assistant, who is not a qualified physiotherapist, but who works under the direction of the SRU physiotherapists, helping patients with exercises, walking practice and so on. In addition to physiotherapy, Bill is receiving help from a speech and language therapist and his speech is improving, although slow progress is making Bill frustrated and angry at times. The two occupational therapists who work on the SRU have also been working with Bill on improving his ability to perform activities of daily living such as dressing, feeding and washing.

Bill's wife, Marie, visits Bill each evening after work and comes to see him Saturday and Sunday afternoons. She is looking more tired with each visit. On each occasion Marie checks with the nurses on Bill's progress, although rarely gets to see any of the physiotherapy staff, due to the timing of her visits.

Since Bill was first admitted to the SRU, Sasha has assessed him on a regular basis to monitor the recovery of his movement and functional abilities and to decide upon appropriate treatment. Sasha has been working collaboratively with both the nurses and the occupational therapists in encouraging Bill to take particular care of his right arm. Because of Bill's diminished sensation to the right side of his body this makes him unaware of times when his arm is in a potentially damaging position, such as when it is dangling over the side of the chair. Sasha has been considering the most appropriate strategies for assisting Bill to become more mobile and to encourage him to regain the use of his affected arm and hand; she has discussed her assessment and proposals with other SRU staff involved in Bill's care and with Bill. They have agreed, for example, that furniture surrounding Bill's bed should be arranged in a way that encourages him to look across to his right side so as to be more aware of his right arm and hand. Bill's bedside cabinet and table have been placed on the right side of his bed, so that he has to reach over to that side if he wishes to pick something up. Now that Bill can walk with the help of two people, it has been agreed that he should walk short distances whenever possible. Bill is now able to walk to the toilet rather than using a commode, although he is unable to do this if two members of staff are not available to help him. Bill is desperately keen to be able to manage this by himself.

The stability of a shoulder joint relies heavily on normal activity in the surrounding muscles. The partial paralysis of the muscles surrounding Bill's right shoulder joint make it very vulnerable to damage, and everyone involved in his care is aware of the need to be very careful not to traumatise the shoulder whenever they assist Bill. A painful, inflamed shoulder needs to be avoided at all costs.

QUESTIONS

■ The physiotherapists know that to maximise the potential for recovery of movement and function Bill needs to be encouraged at every appropriate opportunity to use his right arm, especially in functional, everyday tasks. Why is this information of relevance to other members of the team?

■ Whose role is it to help Bill to walk to the toilet?

■ Bill is getting desperate to manage this task independently; what could be the consequences of staff regularly being unavailable to help him?

■ Can you think of examples when the people involved in Bill's care could cause damage to his right shoulder?

■ What are the potential short-term and long-term problems that could arise from Bill having a painful shoulder? Note: you should consider the consequences for Bill and his carers.

■ Who else, in addition to the interprofessional team, needs to be made aware of the potential for causing damage to Bill's shoulder?

■ What support/advice could the team offer Marie at this stage?

Sasha aims to treat Bill twice a day. Treatment sessions last approximately one hour and usually take place in the SRU's rehabilitation gym but are sometimes carried out in the ward, particularly if Sasha has some practical advice or information to share with other team members. Joint treatment sessions, with nurses and occupational therapists for example, give everyone the opportunity to discuss rehabilitation issues and to plan a coordinated approach to patient care.

During treatment Bill is helped to perform functional tasks, specific therapeutic exercises and movement patterns, in order to help him regain movement and function. Two weeks after his stroke Bill's physiotherapy sessions include a variety of activities, designed to tackle his main movement problems. These have been identified in a detailed assessment, carried out over several sessions by Sasha, in consultation with Bill, whose own priority is to walk independently again. He would also like to be able to use his right hand properly, but he is currently more worried about his walking and his inability to speak clearly. The speech and language therapist continues to see Bill regularly and has given him some strategies to help clarify his speech, including encouraging him to speak more slowly than he normally would. Sasha, the occupational therapists and the nurses are aware of this advice and are gently trying to reinforce it in their own sessions.

As Bill is keen to walk, each physiotherapy session includes some activities which work towards this, although specific exercises and functional activities aimed at recovery of more normal movement and function in Bill's arm are also incorporated into each session. Bill is practising walking in parallel bars, with guidance and feedback from Sasha, and is steadily increasing the length of time he can stay on his feet before fatiguing. Bill has been given some exercises to target weakness in specific muscles which are contributing to his abnormal walking pattern. The physiotherapists are particularly concerned at the marked weakness in the muscles that lift up the foot at the ankle and which prevent the toes from dragging on the floor. A joint therapy session has been arranged between Sasha and one of the occupational therapists, to consider whether Bill might benefit from a splint to prevent his foot from dropping down during walking. Bill is frightened that he is going to trip and fall and a splint might remove this anxiety. The splint can be worn during walking practice, but be removed between walking sessions to enable Bill to build up his muscle strength. Hopefully, in this way, the splint may only be required as a temporary measure, although if the muscle strength does not return, Bill may need to wear a splint to prevent foot drop in the long-term. Sasha has some knowledge of splints but recognises the occupational therapist is more skilled in making splints to suit the needs of individual patients. The assessment should identify whether Bill requires a tailor made splint or whether he could be supplied with a commercially available splint, in which case a written referral will be made to the hospital's orthotics department.

Bill is making good progress and is starting to ask when he might be able to go home. The team has been thinking about this and have discussed Bill's case at an interprofessional meeting. Although the team feels that Bill is not yet independent enough to go home, they are considering what services might need to be put in place when Bill is eventually discharged from the SRU. Sasha thinks it is important that Marie should come along to see what is being done in the physiotherapy sessions and how Bill is progressing. Despite leaving Marie several messages at the SRU reception desk, Marie has not yet been in touch.

QUESTIONS

- Why might the physiotherapist think that Marie should come to a physiotherapy session?

- What could be preventing Marie from contacting the physiotherapist?

- What are the barriers to effective communication in this case?

- Is there anything that Sasha could consider doing to improve the situation?

The case study provides a small snapshot of some aspects of the physiotherapist's role in Bill's rehabilitation and illustrates how the interprofessional team might interact at various points in Bill's recovery. It illustrates that while physiotherapists might concentrate on specific activities such as regaining muscle strength, joint range of movement and functional patterns of movement, the holistic management of Bill's rehabilitation is shared between the whole team. To be effective, the team needs to involve Bill and Marie in planning, implementing and evaluating the rehabilitation process.

Decisions regarding Bill's discharge home, and plans for his future care needs, will also be made by the team, in conjunction with Bill and Marie. Bill may require ongoing treatment and be referred by Sasha to a physiotherapy outpatient department. Alternatively he may be referred to a community physiotherapist who can see Bill at home. Bill may also need ongoing input from other professionals, such as the speech and language therapist, and he may require advice form a social worker, for example regarding benefits which he might be entitled to claim. Marie's needs will also have to be carefully considered as she currently has a full-time job. It is very difficult to predict the extent of recovery following a stroke and Bill might be able to return to his job as a bus driver, but only if he regains a high level of functional ability. However, recovery can be slow and many patients who have had a major stroke do not return to full function.

Effective communication systems need to be in place for as long as necessary between members of the interprofessional team, and Bill and Marie, so that Bill's progress can be monitored and any new problems recognised and managed as soon as possible. Hopefully, Bill will continue to recover steadily and his attendance at the rehabilitation unit or input from the community physiotherapist will eventually cease. In the long-term, Bill and Marie should be given the opportunity to contact a physiotherapist if they need further help and advice.

Professional role boundaries in a changing NHS

Where does the uniqueness of being a physiotherapist end and interprofessionalism begin? The question is not a new one. Potts (1996) identified that health professionals will be challenged by having to justify why so many individual groupings, all of them protective of their professional boundaries, are required for delivery of care and rehabilitation. The NHS Plan articulates clearly that traditional role boundaries are expected to give way to greater flexibility within teams, with staff working under agreed protocols 'that make the best use of all the talents of NHS staff and which are flexible enough to take account of patients' individual needs' (DoH 2000b: 83). This is seen as one of the foundations for improving the quality of patient care and providing greater opportunities for staff development.

The beginning of the 21st century is proving to be an exciting time for AHPs and it is imperative that the professions do not fail to make good use of opportunities presented to them under the NHS Plan, by way of being 'central to the modernisation programme... set in train' (DoH 2000b: 3). The physiotherapy profession has come a long way since those four nurses took protection of their profession into their own hands and established the Society of Trained Masseuses. Physiotherapy is set to continue to evolve and in doing so it is not inconceivable that, over time, a new breed of therapist will begin to emerge as a result of the extension of clinical skills and the blurring of professional boundaries.

References

Blackledge C. (2003) Widening the scope of practice. *Physiotherapy Frontline* 9(22): 7.

CSP (Chartered Society of Physiotherapy) (2000) *Core Standards of Physiotherapy Practice*. London: Chartered Society of Physiotherapy.

CSP (2002) *The Curriculum Framework for Qualifying Programmes in Physiotherapy*. London: Chartered Society of Physiotherapy.

CSP (2004) History of the Chartered Society of Physiotherapy http://www.csp.org.uk/thecsp/about/history.cfm Accessed January 2004.

DoH (Department of Health) (2000a) *Meeting the Challenge: A Strategy for the Allied Health Professions*. London: Department of Health.

DoH (2000b) *The NHS Plan: A Plan for Investment, A Plan for Reform*. London: Department of Health.

HPC (Health Professions Council) (2004) Registrants – Registration – what's in it for me? http://www.hpc-uk.org/registrants/benefits.htm Accessed February 2004.

Potts J. (1996) Physiotherapy in the next century: opportunities and challenges. *Physiotherapy* 82: 150–5.

10

Police

Peter Kennison and Robin Fletcher

Introduction

In order to understand the nature and scope of policing it is necessary to con-centrate on i) what it is that the police actually do and how they go about doing it; and ii) the working relationships police have with other agencies. Systems in good working order cause few difficulties. However, when systems fail their shortcomings are brought into sharp relief. When failure involves a vulnerable child the lessons learned can be particularly painful. This chapter considers a dramatic failure in child protection in the sad case of Victoria Climbié.

The police have a tradition of working with others to prevent and detect crime. In this chapter we discuss interprofessional working within the context of interagency partnerships. In England and Wales the lead agencies with responsibilities for children are the social services, the police and the health service. All these agencies hold a duty of care under the Children Act 1989 to protect children, however in Victoria's case this fell short when communication and cooperation between agency partners was ineffective.

When the police fail to act in a manner that satisfies public and media expectation they are called to account. This expectation, however, raises two issues. Firstly what exactly is the role of the police and secondly to whom are they accountable? It is therefore a surprise to discover that, despite the vast costs of running the police service, its function is not easily defined. This is in spite of a number of attempts to determine core activity and define the role of the police in modern society (ISTD 1993, Home Office 1993a, 1993b, 1995, Posen 1994).

The Role of the Police

Sir Robert Peel set out the primary objective of modern policing when, in 1829, he said:

> It should be understood at the outset that the principal objective to be attained is the prevention of crime.
>
> (cited in Alderson 1979: 198)

This was to be achieved by using uniformed officers to patrol the streets (Critchley 1967, Emsley 1996, Alderson 1979) and by their mere presence deter potential offenders (Reiner 1992). This simple concept of policing prevails today with many calls for a return to uniformed foot patrols together with the expansion of community policing, despite evidence to suggest such activity is ineffective (Kelling *et al*. 1974, Morgan and Newburn 1997).

Research by Hough (1985) and Bayley (1994, 1996) identified that the majority of police work is responding to calls for assistance from the public rather than dealing with crime. Furthermore Bayley's research acknowledged that most policing activity is involved with restoring public order with as much as 31 per cent of police time being spent providing some form of social service.

These findings give some idea of the role of the police. Undoubtedly they are law enforcers (Kinsey *et al*. 1986) whose traditional juridical approach to crime has been one of arrest, prosecution, and incarceration. However in the last three decades this model of policing has gradually given way to a process of managing people within the community following the actuarial justice theories of Feeley and Simon (1992, 1994). This has emerged as a result of government policies that encourage multiagency and partnership practices (Home Office memos 8/84 and 44/90) to tackle causational issues within a less punitive criminal justice system.

The police are also engaged in the maintenance of public order (Wilson 1968) both with antisocial behaviour affecting the quality of life of the community, and in the broader sense of major civil disobedience (O'Byrne 1981). But perhaps the least understood role is that of social service provider. The police have been called the only instantly contactable 24-hour service dealing with any problem (Bittner 1991). The variety of police work is summed up in the following way:

> The Police frequently are the only 24-hour service agency available to respond to those in need. The result is that the police handle everything from unexpected child births, skid row alcoholics, drug addicts, emergency psychiatric cases, family fights, landlord-tenant disputes, and traffic violations, to occasional incidents of crime.
>
> (Morgan and Newburn 1997: 79)

As an example, during the Christmas holiday period 2002, Nottinghamshire Police estimated that one in five 999 calls for assistance was not an emergency. Calls for assistance included resolving a fight between two squirrels in a garden, advice on how to cook a turkey, and how to set up a satellite dish (Hail 2002).

The 1962 Royal Commission highlighted the disparate manner in which individual forces in the towns, shires, and cities had developed, and the way in which they responded to the public as 'an accident of history rather than the result of organisation' (cited in Oliver 1997: 14). The Commission made a number of recommendations to improve efficiency. The number of forces was reduced from 117 to 49, and again in 1972 to the present number of 43 (Emsley 1996). There was a change in the primary objective of the police (Critchley 1967) from Peel's crime prevention to the enforcement of law and order to be measured by crime statistics (Critchley 1978). Ironically these recommendations were being made at a time when another review, the Cornish Committee on the Prevention and Detection of Crime (Home Office 1965), began to establish crime prevention as a subject in its own right (Weatheritt 1986).

Policing styles

The Commission created a Police Research and Planning Branch (Critchley 1967) to examine police activity and provide new policing options. Since then a number of different policing styles have been developed in the attempt to provide a service suitable for an increasingly complex and diverse community.

The first policing system to be developed was the Unit Beat Policing model (Home Office 1967, Emsley 1996) which effectively created a two-tiered system of policing. On one level police officers patrolled in vehicles, responding to incidents quickly, a style often referred to as fire brigade policing (McLaughlin and Muncie 1996). For this police officers were directed to incidents by anonymous centralised controllers who had no understanding of local culture, values, practices or the historical contextualisation of previous linked events.

On the second level residential police officers worked on foot, maintaining community contact (Emsley 1996) acting like the old style village bobby (Banton 1973). It was intended that these officers would retain the confidence of the community through personal contact and develop the necessary information flow to ensure local policing satisfied the requirements of the community.

The separation of police skills began with the Unit Beat system and continued with the creation of specialist departments within the police force headquarters (Crawford 1998). The centralisation of experience was considered a more effective use of resources but it led to a withdrawal of frontline policing from the community, and the notion of patrol as a preventative method declined (Kettle and Hodges 1982, Weatheritt 1986). As a consequence the police resorted to tactics that further alienated them from the community, with devastating effects in Brixton, South London.

The 1970s and 1980s also witnessed a major increase in public disorder. Pope and Weiner (1981) categorised the causes of this into four groups.

- Industrial Disputes – (for example, the miners strikes of 1972/74/84) reflecting problems of unemployment and low pay and the demise of nationalised industries.

■ Demonstrations and Counter Demonstrations – (for example, CND; National Front; Anti-Vietnam war marches), the vocal and physical support of ideological extremism.

■ Recreational Meetings – (for example, football hooliganism; confrontation between mods/rockers/skinheads) as displays of disaffected youth.

■ Spontaneous Attacks on the police in inner city areas (for example, Notting Hill; Brixton; Broadwater Farm).

Whilst the first three categories are examples of the political and social instability of society at particular times, the fourth category is indicative of a loss of respect for the police, who stood accused of racism, sexism and heavy handedness in dealing with the public (Lea and Young 1993, Hall *et al.* 1978, Solomos 1993). This was a low point of police community cooperation, particularly as the police response was to become increasingly militaristic with the use of riot equipment.

The Importance of Scarman and Macpherson

In 1981 the tranquillity of British society was shattered by rioting in Brixton, South London and in other major cities. The inquiry into these events by Lord Scarman (1981) uncovered a deep resentment of the police. A serious increase in street crime had resulted in the police adopting stop and search tactics that Lea and Young (1993) considered more akin to an invasion force, rather than public servants responding to community needs.

Scarman's recommendations were to have a far-reaching impact on how policing was to develop in the latter half of the 20th century. Scarman's main recommendation was to re-establish contact with the community and to respond to its needs. This was to be achieved by adopting a more flexible style of policing that embraced Alderson's (1979) village in the city concept. It was to be the first of many attempts to return to the principles of foot patrols and community policing as crime prevention measures. A key component of which is police/public consultation. This philosophy was considered to be so important that it was incorporated into the Police and Criminal Evidence Act 1984 (PACE), placing a requirement on the police to create and maintain Police and Community Consultation Groups (PCCG). The idea being that a formalised group of this nature would exchange information to help direct the police to deal with problems the community wanted solving, rather than dealing with problems the police thought important. PACE also introduced a code of practice which afforded, for the first time, rights of persons being stopped and searched and of prisoners detained at police stations.

The concept of information exchange has since been promoted as a necessary ingredient in reducing crime and antisocial behaviour (Scarman 1981; S105 PACE 1984; Home Office 1991; S96 Police Act 1996; HMIC 1998). More recently the Crime and Disorder Act 1998 together with recommendations by Sir Macpherson (1999) have established the need to develop a multi-agency process that brings together relevant agencies in order to encourage sharing of information and development of holistic problem solving solutions.

Local accountability

The creation of PCCGs brought with it the dimension of accountability. One of the problems highlighted by Scarman was a lack of local accountability for police action.

The traditional method of local accountability was through a tripartite process involving the Chief Constable, Home Secretary and a Watch Committee (later Police Authorities). Theoretically each had equal status however the Chief Constable maintained a degree of independence that allowed autonomy over tactical decision making. Higher central funds gave the Home Secretary a greater say over policing at the expense of reducing local influence.

Local influence was becoming increasingly important as politicians began to recognise many Law and Order issues affected minority and disadvantaged groups (Lansley *et al.* 1989, Hain and Hebditch 1978), solutions for which would often work only in a local context. The following two decades witnessed radical changes in policing philosophy and placed the community at the centre of proposed solutions. The creation of the Five Towns Initiative in 1986 and the Safer Cities Programmes in 1988 (Crawford 1998) were government sponsored moves toward developing multiagency solutions embracing the community as active partners.

By the end of the 1980s multiagency cooperation had generated a multitude of initiatives and led to a government review of partnership activity. The Morgan Report (Home Office 1991) concluded that local authorities should play a greater role in promoting concepts of crime prevention and community safety (Hughes 1998). The majority of the recommendations made by Morgan were ignored by the Conservative government, but were to re-emerge later in the Crime and Disorder Act 1998 under New Labour.

New managerialism

Whilst community partnership encouraged one form of accountability, in the 1980s, the police, along with other public sector organisations, became subject to the managerial philosophy of Value for Money (now known as Best Value) promoting private sector management practices to achieve greater efficiency. Osbourne and Gaebler (1993) identified that in doing so the government shifted from being an impartial service provider to an administrative body setting goals and objectives. Instead of being measured on its ability to react to incidents the police were to be given targets to achieve (Hughes 1994).

Target setting was re-enforced by the Police and Magistrates Courts Act 1994 which introduced Key National Objectives (KNO) and Key Performance Indicators for all police forces. The police or their authorities did not, at first, see the introduction of KNOs as problematic as they appeared to address issues already on the local agenda. KNOs required that police performance was to be measured by the number of arrests and prosecutions together with reported crime statistics. This approach contrasted with that taken during the previous decade where tackling causational issues through holistic prevention was considered appropriate and where performance criteria were based on partnership and multiagency working.

The Crime and Disorder Act 1998

Within months of being elected to office the 1997 Labour government introduced the Crime and Disorder Act 1998 as the major thrust of its crime reduction programme (Home Office 1998). It had two key elements. The first created a Responsible Authority, consisting of the local authority Chief Executive and the local senior Police Commander. This was consistent with Morgan's (Home Office 1991) recommendation that the local authority play a major role in reducing crime. The second element required public consultation, particularly with those groups identified as hard to reach (Home Office 1998).

This was intended to make police and local authorities accountable to the community for the reduction of crime and antisocial behaviour and this required cooperation to seek holistic solutions in partnership with others. The measure of success was to be an improved quality of life for the community, identified by qualitatively based performance criteria embracing the aims and objectives of all participating partners.

There are two groups of agencies under the Crime and Disorder Act (1998). Statutory agencies include the police, local authority, the fire brigade, social services, health, and education while among the voluntary agencies are victim support services, the business sector, and other community groups. The type of service available will vary but in general agencies are involved in, among other things, the provision of housing, welfare, benefit, education, health, policing and jobs.

What are partnerships?

The government of the early 1980s recognised that crime was a problem for all and that many sociological issues beyond the control of the police needed to be tackled. Partnerships can be traced to Circular 8/84 which identified crime prevention as a task for the whole community (Home Office 1984), suggesting the police alone could not tackle crime. Working in partnership to fight crime has since become standard policing.

Changes in legislation have spread the burden of crime prevention, crime reduction, and community safety into a wider forum, making it a statutory requirement for the police to work as equal partners with local authorities. Partnership culture was introduced by the Crime and Disorder Act 1998. Partnerships are considered to be:

> The set of characteristics that differentiate provision agencies including legislative framework, powers and responsibilities, degrees of electoral accountability, codes and practices, career paths and so on.
>
> (Balloch and Taylor 2001: 36)

Crawford considers non-business partnerships by suggesting that:

> Partnerships – especially within the field of crime control and criminal justice – by their nature draw together diverse organisations with very different cultures, ideologies and traditions which pursue distinct aims through divergent structures, strategies and practices.
>
> (1998: 171)

An example of an effective partnership introduced within the legislation is Youth Offending Teams. Youth Offending Teams bring together police, social workers, education workers, youth workers, and probation officers to deal with young people who commit crime.

Partnership working presupposes participating agencies function well and will work effectively with one another, however, partnerships are not without their difficulties. There are problems of culture and power relations where some agencies assume control and influence by exerting their own group norms, beliefs, socialisation, understandings, and goals on others to the detriment of the partnership.

The Case of Victoria Climbié

The inquiry into the death of Victoria Climbié highlighted a number of problems arising from ineffective working relationships between personnel within the police, health, and social services. Some of these are identified below.

CASE STUDY

Ten months of tragedy – the tragedy of Victoria Climbié

Victoria, a black child born on the Ivory Coast was entrusted into the care of Marie-Theresa Kouao an aunt (sic) by her parents who wanted a better life for her in England. She arrived in the UK from Paris on 24 April 1999 with Kouao. Victoria's identity had been subverted with Victoria being treated by outsiders as the daughter of Kouao, rather than her niece.

On arrival and travelling as EU citizens they went to accommodation in Acton but later moved to a hostel in Harlesden. During later visits to Ealing Social Services the staff noticed a difference in dress between mother and daughter with the latter being far scruffier (Laming 2003). By May 1999 there was evidence to suggest Victoria was already suffering from neglect.

Within two months of arrival other people began to notice injuries on Victoria especially the scars which Kouao explained as resulting from a fall on an escalator. Kouao met Carl Manning on 14 June 1999 and three days later a friend of Kouoa who met the pair in the street was sufficiently concerned at Victoria's appearance and behaviour that she telephoned Brent Social Services twice, anonymously. This was the first social services contact made however by the end of this tragic affair further contacts were made with Haringay Social Services, Enfield Social Services and the Tottenham Child and Family Centre (Laming 2003) but all to no avail.

Child Protection Teams

In 1987 the Metropolitan Police introduced Child Protection Teams (CPTs) comprising police officers working in partnership with social workers and other relevant professionals on joint investigations. CPTs deal with child protection issues where prosecution and conviction are seen as less important than establishing truth and preserving the interests of child victims (Fido and Skinner 1999). CPTs operate on a borough basis, usually from one location.

CASE STUDY continued

Victoria's first visit to hospital occurred when she was taken to the Central Middlesex Hospital on the 14 July 1999 where she was seen for injuries which were later described to be non-accidental (Laming 2003). Concern was such that she was referred to the paediatric registrar who recorded that Victoria had numerous injuries on her body. Brent Social Services were informed of Victoria's admission to hospital for observation and further examination. The next day a doctor diagnosed scabies as the cause of the injuries and Victoria left hospital. One week later, and concerned about facial scalding, Kouao took Victoria to the North Middlesex Hospital. Victoria spent 13 nights in the paediatric ward. On her third visit to hospital on 25 February 2000 Victoria was declared dead aged eight years and three months.

Laming (2003) showed that there was a lack of initial investigation procedures during the early stages of this inquiry. The initial response was to give the case low priority even though evidence suggested serious physical injury. The victim was in hospital and in agreement with social services Victoria was placed under police protection. The officer went off duty and failed to visit Victoria, a factor which Laming suggested was a grave error of judgement because had she visited she would have found 12 key pieces of information, which would have given her cause for concern for the safety of Victoria.

By the time of Victoria's death she had been to or brought to the attention of no less than five social service agencies (two of which were in the same borough) and two separate hospitals, which she visited on three occasions. It can be a common misconception that the prevention and detection of crimes is not a function of health practitioners and whilst treatment takes priority, health professionals often see crime as a matter for the police. This does not reflect a culture of partnership but that of an isolated group operating under difficult circumstances.

QUESTION

■ What are your responsibilities in reporting suspected cases of deliberate harm to the police?

Confusion of roles and responsibilities

The Laming Report illustrates serious failings of the police at all levels and across jurisdictions. In the case of suspected injury or harm to a child the police are the lead investigative agency, responsible for making enquiries, collecting information, and evaluating evidence for criminal prosecutions.

The police submit evidence in case files to the Crown Prosecution Service who decide, amongst other things, if there is sufficient evidence to progress a prosecution.

In Victoria's case as far as the police were concerned social services were the lead agency in child protection matters, a position which Laming criticised. As a result roles and responsibilities were blurred. Although social services were acknowledged to have an important role in leading the coordination of various sources of information, as Laming pointed out 'the police are the lead agency in a criminal investigation' (2003: 306) and in his view they should have conducted a parallel investigation into the crime reported against her.

Laming (2003) noted child protection officers had been unsure regarding their exact responsibilities within the context of CPTs and the investigation of suspected deliberate harm to a child. Had this uncertainty been discussed by all concerned a clearer understanding of the roles, responsibilities, and boundaries of each professional might have facilitated more effective interprofessional working practices.

QUESTION

■ What factors might result in confusion regarding the roles and responsibilities of different professional groups?

Training and work experience

Laming (2003) highlighted the lack of detective training and experience in the relevant CPTs. In both of the two borough CPTs there was only one qualified detective with sufficient experience and training to deal with child protection matters.

For effective interprofessional working, a combination of personal and professional confidence, together with competent communication skills are required to enable individuals to challenge the views of other professionals. The initial referral of Victoria's case to the police indicated that she had suffered bruises to a number of areas of her body in addition to infected fingers and bloodshot eyes. However, on the following day the police officer concerned was notified that the paediatrician attributed all of Victoria's injuries to scabies. Laming (2003) criticised the police officer for accepting this explanation without question and cited this as a factor contributing to an inadequate investigation. This was compounded by what he referred to as a 'profound reluctance to challenge the diagnosis of a consultant paediatrician' (Laming 2003: 302). Had the doctor been questioned, it would have become clear that the diagnosis of scabies did not account for all of the injuries sustained by Victoria. Laming (2003) acknowledges the role of medical staff in providing information on injuries together with an opinion regarding their cause, however, he attributes the primary role in determining the significance and interpretation of such injuries to specialists in child protection. That is, social workers and child protection police officers who have the benefit of forensic evidence and information about a child's wider social circumstances.

QUESTION

■ What factors might inhibit a junior member of one profession questioning the views of a more senior member of another profession?

Deficiencies in both supervision and training were highlighted within the Laming Report (2003). Had the junior officers been more closely supervised by their senior officers mistakes might have been avoided.

Laming (2003) recommended that all child protection officers receive training in order to develop the confidence and skills required to challenge the views of others. Interprofessional education, whereby different professionals learn together with the object of developing collaborative practice (CAIPE 1997) would appear to be a suitable approach in facilitating the knowledge, skills, and attitudes required to work in interprofessional teams within the context of child protection.

Group behaviour – the problems of culture

While individual failures are important, it is also necessary to consider group dynamics. Group behaviour will be dependent on group norms, beliefs, understandings, and shared goals. There can be internal conflict when group goals differ from those of the organisation. Organisational goals are set by those who are established at the top of hierarchies. The group dynamics of cultural structures or vertical hierarchies reflect the differences of each cultural group.

During the Laming inquiry, although police representatives stated there were many examples of good working relationships with social services, examples of poor relationships were also evident. Some within the police service reported feeling some workers in social services held stereotypical views of the police, perceiving them to be too heavy-handed and more concerned with securing a conviction than with the interests of the child. Whereas some in the police service perceived social service staff as inflexible and unprepared to negotiate mutually convenient times and places for strategy meetings. Laming (2003) considered there was no real sense of equality within the relationship between the two agencies and he criticised the police for failing to challenge this. According to Laming (2003) child protection strategy meetings should not be viewed as the remit of one agency with professionals from other agencies invited to attend. They should be a shared multiagency responsibility.

QUESTIONS

■ What stereotypical views might be held regarding the police?

■ Think of other professional groups that you might be required to work with and consider what stereotypes might be held regarding these professions?

Mutual respect is identified by Stapleton (1998) as a critical attribute of collaborative working. Mutual respect is facilitated through open and honest communication which enables each of the professionals involved in an inter-professional endeavour to develop an understanding of one another's perspectives. Had the perceptions of inequality, inflexibility, and stereotyping been openly discussed this may have provided a platform for mutual understanding, more flexible patterns of working, and a more equal distribution of power.

CASE STUDY continued

On 12 January 2001 Marie-Theresa Kouao and Carl Manning were convicted and jailed for life, for the murder of Victoria (Anna) Climbié. The results of the post mortem showed she had died from hypothermia which had arisen in the context of malnourishment, a damp environment and restricted movement (Laming 2003). She had 128 separate injuries showing that she had been beaten with a range of both sharp and blunt instruments. The last days of her short life were spent living in a cold unheated bathroom, bound hand and foot inside a bin bag lying in her own urine and excrement. To some involved this had been the worst case of child abuse they had ever seen.

There were at least 12 key occasions when the relevant services had an opportunity to intervene (Laming 2003). These warning signs occurred when Victoria had been taken or been referred to hospital accident and emergency units, social services departments or to the police. Those responsible failed to work together effectively and never seriously reviewed the individual circumstances. As a result Victoria was left to die abandoned, unheard, in agony and alone. Laming suggests this was a gross failure and was inexcusable.

Conclusion

This chapter has outlined the role of the police and considered their responsibilities in terms of child protection. Police accountability is complicated and diffuse. In the early days the role of police shifted from prevention to that of law enforcement and then to the actuarial justice approach, involving the management of people. Within this latter role prominence was paid first to the maintenance of public order and then to a return of community based policing methods responding to the needs of the community whilst working in partnership with other agencies in solving common problems. New managerialism introduced key national objectives and key performance indicators designed to enhance police working that also sought to improve the quality of life for the community.

In the case of Victoria Climbié the prosecution rested with the police yet they perceived this not to be their decision but that of social services. The case illustrates individuals from different agencies working separately with little consultation demonstrating that communication across agencies was inadequate.

The police had developed CPTs to help protect children, originally an impressive model of good practice but which failed because people with inadequate investigative skills, little practical work experience, and poor training staffed them. Blurred individual roles, disjointed lines of accountability, ineffective internal communication, supervision and management further compounded the problem. Finally there was failure by a number of individuals from a variety of professional backgrounds, further complicated by the role of the group dynamic of organisational cultures.

If true partnerships are to function effectively accurate information sharing is the key to reliable problem solving and decision making. In the case of Victoria Climbié had all the information been pooled in what Laming describes as a multiagency assessment tool then mistakes could have been avoided.

References

Alderson J. (1979) *Policing Freedom*. Plymouth: Latimer Trend and Co.

Banton M. (1973) *Police-Community Relations*. London: Collins.

Balloch S. and Taylor M. (2001) *Partnership Working*. Bristol: The Policy Press.

Bayley D.H. (1994) *Police for the Future*. New York: Oxford University Press.

Bayley D.H. (1996) What do police do. In Saulsbury W., Mott J. and Newburn T. (eds) *Themes in Contemporary Policing. Independent Inquiry into the Roles and Responsibilities of the Police*. London: Police Foundation Policy Studies Institute, pp. 29–41.

Bittner E. (1991) The functions of the police in modern society. In Klockars C.B. and Mastrofski S.D. (eds) *Thinking About Police*. New York: McGraw-Hill, pp. 35–51.

CAIPE (Centre for the Advancement of Interprofessional Education) (1997) *Interprofessional Education – A Definition*. London: CAIPE Bulletin **13**.

Critchley T.A. (1967) *A History of Police in England and Wales*. London: Constable and Company.

Critchley T.A. (1978) *A History of the Police in England and Wales* (2nd edn). London: Constable and Company.

Crawford A. (1998) *Crime Prevention and Community Safety*. London: Longman.

Emsley C. (1996) The History of Crime and Crime Control Institutions c1770–c1945. In Maguire M., Morgan R. and Reiner R. (eds) *The Oxford Handbook of Criminology*. Oxford: Clarendon Press, pp. 149–82.

Feeley M. and Simon J. (1992) The new penology: notes on the emerging strategy of corrections and its implications. *Criminology* **30**(4): 449–74.

Feeley M. and Simon J. (1994) Actuarial justice: the emerging new criminal law. In Nelken D. (ed.) *The Futures of Criminology*. London: Sage, pp. 173–201.

Fido M. and Skinner K. (1999) *The Official Encyclopaedia of Scotland Yard*. London: Virgin Press.

Hail B. (2002) Hello, 999? Squirrels are fighting in my garden. *Daily Mail*, 28 December: 3.

Hain P. and Hebditch S. (1978) *Radicals and Socialism*. Nottingham: Institute for Workers Control.

Hall S., Chrichter C., Jefferson T., Clarke J. and Roberts B. (1978) *Policing the Crisis: Mugging the State and Law and Order*. London: Macmillan.

HMIC (Her Majesty's Inspectorate of Constabulary) (1998) *Winning the Race*. London: HMSO.

Home Office (1965) *Report of the Committee on the Prevention and Detection of Crime* (the Cornish Report). London: HMSO.

Home Office (1967) *Police Manpower, Equipment and Efficiency*. London: HMSO.

Home Office, Department of Education and Science, Department of the Environment, Department of Health and Social Security and Welsh Office (1984) *Crime Prevention* (Home Office Circular 8/1984). London: Home Office.

Home Office (1990) *The Success of the Partnership Approach* (Circular 44/1990). London: Home Office.

Home Office (1991) *Safer Communities: The Local Delivery of Crime Prevention through the Partnership Approach* (the Morgan Report). London: Home Office.

Home Office, Northern Ireland Office and Scottish Office (1993a) *Inquiry into Police Responsibilities and Rewards* Cm 2280 (the Sheehy Report). London: HMSO.

Home Office (1993b) *Police reform; A Police Service for the Twenty First Century* Cm 2281. London: HMSO.

Home Office (1995) *Review of the Police Core and Ancillary Tasks: Final report* (the Posen Report). London: HMSO.

Home Office (1998) *Crime and Disorder Act Guidelines.* London: HMSO.

Hough M. (1985) Organizations and resource management in the uniformed police. In Heal K., Tarling R. and Burrows J. (eds) *Policing Today.* London: HMSO.

Hughes O.E. (1994) *Public Management and Administration.* New York: St Martins Press.

Hughes G. (1998) *Understanding Crime Prevention.* Milton Keynes: Open University Press.

ISTD (1993) *Changing Police; Business or Service?* London: ISTD.

Kettle M. and Hodges L. (1982) *Uprising.* London: Pan.

Kelling G., Pate T., Dieckman D. and Brown C. (1974) *The Kansas City Preventive Patrol Experiment: A Summary Report.* Washington DC: Police Foundation.

Kinsey R., Lea J. and Young J. (1986) *Losing the Fight Against Crime.* Oxford: Blackwell.

Laming Lord (2003) *Inquiry into the Death of Victoria Climbié.* London: The Stationery Office.

Lansley S., Goss S. and Wolmar C. (1989) *Councils in Conflict.* London: Macmillan.

Lea J. and Young J. (1993) *What is to be Done About Law and Order.* London: Pluto Press.

McLaughlin E. and Muncie J. (1996) *Controlling Crime.* London: Sage.

MacPherson W. Sir (1999) *The Inquiry into the Matters Arising From the Death of Stephen Lawrence.* London: HMSO.

Morgan R. and Newburn T. (1997) *The Future of Policing.* Oxford: Clarendon Press.

O'Byrne M. (1981) The Role of the Police. In Pope D.W. and Weiner N.L. (eds) *Modern Policing.* London: Croom Helm Ltd, pp. 11–21.

Oliver I. (1997) *Police, Government and Accountability.* London: Macmillan Press.

Pope D.W. and Weiner N.L. (eds) (1981) *Modern Policing.* London: Croom Helm Ltd.

Posen I. (1994) *Review of Police Core and Ancillary Tasks.* Paper presented to ACPO conference March 1994.

Reiner R. (1992) *The Politics of Police.* London: Harvester Wheatsheaf.

Scarman Lord (1981) *The Brixton Disorders 10–12 April 1981; report of an inquiry by the Rt. Hon. The Lord Scarman O.B.E.* London: HMSO.

Solomos J. (1993) *Race and Racism in Britain.* London: Macmillan.

Stapleton S.R. (1998) Team-building: making collaborative practice work. *Journal of Nurse-Midwifery* **43**: 12–8.

Weatheritt M. (1986) *Innovations in Policing.* London: Croom Helm Ltd.

Wilson J.Q. (1968) *Varieties of Police Behaviour.* Cambridge, Massachusetts: Harvard University Press.

CHAPTER 11

Probation

Jane Lindsay

Introduction

The probation service has its origins in the 19th century and like other public services, is being rapidly transformed as part of the current modernisation agenda. Established under The Criminal Justice and Court Services Act (2000), the National Probation Service for England and Wales assists the 'courts in sentencing decisions and providing for the supervision and rehabilitation of persons charged with, or convicted of offences' (Home Office 2001: 2). The National Probation Service aims to:

(a) protect the public,
(b) reduce re-offending,
(c) provide for the proper punishment of offenders,
(d) ensure that offenders are aware of the effects of crime on the victims of crime and the public,
(e) rehabilitate offenders.

(Criminal Justice and Court Services Act 2000, s2.2)

Recent changes require probation staff to work collaboratively with statutory and voluntary agencies including police, prison, health, victim support, social services and housing. The probation service also works in partnership with voluntary agencies that provide specialist rehabilitation services for offenders.

This chapter outlines how the probation service is developing approaches to effective working with both other professionals and offenders. Three key themes of protecting the public, reducing re-offending and working with victims of crime are presented and discussed, along with the organisational structure, the key roles and the ethical framework of probation work. Inter-professional policy initiatives are outlined together with the implications for collaborative working. The chapter concludes with an overview of some of the challenges and visions of working interprofessionally to promote community justice.

The National Probation Service for England and Wales: the organisational structure

From June 2004, the probation service forms part of the National Offender Management Service (NOMS). NOMS brings together both the prison and probation services into a new body charged with managing all offenders both in the community and in prison in order to ensure that offenders are punished, and that their re-offending is reduced (Home Office 2004). NOMS will promote *end-to-end* management of offenders, which means progress offenders make in prison should be built on in the community. NOMS is an agency of the Home Office led by a Chief Executive. A National Offender Manager reports to the Chief Executive and is responsible for reducing re-offending, managing the budget for offender services and leading a team of Regional Offender Managers (nine English regions and Wales). One of the objectives of NOMS is to ensure greater value for money and more use of private and *not-for-profit* sectors in prison and the community. This may lead to increased opportunities for other agencies to contribute directly to supervising offenders in the community and increased interprofessional work.

Within the probation service, organisational structures vary. Staff are often grouped in teams with specialist functions including: preparation of court reports, case management of offenders, delivery of intervention programmes, and supervision of community punishments. Some staff are seconded to work in Youth Offending Teams, prisons, and other public protection and crime prevention or reduction partnership agencies.

Probation staff include a number of different professional groups, including probation officers, probation service officers and psychologists. Before 1997 a probation officer was required to be a qualified social worker. Preparation now consists of a combined academic and professional qualification. Probation officers are responsible for case management, risk assessment and management, and with delivering programmes of intervention for offenders. Probation service officers undertake tasks such as court work, group work, individual casework, supervising community punishments and working as hostel officers.

A recent survey suggested that probation has yet to achieve widespread public recognition. Half of those surveyed claimed to know 'hardly anything or nothing at all about the service' (National Probation Service/MORI 2002: 5).

The level of awareness and understanding of the probation service among black and minority ethic communities was even lower. Only 11 per cent of respondents considered the service to be concerned with reducing re-offending and just two per cent perceived punishment of offenders and protection of the public to be a function of the service (*ibid*). Perhaps the service's rebranding as part of NOMS may change public perceptions.

An outline of key probation roles and tasks

The probation service works primarily with those aged 18 and over convicted of offences. Probation workers provide courts with assistance in determining appropriate sentences to pass and supervise those serving community sentences and people released from prison on licence. Young offenders, aged under 18, are dealt with by multiprofessional Youth Offending Teams (YOTs) which include representation from the police, probation service, social services, health, education, drug and alcohol misuse services, and housing officers (for more information about YOTs see http://www.youth-justice-board.gov.uk/youthjusticeboard).

The National Standards for the Supervision of Offenders in the Community (Home Office 2000) set out the framework for a consistent approach when working with offenders. Hopley (2002) argues such consistency combined with evidence of effectiveness enhances public confidence. Probation staff are required to secure offender compliance with the requirements of their orders and to take enforcement action in cases of failure to comply, normally by taking offenders back before the court.

Community Justice: An ethical framework for probation work?

The service's national policy (NPS) sets out a vision and an ethical framework for probation work, articulating an aspiration to:

> change the image of the Service from that of 'well meaning but amateurish' to that of 'hawk-like professional', sharp and keen eyed ... [in the] ...oversight of offenders, in the knowledge and analysis of research to inform the development of effective offender programmes and in organisational practices.
>
> (NPS 2001: 8)

Eleven key values flow from this vision (Table 11.1). Nellis (2001, 2002) argues that these value statements blur *the ends and the means,* promote *coercive rehabilitation* and are *pervaded with managerial utopianism*. Within the service there is concern about the *correctional* agenda and the emphasis on punishment. Nellis suggests probation values become community justice values, and argues that all in the community should be involved in the pursuit of ensuring community safety, restorative justice, and reducing the excessive use of imprisonment. Lacey (2002) points to the centrality of justice and human rights highlighting a need for the recognition of humanity and mercy. A *community justice* approach to values would enhance interprofessional work in probation as it points to the interdependency of a common pursuit of justice.

Table 11.1 The Values of the National Probation Service (NPD 2001: 8)

- **Victim awareness and empathy** are central
- **Protection of the public is paramount** particularly where there are specific, known victims of violent and sexually violent crime
- **Law enforcement** taking positive steps to ensure compliance but, where this fails, acting quickly to instigate breach or recall proceedings
- **Rehabilitation of offenders**, working positively to ensure their restoration
- **Empiricism,** basing all offender and victim practice on evidence of what works
- **Continuous improvement**, always pursuing excellence
- **Openness and transparency**
- **Responding to and learning to work with difference** to achieve equality of opportunity for NPS staff and service users
- **Problem solving** as a way of resolving conflict and doing business
- **Partnership,** using a highly collaborative approach to add value to the capacity of the NPS to achieve its expected outcomes
- **Better Quality Services** so that the public receives effective services at the best price.

Protecting the public

Assessing and managing risk and working together

Central tasks in the protection of the public are the assessment of risk and the management of this risk in the community. Kempshall (2002) argues the emphasis on risk and protection reflects a general public anxiety about the dangers posed by offenders and leads to a defensive attitude to risk with an emphasis on precaution and prevention.

The background to recent developments in interprofessional work to manage risk lies in the reporting in the 1990s of several high profile cases of offences committed by individuals already known to professionals in different agencies. Concern relating to the risks they posed had been identified prior to the offences being committed and this drew attention to a critical need for effective interagency working (Home Office 2003). Legislation, which can be seen as a response to these concerns, was introduced and placed obligations on different agencies to manage risk and share information (for example, the Sex Offenders Registration Act 1997, the Crime and Disorder Act 1998 and the Criminal Justice and Court Services Act 2000). This legislation aims to develop a framework for sharing information and assessing and managing risk in a strategic and interprofessional way.

Multi-Agency Public Protection Panels (MAPPs) were established under sections 67 and 68 of the Criminal Justice and Court Services Act. The Act and accompanying guidance requires the police and the probation service to work together to protect the public from offenders thought to pose a serious risk. Each probation and police area is required to liaise with the prison service and negotiate the involvement of social services, local authority housing and the health service to contribute to the local MAPP. Exchange of confidential information between agencies must comply with the provisions of the Data Protection Act 1998 and the Human Rights Act 1998.

Only those offenders who are seen to pose the greatest risk to the public are presented to the local MAPP. Information about the offender is shared in order to inform the risk assessment and to contribute to a joint plan to effectively and safely manage the risk. Social services are the lead agency for cases of risk to children and other vulnerable groups and contribute to the prevention of abuse, the assessment and protection of children at risk, and in the rehabilitation of offenders. Health service personnel provide advice about the appropriateness of health interventions, including mental health interventions, and housing departments advise on the safest housing options available for offenders returning to the community. The prison service provides information to the probation service and police about those who are being released.

The majority of those considered by MAPPs are supervised by the probation service which is required to liaise with other agencies in seeking the robust management of risk and the use of effective interventions to reduce that risk.

═══════════════════════════ **ACTIVITY** ═══════════════════════════

Multi-Agency Public Protection Panels:

■ Locate the Home Office Internet site. (http://www.probation.homeoffice.gov.uk/output/page30.asp)

■ Look up your local area report. Identify which agencies contribute to the local MAPP.

■ What roles and responsibilities are given to each agency?

■ Does the report detail the costs of local arrangements?

■ What do you consider to be the costs and benefits of MAPPs?

■ How are victim's interests taken into account by your local MAPP?

The Probation Service approach to working with offenders to assess and manage risk. Probation offices work with offenders to:

■ attempt to identify the factors that led to their offending,

■ assess the risk they pose,

■ take action to ensure public protection, and

■ match offenders to programmes which are most likely to reduce their risk of re-offending.

The Offender Assessment System (OASys) developed jointly by the prison and probation service was introduced nationally in 2003 and is used to assess:

■ how likely an offender is to re-offend,

■ the risk of serious harm should further offences occur,

■ to whom the risk of harm is posed and under what circumstances, and

■ an offender's ability and motivation to change their behaviour.

(Home Office 2002a)

It also helps identify and classify offending related needs, including basic characteristics and cognitive behavioural problems. The completed assessment informs sentencing, risk management, and decisions about an intervention programme.

In using OASys probation staff interview the offender, draw on material from records and court papers, and may obtain information from relevant people including the victim, and other professionals. The result of an OASys assessment sometimes suggests a need for a further assessment (for example, in relation to mental health problems, domestic violence, sex offending, alcohol or drugs, or basic skills) that may be carried out by probation staff or by other specialist professionals. The resultant profile and key areas for targeting in any intervention plan are highlighted. Risks are categorised as being: risk of serious harm to others; risk to children; and/or risk to the individual offender. The probation intervention plan (supervision plan) must include how identified risks are going to be addressed and may include multiagency arrangements such as referral to a MAPP and liaison with social services or mental health professionals.

CASE STUDY: PRE-SENTENCE WORK

(a) A referral from court

John, a white male in his early 30s, appeared in the Magistrates Court for an offence of Assault Occasioning Actual Bodily Harm. The victim of the offence was his partner Mary. John had one previous conviction for assault (one year ago) and a conviction for Drinking and Driving (two years ago). His case was adjourned for a pre-sentence report with John released on bail to live with his mother and with a bail condition not to contact Mary. A probation officer, Nina, was assigned to write the report.

(b) Women's safety work – services to victims

Nina referred the case to Jennie, the domestic violence women's safety worker who arranged to see Mary to assess her need for support. Mary explained that she was pregnant and has two young children, aged three and six. Mary had thought about leaving John but was frightened he would not accept this. Jennie outlined some options, discussed things Mary might do to keep herself safe, provided her with information about women's support services, and informed her where she could get legal and housing advice. Jennie also advised Mary to share her concerns with both her doctor and community midwife.

Jennie asked Mary if she would be prepared to contribute to John's assessment. She assured Mary that any information provided would remain anonymous although Jennie would be bound to inform social services if Mary said anything that suggested the safety of children was compromised. She explained that the probation officer would be contacting social services. Mary agreed to contribute.

CASE STUDY continued

Jennie used a semi-structured interview schedule designed to contribute to the probation officer's risk assessment together with a questionnaire designed to contribute to the overall evaluation of the men's domestic violence programme. Mary stated that John had been violent and abusive to her for several years, especially when he had been drinking. He prevented her from seeing her mother and other members of her family, and had recently attempted to strangle her on two occasions. Mary explained that John said he would kill her if she left him. Jennie advised her to contact the police whenever she felt threatened by John. Jennie then provided Nina with a summary of the interview.

In discussion with the police community safety unit Nina discovered that the police had responded to 15 *domestic call outs* to John and Mary's home in the past year. Nina informed them about Mary's current concerns and they agreed the safety unit would advise operational units to respond as a priority to any reports of incidents at Mary's address. Nina also contacted social services to see if they were working with the family and to tell them about probation service involvement. Social services had been informed by the police about the offence and knew the family. They were aware that Mary was pregnant when John assaulted her and were concerned that both the other children had witnessed the assault.

(c) The assessment of the offender

Nina reviewed the court papers and probation records together with the information from the women's safety worker and from Mary. Nina then interviewed John using the OASys assessment form and a domestic assault risk assessment tool. John admitted assaulting Mary but maintained that he had only been abusive to her once. He blamed Mary for provoking him saying he would never be violent to Mary again and that he wanted the relationship to continue. The OASys assessment tool indicated factors related to relationships and alcohol use as key areas associated with risk of re-offending. Nina assessed John as posing a high risk of violence to Mary. She told John that she was considering proposing a community sentence with a condition that he attend a Domestic Violence programme and a programme with an alcohol counsellor. She explained the plan for supervision to John who agreed that it might be of help. She then prepared a pre-sentence report for the court reviewing sentencing options and making a proposal for sentencing.

Probation officers assist the court to decide on a suitable sentence for an offender by preparing a pre-sentence report. In a domestic violence case the probation officer should refer the case to a specialist women's safety worker.

Probation work in domestic violence is part of a developing integrated approach to providing support to victims of abuse and their children. In this case, the police had already contacted social services when they arrested John because the children had witnessed the offence. Women's safety workers (who can be directly employed by the probation service or by other community agencies who contract with the probation service to provide this service) liaise with other agencies to provide support to women and children living in contexts of domestic abuse. They can help women access specialist services, such as legal advice, refuge provision, children's services and housing advice. They contribute to promoting safety by supporting women to construct a realistic safety plan for themselves and their children. They can also explain court processes and provide realistic information about the types of intervention available to offenders.

Whilst the needs of women and children are often similar the safety of children is always paramount. An important point to note here is that when there are concerns about the safety of the child confidentiality is limited and concerns must be reported to social services. Information provided by women victims is never disclosed directly to offenders as this may increase the risk to women and children.

QUESTIONS

■ What are the main risks in this case? Who is at risk and why?

■ What do you consider might reduce these risks?

■ Which professionals should be involved?

Reducing offending

Working together to reduce offending: Crime and Disorder Partnerships

The probation service is a member of local Crime and Disorder Partnerships set up to develop community safety strategies by working together to protect the public (Crime and Disorder Act 1998, s5 and 6). Members of these partnerships include the police, local authorities and a range of representatives from local community services, for example, education, social services, youth services, neighbourhood watch, victim support and local employers. Partnerships are required to conduct and publish an audit of local crime and disorder problems, determine priorities for action, devise and publish a strategy, and monitor and review progress. Working in partnership with other agencies has advantages and disadvantages. Hester (2000) suggests voluntary and community sector organisations involvement in partnerships creates links with police and local authorities and helps form networks. However negative effects, such as staff time to attend frequent meetings, were also reported. Some respondents felt that their contribution was limited because of 'a perceived tokenism by some statutory agencies' (Hester 2000: 1). One way of resolving this could be to involve smaller agencies in planning and action when they have a specialist contribution to make but this could increase tokenism.

ACTIVITY

Finding out about your local Crime and Disorder Strategy:

■ Ask for a copy of your local strategy from your local authority.

■ Who contributed to this strategy? What agencies and who in the agency – what positions do they hold?

■ Examine the priorities for action. Do they concur with your view of crime in your area?

The probation service's direct work with offenders to reduce offending is based on evidence of effectiveness of interventions, an initiative known as What Works. Guidelines for evidence based practice set out key principles including:

- the risk principle matching offenders to programmes that reflect the seriousness and persistence of their offending,

- the needs principle targeting offenders' needs related to their offending and seeking to change factors which led to the crime,

- the responsivity principle helping offenders to respond to the intervention by engaging their active participation using approaches and methods to which they can respond.

(Chapman and Hough 1998)

Emphasis is placed on developing a community based multi-modal approach to intervention that is skills-oriented and models pro-social behaviour. This initiative is believed to be the 'largest experiment in effective correctional practice ever undertaken anywhere in the world' (Raynor 2002: 182). A range of individual and/or group programmes are being developed which offenders undertake as part of their programme of supervision. Known as *pathfinders*, the programmes are rigorously evaluated by independent researchers to determine their effectiveness in reducing re-offending. Once formally approved by the Correctional Services Accreditation Panel, a programme forms part of a menu of approved interventions, known as the core curriculum offered to offenders. Examples include: cognitive behavioural programmes, aggression replacement training, the drink impaired driver programmes, and community sex offenders programmes. Common themes in all programmes are:

- enabling offenders to accept full responsibility for their offending,

- enhancing offenders' understanding of their patterns of thinking, feeling and behaviour which can lead to offending,

- examination of what each offender did to create opportunities to offend and what he or she can do in the future to avoid this,

- raising awareness of the effects on victims as offenders can use *thinking errors* to psychologically convince themselves their behaviour is acceptable, and

- helping offenders learn to recognise high-risk situations when they may offend and providing opportunities to practice steps to take to avoid this.

Programmes are evaluated to assess if there is a reduction of re-offending over a period of two years following an intervention programme when compared with control groups who had not had these opportunities (findings are available on www.homeoffice.gov.uk/rds/pubsintol.html). Each offender's programme of supervision may include one or more accredited programmes. Programmes are delivered by specially trained programme tutors, who may be probation staff, or staff from partner agencies (for example Drug and Alcohol Service staff).

CASE STUDY continued: SUPERVISING OFFENDERS IN THE COMMUNITY

John is sentenced to a Community Order for two years with requirements that he attends the Domestic Violence programme and addresses his alcohol problem. John is given his first appointment at court to report to meet his Case Manager (a probation officer) to start his programme of supervision.

At the first meeting with the Case Manager, the requirements of the order are explained together with what will happen to John if he fails to keep scheduled appointments. The Case Manager reviews the pre-sentence report and OASys assessment and draws up a supervision plan.

John tells the Case Manager that he has moved back home with Mary and he has promised to stop drinking and never to assault her again. The Case Manager discusses this with him, asking him to identify what steps he plans to take to stop behaving in a controlling and violent way. The Case Manager also makes an appointment for John for alcohol counselling with a partner agency to start the following week. After the meeting the Case Manager lets the Police Community Safety Unit, social services and Jennie (the women's safety worker) know that John has moved home again.

Jennie contacts Mary, confirms John's story, discusses safety planning and also ensures that Mary understands that there is no guarantee that the programme will be a success. Jennie offers to keep Mary informed about John's attendance on the Domestic Violence programme and advises her to contact the police immediately if she feels under threat.

On John's next two appointments, the Case Manager works with John to prepare him for the Domestic Violence programme and completes pre-programme evaluation measures. A programme tutor from the Domestic Violence programme attends one of these meetings and explains some of the methods used on the group work part of the programme.

For the next 28 weeks John will attend the Domestic Violence group work programme. He also attends weekly meetings with the alcohol counsellor. The Domestic Violence group work programme provides weekly reports to the Case Manager and the women's safety worker about John's progress. He will meet with his Case Manager once a month to review the programme of intervention. A programme facilitator from the Domestic Violence programme will attend the midway meeting and end of programme meeting with John and the Case Manager to report back on his progress in the group.

After John has finished the group work programme, he will then undertake one-to-one work with the Case Manager to consolidate his learning.

During this period Jennie will keep in touch with Mary and let the Case Manager know about any concerns. She will keep in contact with Mary after the programme has finished to provide support and to get feedback from Mary to help the probation service evaluate the programme.

============================ **ACTIVITY** ============================

Review the information provided in the two extracts provided of this case example and consider the following questions:

■ What agencies will John and Mary be in contact with during the period John is on a Community Punishment Order?

■ What concerns or risks can you identify in this situation?

■ How do you think information should be shared in case of any concerns of emerging risks?

■ Who should take responsibility for sharing information?

■ What problems can you identify about sharing information in this case?

■ What benefits might come from sharing information and working together?

Working together to support victims of crime

Victim services and support have recently been highlighted as part of the criminal justice agenda that aims to ensure victims' interests become central to the Criminal Justice System (Home Office 2002b). Government policy aims to develop a national framework for collaborative working among agencies within the Criminal Justice System to promote victims' rights and safety. The probation service offers information and support to victims of sexual or other violent crime when an offender is sentenced to 12 months or more in prison. Victims are given an opportunity to contribute to key decisions (such as move to open prison conditions, temporary release, or release on licence) and to request conditions be placed on those released from prison. Safety advice to victims of offenders on specific programmes of intervention, such as the domestic violence programme is also provided.

The probation service liaises with victim support, the police, and other specialist agencies. Working with victims and victims' organisations is a sensitive area of work in which probation workers attempt to build in order to promote victim safety (Lindsay and Brady 2002).

In all programmes of intervention with offenders a clear focus is kept on the effects of crime on victims with the aim of requiring offenders to face up to the impact of their actions on others. Restorative justice approaches are also being developed to enable offenders to make direct amends to the victims and communities (see Home Office 2003).

Working together interprofessionally – challenges and visions

This chapter has highlighted the need for coordination between agencies working with offenders and for collaboration between probation workers and other professionals in order to protect the public, to reduce re-offending, and to work with victims of crime. It is increasingly recognised that the development of the effective practice initiative (What Works) to reduce re-offending and to rehabilitate offenders requires the development of purposeful working relationships between agencies and professionals.

Contributing to local crime and disorder strategies and being part of multi-agency public protection panels, at area and local levels, are relatively new requirements for probation staff. Processes and protocols are in place, but the development of skills and approaches to collaborative interprofessional work and research on the effectiveness of these approaches is needed. Promising initiatives include the deployment of probation staff to work in multiprofessional teams, Youth Offending Teams, public protection teams and the new Joint Justice Centres. Such initiatives are leading to *trans-disciplinary work* (Garner and Orelove 1994 cited in Payne 2000) with probation workers training on work normally associated with other occupational groups such as social workers or police officers.

The potential of a coordinated approach to community justice can be glimpsed in the efforts of active and purposeful networking of individuals from different agencies (Payne 2000). Legislation, protocols and procedures for interagency working legitimate and require such contact. Effective collaborative working requires professionals to learn about each other's perspectives, priorities, responsibilities and remit. It also requires probation staff to share information with, and recognise the contribution of, other professionals when working with offenders. Professionals working together need to recognise power relationships which can result in conflicts of interest between professionals. Interprofessional relationships need to be nurtured (Hudson *et al.* 1999). Trust needs to be earned by principled conduct and pro-active communication to promote understanding and to acknowledge, address and resolve any difficulties that may arise. Forging productive collaborative relationships requires significant investment of time, energy, and human resources. The potential returns on such investment are high. It is only by working with other professionals effectively that the aims of the service can be met and the vision of community justice can be realised.

References

Chapman T. and Hough T. (1998) *Evidence Based Practice. A Guide to Effective Practice.* London: Home Office HM Inspectorate of Probation.

Hester R. (2000) *Crime and Disorder Partnerships: Voluntary and Community Sector Involvement.* London: Home Office.

Home Office (2000) *National Standards for the Supervision of Offenders in the Community,* London: Home Office.

Home Office (2001) *Probation Circular 25/2001.* London: Home Office.

Home Office (2002a) *Offender Assessment System OASys User Manual.* London: Home Office.

Home Office (2002b) *A Better Deal for Victims and Witnesses.* London: Home Office.

Home Office (2003) *Multi-Agency Public Protection Arrangements: Annual Report 2001–2.* London: Home Office.

Home Office (2004) *Reducing Crime – Changing Lives, The Government's Plans for Transforming the Management of Offenders.* London: Home Office.

Hopley K. (2002) National standards: defining the service. In Ward D., Scott J. and Lacey M. (eds) *Probation: Working for Justice* (2nd edn). Oxford: Oxford University Press, pp. 297–307.

Hudson B., Hardy B., Henwood M. and Wistow G. (1999) In pursuit of inter-agency collaboration in the public sector. *Public Management* 1(2): 231–49.

Kempshall H. (2002) Risk, public protection and justice. In Ward D., Scott J. and Lacey M. (eds) *Probation: Working for Justice* (2nd edn). Oxford: Oxford University Press, pp. 95–110.

Lacey M. (2002) Justice, humanity and mercy. In Ward D., Scott J. and Lacey M. (eds) *Probation: Working for Justice* (2nd edn). Oxford: Oxford University Press, pp. 25–38.

Lindsay J. and Brady D. (2002) Nurturing fragile relationships: early reflections on working with victims of domestic violence on the national probation service's Duluth Pathfinder research programme. *Issues in Forensic Psychology* **3**: 59–71.

National Probation Service (2001) *A New Choreography: Integrated Strategy for the National Probation Service.* London: National Probation Directorate.

National Probation Service/MORI (2002) *Perceptions of the National Probation Service.* London: National Probation Service.

Nellis M. (2001) Community values and community justice. *Probation Journal* **48**: 34–8.

Nellis M. (2002) Community justice and the new probation service. *Howard Journal* **41**(1): 59–86.

Payne M. (2000) *Teamwork in Multi-professional Care.* Basingstoke: Macmillan.

Raynor P. (2002) What works: have we moved on? In Ward D., Scott J. and Lacey M. (eds) *Probation: Working for Justice* (2nd edn). London: Oxford University Press, pp. 166–84.

Radiography

Jan Chianese and Ken Holmes

History of radiography

In November 1895, German physics Professor Wilhelm Conrad Roentgen was acclaimed for discovering an invisible ray which he called X-rays. On 22 December 1895, he produced a radiograph of his wife's hand, traditionally recognised as the first X-ray picture and he received the first Nobel Prize for Physics in 1901. The discovery of X-rays led to the development of the early radiographers and by January 1896 X-rays were being used for the diagnosis and setting of broken bones and in the location of foreign bodies (Mould 1980).

Discovery of the therapeutic effects of X-rays in the treatment of cancer is attributed to Sjogren in 1899. In the same era radium therapy was developed and, unlike the electrically produced X-rays, radium therapy used the naturally occurring gamma radiation emitted by radium. Radium therapy was reported as being used successfully as early as 1903, only five years after the discovery of radium was announced by Bemont, Pierre and Marie Curie (Mould 1980). Interestingly, Pierre and Jacques Curie discovered the piezo electric effect in crystals which is a component of ultrasound equipment used for imaging purposes in more recent times.

The early users of both X-rays and gamma radiation were unaware of the risks from the ionising radiation they administered. Knowledge and understanding of the potential for cancerous changes and burns would only emerge later and pioneers in the craft had no knowledge of the need for protection from radiation.

Indeed they often used their hands to judge the strength of an X-ray beam and to hold patients still during procedures, including, at that time, the treatment of such common complaints as ringworm, acne, and arthritis.

The importance of protection from repeated exposure to ionising radiation only received international recognition in 1929 after a number of radiographers, physicists, chemists, radiologists, technical workers, nursing staff and others working with X-rays died from radiation induced injury. Memorial stones now commemorate these martyrs to the advancement of the science (Moodie 1970).

The Society of Radiographers was registered as a limited company on 6 August 1920 in order to advance the science and to control the development of the profession (Moodie 1970). By February of the following year the first qualifying examination had been taken by students and for the next 66 years the Society of Radiographers was responsible for the syllabus and entry requirements for the practice of diagnostic and therapeutic radiography.

The first degree course for radiographers was validated and delivered in Dublin in 1987 and led to all graduate education for diagnostic and therapeutic radiography practitioners in the United Kingdom (UK) and Ireland by 1993. Having successfully completed an approved educational programme the newly qualified radiography practitioner forms one tier of a recently introduced four-tier system. A radiography practitioner can develop specific specialist skills to become an advanced practitioner and then, after further specialist training, a consultant practitioner (CoR 2003). To these has been added the assistant practitioner who can undertake simple X-ray examinations in diagnostic imaging or assist radiotherapy radiographers in radiotherapy treatments and associated procedures (DoH 2003). Reporting on radiographic images was restricted to medical practitioners following a Society of Radiographers council resolution passed in 1924. The same resolution made it clear that doctors were responsible for prescribing radiotherapy treatment, and confirmed that radiographers could only accept requests for radiographic images from suitably qualified medical practitioners (Moodie 1970).

In the UK the law requires that the title radiographer can be used only by someone whose name is on the national register of radiographers held by the Health Professions Council (HPC), and radiographers must be registered with the HPC before they can work in the National Health Service (NHS). The HPC and the Society of Radiographers are jointly responsible for accreditation of educational programmes for radiographers.

Two distinct types of radiography professionals have evolved: diagnostic radiographers are primarily involved with the production of images used as tools to aid diagnosis; and radiotherapy radiographers are concerned with the administration of ionising radiation treatments. Currently students of both undertake a three-year full-time (or equivalent) programme of study in preparation for registration and subsequent practice. The programme comprises of equal time spent in the hospital environment and in the university. Many aspects of learning are shared by diagnostic and radiotherapy students but the clinical components are separate and require placements in different hospital departments.

The Society of Radiographers Code of Professional Conduct (CoR 2002a) comprises ten statements that guide and inform the professional practice of radiography.

Radiography practice continues to evolve and radiographers need to engage with developments in equipment as well as with changes in treatment protocols. All qualified radiographers are expected to evaluate and adopt new practices where these provide benefits for patients and clients as well as undertake continuous professional development (CPD) and life long learning (CoR 2002a).

Developments in imaging technology together with an increasing demand for imaging services has led to an increase of more than seven per cent in the number of diagnostic radiographers employed in the NHS between 1999 and 2003 (DoH 2003). Since the introduction of all graduate education the role of radiographers has become extended beyond the 1924 restrictions. Suitably trained diagnostic radiographers now have discretion to perform additional images, can undertake diagnostic examinations, and can report on the images produced from these procedures within set protocols (DoH 2002d). The College of Radiographers has recognised the need, following appropriate education and training, for radiotherapy radiographers to extend their role within the clinical oncology setting to develop specialist areas of work previously outside of their remit. This includes counselling, providing information and support for patients with cancer, and prescribing medication for common side-effects of radiotherapy treatment (CoR 2001).

Working with radiation

X-rays and gamma radiation are known as ionising radiations and can cause damage to cells and tissues. Minute doses of ionising radiation, whether naturally occurring or man-made, have the potential to cause cancers although the additional cancer risk from exposure to low doses is effectively undetectable in the population (NRPB 2003). The use of ionising radiation is controlled by European legislation under the Ionising Radiations (Medical Exposure) Regulations (IR(ME)R 2000) which sets out the education and training required for radiography practice. In addition, it determines the role of practitioners within radiology and radiotherapy service (IR(ME)R 2000 Regulation 11 and 12). Radiographers need to be able to understand, discuss and convey technical information about the risk of radiographic procedures in a way that is both clear and reassuring to patients.

CASE STUDY

Thandie Washington is a 54-year-old white woman who is a full-time working mother of two teenage children. She has been recalled for a second mammogram following a routine screening the previous week.

It is the use of ionising radiation that links the diagnostic radiographer, who produces images for diagnostic reasons, with the radiotherapy radiographer, who uses ionising radiation for curative or palliative purposes. The presented case study is used to trace one patient's journey from diagnosis to treatment and highlights some areas of interprofessional working.

The role of the diagnostic radiographer

The main methods of imaging undertaken by diagnostic radiographers involve the use of X-rays. Diagnostic radiographers are required to produce high quality images of the body as one aspect of the diagnostic process. Effective diagnostic imaging relies on the ability of the radiographer to establish quickly a working relationship with the patient. The radiographer will need to discuss the examination and its consequences, answer questions about the procedure and try to put the patient at ease. This may include explaining the radiation risk to the patient and the benefits to be gained by accurate diagnosis of her or his symptom(s) or condition. While all radiographers have knowledge of the application of most radiographic techniques, some will specialise in for example, nuclear medicine using radioactive isotopes, ultrasound and scanning with magnetic resonance imaging (MRI), and computerised tomography (CT). As well as working in the general imaging departments found in most hospitals, diagnostic radiographers work in accident and emergency departments and may work in specialist centres such as breast care units where mammograms are performed, and on hospital wards using portable imaging equipment. In these different environments diagnostic radiographers work alongside radiologists (consultant doctors who specialise in radiological medicine), nurses, technicians and other medical staff.

CASE STUDY continued

Thandie is worried about being recalled to the imaging department as she found the first examination uncomfortable and she thinks if she has been asked back there must be something wrong.

QUESTIONS

- What fears might someone who is recalled to the imaging department have?

- How might the diagnostic radiographer respond to these concerns and what dilemmas might there be for them?

- What sort of information would be helpful to the patient in such circumstances and how would this best be given? (Think about the potential difficulties in terms of the patient's anxiety, if they had limited understanding, a hearing impairment or literacy skills)

It is recognised that women recalled for a second mammogram are likely to be worried so Catriona, the diagnostic radiographer, sits down with Thandie, listens to her concerns, and explains that a second examination is necessary because the first image failed to provide sufficient information. Often this is because it is not always easy to position the patient so that all of the area that needs to be imaged is captured or, as in Thandie's case, because there is some ambiguity in the image. It is not unusual for women to be invited back and it does not necessarily mean there is anything wrong. Catriona explains to Thandie why it is necessary to get firm pressure on her breast tissue between the plates of the machine in order to get a good image but that this pressure will be built up gradually so that Thandie can adapt to it. Catriona tells Thandie that, unlike the first visit, the image will be processed while she waits in the department so that she will be able to discuss the results with a member of the breast care team. Catriona ensures that Thandie's questions about the procedure are answered before taking the X-ray image.

In order to reduce the number of errors in diagnosis all images are reviewed independently by two members of the radiography team (this will be either two radiographers or a radiographer and a radiologist) who then compare results before a diagnosis is made. After obtaining a suitable image Catriona identifies an area of microcalcification which is indicative of cancer. She passes her report to the consultant who confirms that the image is strongly suggestive of cancer of the breast.

Communicating the results of mammogram examination to a patient is part of what the breast care team do. The breast care team normally includes a specialist breast care nurse, a radiographer and a doctor. Each member of the team is skilled in communication and able to answer questions about prognosis, treatment options, and further imaging procedures.

In Thandie's case treatment will depend upon the precise site of the cancer and whether or not there has been any spread of the disease to other parts of her body (metastatic spread). Most patients will undergo radionuclide imaging in an attempt to detect metastatic spread from the primary cancer to bone early in the progression of the cancer and before it is visible on plain radiographs. From further tests it is confirmed that Thandie's disease is confined to her breast.

The role of the radiotherapy radiographer

Unlike diagnostic imaging, radiotherapy makes therapeutic use of the destructive power of high energy ionising radiation to kill cancer cells in a precise and controlled manner. Radiotherapy radiographers work in oncology departments, sited mainly either in purpose built hospitals, or in specialist units within large general hospitals. Radiotherapy is a treatment that is used in the attempt to eradicate cancer cells as a cure or to relieve symptoms of particular cancers such as, pain from cancer spread to bone or breathlessness from lung cancer. Radiotherapy is also often used alongside surgery and/or cytotoxic chemotherapy. The most common type of radiotherapy equipment is the linear accelerator, which produces photon energies in the order of millions of electron volts compared to the thousands produced by general diagnostic X-ray machines.

Nevertheless, radiotherapy radiographers also work with diagnostic X-ray equipment to produce images but only for the purpose of planning radiotherapy treatments. Most radiotherapy departments use simulators to mimic the movements of the linear accelerator and this enables the radiotherapy radiographer to visualise the potential pathway of a therapy beam prior to the start of treatment. Many linear accelerators now have the facility to produce images while treatment is taking place. These snapshot images, called portal images, help reinforce the checks that verify the target area of the cancer is being treated. Radiotherapy radiographers can also make use of CT and MRI scanning, as well as ultrasound equipment, to assist treatment planning in some circumstances.

Following discussion with the oncologist (a consultant doctor who specialises in cancer treatment) about her treatment options agreement is reached that Thandie will have surgery followed by a course of radiotherapy. The aim of surgery is to remove the cancer together with some surrounding tissue while the aim of the radiotherapy treatment is to kill any remaining cancer cells.

Following recovery from the surgery Thandie arrives at the pre-treatment suite at the oncology centre. The simulation and/or planning of a patient's treatment before it starts is normally the first point of contact between the radiotherapy radiographer and the patient. Usually the patient has many questions at this stage and it is one of the roles of radiotherapy radiographers in the pre-treatment suite to take the patient step-by-step through the process, answering their questions and making arrangements for the first treatment appointment.

Lara, the radiotherapy radiographer, talks to Thandie explaining the process of the simulation and the treatment to follow. Thandie has many questions but is unlikely to understand all aspects of the treatment because there is a lot of information to take in and because she is very nervous.

Lara helps Thandie assume the correct position on the simulator couch and explains that she needs to hold her arm a particular way while measurements are taken together with X-ray images and these are passed to the planning team. The planning team incorporates medical physics technicians, physicists and (usually) dedicated radiotherapy radiographers. Lara reinforces the information given at the beginning of the procedure, answers Thandie's questions, and takes her to meet a member of the team on the unit where she will receive treatment.

A team of radiotherapy radiographers operate a linear accelerator that delivers radiotherapy in a treatment room. Due to the high energy of the radiation used radiographers cannot stay in the room with the patient during treatment. It is essential that the patient remains still during radiotherapy treatment so that the beam remains directed to the correct part of the body. The radiographer has an important role to play in gaining the trust of the patient so that she or he will remain in the correct treatment position for the few minutes each treatment is administered.

Radiotherapy radiographers are now becoming more involved in ensuring patients give informed consent for treatment. This includes informing the patient of the potential effects of radiotherapy and about how to look after themselves during treatment. Because they see the patient each day of treatment radiotherapy radiographers are well placed to monitor skin reactions and other side-effects. They can also work with, for example, specialist oncology or breast care nurses, dieticians, counsellors and oncologists to advise on skin care, diet and the prescribing of medications to minimise the side-effects. Radiographers who have extended their roles may be in a position to offer counselling or to prescribe certain medications for side effects such as nausea and dysphagia (difficult or painful swallowing).

On the first day of treatment, a member of the radiotherapy radiography team explains to Thandie what will happen at the start and during treatment. Thandie goes into the treatment room with the radiographer and finds that the process is similar to the one she experienced in the simulator during treatment planning. Once the lights are dimmed in the room the treatment team ensure that the radiotherapy beams are lined up accurately by using light lasers to help define the treatment area. The printed computerised plan produced by the planning team is used for reference points and reproduces the measurements that coincide with the surface anatomy of Thandie's body. A light beam shines on Thandie's chest to simulate the position of the radiation beam. Once the team is satisfied that Thandie is positioned correctly and that she knows how to contact the team should she feel uncomfortable during the treatment, the radiographers leave the room to switch on the linear accelerator and Thandie's radiotherapy treatment begins. Thandie attends the radiotherapy department for five weeks, she comes each week day and gets to know the regular staff of the treatment team.

QUESTIONS

- If you were undergoing radiotherapy treatment what skills and qualities would you expect the radiotherapy team to demonstrate?

- Why do you think communication between different professionals in such situations is so important?

- What might help or hinder communication between professionals in this sort of situation? (Think about this in terms of practical issues and staff attitudes).

Cancer services are constantly evolving in the attempt to improve patient management and outcomes. Technological developments in imaging and radiotherapy equipment have both improved patient outcomes in the last 20 years (Burnet *et al.* 2000). Cancer is one of the most common diseases in the Western world with 600 new cases diagnosed each day in England alone (DoH 2000a). Workloads in radiotherapy departments are rising annually (IPEM, RCoR, SCoR 2002) and to meet this demand the number of therapeutic radiographers has also increased. Between 1997 and 2001 the numbers rose from 1410 to 1540, an increase of more than nine per cent.

Contemporary roles and responsibilities of radiographers

There is an emphasis in the modern NHS on the accountability of each individual health care professional. All health care professionals are required to provide evidence of maintaining competence to practice and radiographers are expected to engage with CPD and life long learning. The need for radiographers to work collaboratively with other health care professionals in order to meet the needs of patients is recognised. Effective radiographic practice integrates specialist knowledge and understanding, clinical skills with problem solving, and professional judgement with decision making in a complex and changing environment (QAA 2003).

The HPC indicates the standards of knowledge and understanding at each stage of the diagnostic imaging or radiotherapy process. Additionally, personal and transferable skills are also described. The HPC standards state:

> Professional relationships include knowledge of 'Radiographers Professional boundaries' for personal scope and practice and to be able to work, where appropriate, in partnership with other professional, support staff, patients, clients and users, and their relatives and carers. Radiographers need to contribute effectively to the multi-disciplinary team and demonstrate effective and appropriate skills in communicating information, advice and instructions based on their professional opinion.
>
> (HPC 2003: 12)

In the context of caring for cancer patients the Calman-Hine Report (1996) set out some of the basic principles to achieve quality care for patients with cancer, one of these was a recommendation for a provision of seamless care by an interprofessional team. To provide effective and seamless care for patients, radiotherapy radiographers need to have knowledge of adjuvant treatments as well as knowledge of the role of other health care professionals involved in the delivery and aftercare of treatments. Liaison with oncologists, nurse teams (specifically oncology nurses), medical physicists, health care assistants and technicians is often required on a daily basis in radiotherapy and oncology departments. This may extend to involve other health and social care professionals as radiotherapy radiographers may be a first point of contact for many outpatients receiving treatment lasting several weeks.

Role development in radiography

Contemporary roles are best summed up in the recent documents Standards of Proficiency (HPC 2003) and Benchmark Statements (QAA 2003). The proficiency standards set out minimum requirements for admittance to the register while the benchmark statements assist curriculum design and academic review.

A strategy for the educational and professional development of radiographers (CoR 2002b) sets out the principles to underpin the future educational and professional development framework for radiographers. This will enable continuous improvements in the delivery of patient services. It is in response to the government modernisation of the health service (DoH 2000b, 2000c, 2000d).

The four-tier structure includes the assistant practitioner, the state registered practitioner, the advanced practitioner and the consultant practitioner. Development to advanced practitioner and consultant practitioner requires specialist postgraduate study. These roles are defined and discussed within the Advance Letter (Professions Allied to Medicine) 2/2001 which outlines the four core functions of practice as: 'expert practice, professional leadership and consultancy, education training and development, and practice and service development, research and evaluation' (DoH 2001: unnumbered).

The structure aims to encourage radiographers to work collaboratively in interprofessional health care teams. It is therefore essential that radiographers re-define their roles to embrace innovative ways of providing services with the patient at the cornerstone of delivery and care. The strategy promotes widening access, flexible career pathways and development of new roles.

The role of the radiographer in the new national health service:

> The NHS Plan sets out a vision of a modernised NHS with many more staff, working differently. It describes how services will be redesigned around the patient's journey and how this will radically improve the patient's experience. Our strategy to deliver the challenging objective of growing and changing the workforce is called the Skills Escalator.
>
> (DoH 2003: 1)

This requires radiographers to use a strategy of CPD and life long learning to maintain and extend their skills and knowledge, thus enabling progression on the skills escalator towards advanced and consultant practitioner roles and responsibilities. Meanwhile, efficiencies and skill mix benefits are generated by delegating roles, work and responsibilities where appropriate to assistant practitioners. To enable these visionary changes the government is seeking to improve staff morale, make the NHS a model employer, employ another 6500 therapists and other health care professionals, and provide a model career progression through the skills escalator.

References

Burnet N.G., Benson R.J., Williams M.V. and Peacock J.H. (2000) Improving cancer outcomes through radiotherapy. *British Medical Journal* **320**: 198–9.

Calman-Hine Report (1996) http://www.dh.gov.uk/PublicationsAndStatistics/Publications/ PublicationsPolicyAndGuidance/PublicationsPolicyAndGuidanceArticle/fs/en?CONTENT_I D=4071083&chk=%2Bo6fka. accessed February 2003.

CoR (2001) *Radiographic Staffing Standards in Clinical Oncology Departments*. London: CoR.

CoR (2002a) *Statements for Professional Conduct*. London: CoR.

CoR (2002b) *A Strategy for the Educational and Professional Development of Radiographers*. London: CoR.

CoR (2003) Radiography Skills Mix A Report on the Four-Tier Service Delivery Model June 2003 www.doh.gov.uk/radiography/skillsmix-june03.htm accessed January 2004.

DoH (Department of Health) (2000a) *The NHS Cancer Plan: A Plan for Investment; A Plan for Reform*. London: HMSO.

DoH (2000b) *A Health Service for all the Talents – Developing the NHS Workforce.* London: HMSO.

DoH (2000c) *The National Health Service Plan: A Plan for Investment, A Plan for Reform.* London: HMSO.

DoH (2000d) *Meeting the Challenge: A Strategy for Allied Health Professionals.* London: HMSO.

DoH (2001) *Arrangements for Consultant Posts for Staff Covered by the Professions Allied to Medicine pt "A" Whitley Council: Pay for 2001/2002.* London: HMSO.

DoH (2003) Introduction to the Skills Escalator www.dh.gov.uk/PolicyandGuidance accessed August 2004.

HPC (Health Professions Council) (2003) *Standards of Proficiency.* London: HPC.

IPEM, RCoR, SCoR (Institute of Physics and Engineering in Medicine, Royal College of Radiologists, Society and the College of Radiographers) (2002) *Development and Implementation of Conformal Radiotherapy in the United Kingdom.* York: IPEM.

IR(ME)R (Ionising Radiation (Medical Exposure) Regulations) (2000) www.doh.gov.uk/irmer.htm accessed January 2004.

Mould R.F. (1980) *A History of X-rays and Radium.* Birmingham: PC Business Press Ltd.

Moodie I. (1970) *50 Years of History.* London: College of Radiographers.

NRPB (National Radiological Protection Board) (2003) *Ionising radiation damage and cancer* www.nrpb.org/radiation_topics/risks/damage.htm accessed January 2004.

QAA (Quality Assurance Agency) (2003) *Benchmark Statements for Healthcare Programmes (Radiography).* www.qaa.ac.uk/crntwork/benchmark/nhsbenchmark/radio.pdf accessed February 2003.

13

Social Work

Pat Taylor and Adrian Vatcher

Introduction

For 30 years social work in England and Wales has been primarily identified with local authority social services departments that provide information and advice, and arrange services to support individuals, families and groups in local communities. Social workers are a relatively small group amongst their staff, although essential to their work. They work alongside social care and home-care workers, residential care workers and occupational therapists, and are based in locality offices, day centres, residential care homes, hospitals and community projects. Significant numbers of social workers are also employed by voluntary and independent organisations.

Until recently, social workers usually worked in separate professional teams. However, current polices for health and social care services are such that increasingly social workers will be integrated into interprofessional teams. This chapter offers a brief overview of social work and its historical development, outlines the nature of modern social work and offers an insight into the way in which social workers contribute to interprofessional working.

Defining social work

Social work is defined as promoting:

> social change, problem solving in human relationships and the empowerment and liberation of people to enhance well-being. Utilising theories of human

behaviour and social systems, social work intervenes at the points where people interact with their environments. Principles of human rights and social justice are fundamental to social work.

(IASSW/IFSW 2004: 1)

This definition covers a variety of social work practices in different social and political contexts across the world. The commentary on this definition high-lights the role of the profession 'in solidarity with those who are disadvantaged' (*ibid*) in alleviating poverty, promoting social inclusion, identifying a range of interventions from working with individuals to involvement in social policy.

As such social work encompasses a range of activities from individual coun-selling to political action. In the United Kingdom (UK) social work generally involves the following activities.

- Listening, communicating and counselling – engaging with clients to build trusting relationships in order to help people find ways to improve their lives.

- Assessing social needs – helping people to understand their needs and iden-tify ways they might deal with their everyday problems. This might include supporting people to make individual changes, linking them into existing networks of friends and relatives, and/or arranging specific services.

- Giving information, signposting and being an advocate – enabling people to recognise and secure their entitlements and on occasions, speak directly on clients' behalf.

- Coordinating services for clients with complex needs – ensuring these address their needs.

- Acting as a gatekeeper of resources – assessing social needs and deciding whether clients are eligible for a service.

- Making decisions to intervene, within a legal framework, to protect children and vulnerable adults

- Working in the community to encourage the development of services and support relevant to client's unmet needs .

(DoH 1991a, Coulshed and Orme 1998, Trevithick 2000, Adams *et al.* 2002)

Social work is inherently political. It takes place only as a collectively organised response to public concern about complex social problems. Because there is debate about how best to understand and help people, social workers are as likely to be criticised as praised for what they do. They can be seen as too soft on people who should be made to conform, or as agents of social control – too involved in attempting to make people conform.

Society also expects social workers to make difficult decisions when there are no certain outcomes. For example, they may help a frail but fiercely inde-pendent older person continue living in her own home, but if she falls and is injured social services and social workers are called to account.

Similarly, social workers recognise it is generally better for children to be looked after in their own families, and are required to work in partnership with parents to promote children's welfare. So, unless there is clear evidence to the contrary, social workers will usually seek to support a family to stay together during difficult times. However, it is not possible to be certain that children will always be safe and social workers will be criticised for not having removed the child if a non-accidental injury occurs. Despite publicity to the contrary, social workers get things right more often than not (Ferguson 2002).

Social workers tend to claim a specific set of values although it is unlikely these values are unique to social work (Davis and Sims 2003). However, because social workers see the consequences of social disadvantage there is a tradition of political action shown in, for example, the commitment to the principles of anti-discriminatory and anti-oppressive practice. Social workers need to recognise their position within social and political power structures to ensure social work does not reinforce discrimination and oppression. Social workers maintain a debate amongst themselves, with service users and other professionals about how far their work promotes care and/or control; empowerment and/or protection; and dependency and/or oppression (Dalrymple and Burke 1995, Dominelli 2002).

QUESTIONS

■ What values do you bring to your profession?

■ How did these develop?

■ How do they relate to any professional value statements?

Social work organisation – history and current developments

Social work in the UK developed from at least four separate threads, those of charity, philanthropy, mutual aid, and state intervention. These historical influences continue to exert tensions and help to explain different perspectives on its nature and purposes. Charity is part of the Christian tradition and is illustrated in, for example, the visits of (most often) women of comfortable means who tried to alleviate poverty and improve public morals. Philanthropy includes the efforts of social reformers such as Booth in 1889 and Rowntree in 1901 and 1941 who undertook extensive surveys of poverty and social deprivation (Holman 1978). Traditions of mutual aid can be found in the friendly and cooperative societies and in the trade union movement. The tradition of state intervention dates from the 19th century Poor Law which first gave us the concept of a deserving and a non-deserving poor; an idea that continues to exert an influence over social policy (Brenton 1985).

Modern social work began to take shape in the post-war Welfare State with the establishment of local authority Welfare Departments to work with older and disabled people; and Children's Departments to work with children. The Younghusband Committee (1959) and the 1969 Seebohm Committee developed the debate about the social work role within local authorities. Seebohm recommended the setting up of separate social services departments (SSDs) under a dedicated director of social work and this was implemented in 1970.

However, the Labour government's policy of modernising public services since 1996 has meant social workers, along with many other public service professionals, face organisational changes. The Health Act 1999 introduced ways in which budgets could be shared between local authorities and the NHS enabling different services to work closely together in new interdisciplinary teams. There is an expectation that social services departments in England are likely to be phased out.

A key aspect of the Green Paper *Every Child Matters* (Treasury 2003) and the resulting Children Bill (2003) is the proposal for social work with children to be provided within Children's Trusts. The Health and Social Care Act 2001 made it possible to set up Care Trusts where social workers working with adults could work alongside their health colleagues. Some examples of these new ways of working are given below.

- A Children's Trust will bring together education, social work and health services for children. Statutory agencies (including Connexions and Youth Offending Teams) together with voluntary and private agencies will be part of local partnerships within Children's Trusts and provide the impetus for new interdisciplinary teams working collaboratively around different aspects of children's support.

- Intermediate Care teams include social workers, community nurses, home-care support workers, physiotherapists and occupational therapists working together to enable frail older people to remain at home.

- Community Mental Health Teams where integrated teams of mental health social workers, community care support workers, community psychiatric workers and psychiatrists work together to provide an integrated service for people with enduring mental health problems.

Roles and responsibilities which have been primarily the remit of social workers may become increasingly blurred as nurses, teachers, and other professionals work collaboratively to address the needs of the different client groups.

Qualification, registration, and accountability in social work

Qualification as a social worker requires successful completion of a three-year degree programme that in 2003 replaced a two-year diploma. Once qualified social workers are required to register with the General Social Care Council (GSCC). The register of the social care workforce held by the GSCC currently includes social workers but will eventually include other social care workers such as residential and homecare workers.

The Care Standards Act (2000) provides legal protection for the title social worker, from April 2005 only someone with a recognised qualification and registered is legally entitled to call themselves a social worker. The first Code of Practice for social care workers and employers (GSCC 2002) developed to provide public protection requires, amongst other things, that social care workers 'take responsibility for maintaining and improving their knowledge and skills' (GSCC 2002: unnumbered).

The Care Standards Act (2000) established:

- the Social Care Institute of Excellence (SCIE) charged with promoting improvements in services by reviewing research and developing best practice guidelines, and

- the National Care Standards Commission responsible for the regulation and inspection of care agencies including residential services.

Social work with children

Social work with children is principally governed by the Children Act 1989 and a range of secondary legislation and guidance. One of the key ideas which informed the Act was the view that 'the child is a person and not an object of concern' (Butler-Sloss 1987: 254). The Act recognises the relationship between parents and children in terms of responsibility rather than rights; and when parents separate the question is with whom the child has residence or is in contact rather than about custody so placing the child, not the parents or carers first.

The Act requires that courts are bound by the following principles in making decisions:

- children should usually be brought up in their own family,

- the welfare of the child is the paramount consideration,

- delay in hearing a case works against the child's welfare,

- courts must pay attention to a range of specific issues including the child's wishes and feelings; their physical, emotional and educational needs; the ability of their parents or carers to meet those needs; and the likely effects of changing circumstances, and

- courts should not make an order unless making one is better than not making one.

The legal frameworks emphasise the strengths and advantages of family life. They are based on evidence that arranging for children to be cared for away from their families cannot be presumed to make things better and might make them worse (Rowe and Lambert 1973, Millham *et al.* 1986, DoH 1991b).

The Act places a duty on local authorities to promote the welfare of children in need and as far as possible to promote their upbringing in their own family. The Act sets out criteria for deciding which children are in need and imposes duties on the local authority. Social workers assess the needs of specific children who have been identified as possibly being in need taking into account the children's individual characteristics, the ability of their parents to care for them, and the social circumstances of both. This will mean talking to parents and children, and seeking information from others involved. Where possible social workers also: arrange services to support children in need being cared for within their families; arrange for children to be cared for away from their families if necessary; arrange for the return of children looked after away from their families to be returned; and provide alternative long-term care for them if this is not possible. In keeping with the principles of the Adoption and Children Act 2002, plans for many children in this last situation this will involve making arrangements for adoption.

In the spirit of the Children Act 1989 social workers will seek to work in partnership with parents and children in the attempt to find constructive and cooperative solutions to what are often serious and longstanding difficulties. However, if a child is believed to be at risk of harm local authorities can seek legal powers to intervene through a supervision or care order. In these situations the social worker will present detailed reports to the court. Maintaining a sense of partnership with parents at this time can become difficult, and may not always be possible, since the social worker's primary concern must be the welfare of the child.

═══════════════════════ **QUESTIONS** ═══════════════════════

■ What are the sorts of things a social worker may need to do and say to encourage a sense of partnership with parents?

■ What might make this difficult?

Social work with adults

The NHS and Community Care Act 1990 created the modern context for social work with adults. The Act began to address longstanding concerns about the haphazard, confused and variable arrangements resulting from different pieces of legislation aimed at improving services and support. The Act required social services departments to establish care management systems where social workers undertake an initial assessment of need, drawing on the professional expertise of others as appropriate. Then based on that assessment, develop, coordinate and implement a care package of services to meet the agreed needs that is monitored and reviewed. Alongside the care management system wider changes in the NHS and in SSDs were introduced which separated the purchaser from the provider. Local authority social workers became purchasers able to select the best services on behalf of clients. This separation of function represented a radical change for social workers whose role had previously incorporated both assessment and the provision of services. The Act stipulates that 75 per cent of services must be purchased from the private or independent sector.

Unlike health care, which is free at the time of need, social care has always been means tested. This difference has long presented problems for health and social care professionals working together as they try to establish which of a persons needs are social (means tested) or health (free). The social worker as care manager became gatekeeper of resources as social services departments were expected to manage within a limited budget where means tested provision sat uncomfortably with a holistic needs assessment.

Campaigning organisations representing service users such as People First (for people with learning disabilities), Mind (the mental health charity) and the Coalition for Disabled People lobbied for changes to the way that social services departments operate. Direct payments schemes have been implemented for people with long-term care needs who prefer to arrange their own services (Glasby and Littlechild 2002). The policy of helping people remain independent within their own homes has inevitably increased the pressures on informal carers. Their needs have been better recognised with the right for carers to have their needs assessed and a ring-fenced grant introduced to meet carers needs in 2002.

Because of charges for social care services, clients and their families have become reluctant to remove people from free national health service care to means tested residential or community care services. Social workers find they need to resist pressure from hospitals (wanting to clear beds) and try to ensure adequate arrangements are made before frail older people with complex, expensive care needs are discharged. Government plans to regulate care provision include an increasing emphasis on joint working within integrated health and social care teams. By April 2004 each social services department had to introduce a single assessment process (DoH 2002a) that could be administered by different professional groups (nurses, occupational therapists, social workers, homecare managers and so on). This effectively ends the social work monopoly of the care management process. Some pilot studies have combined health care assistant and social care roles (Taylor 2001) creating a generic worker providing basic health and social care tasks for frail elderly clients, thus reducing fragmentation of services.

It will be clear from the above discussion that social work practice is complex and often contradictory. A social worker must understand how the service user fits into their wider social context, what kind of relationships they have with their families, friends and wider social network, where are the strengths in the immediate situation and in the person themselves. Everything a social worker does must take place within the framework of the relevant laws and policies that frame many of the resources available. The case study below is offered to help readers see the process of social work in action.

Social workers first became involved with Dan and his family when the school contacted the local education welfare service. Dan is often late for school in the morning and after lunch. In class, he seems to find concentration difficult and gets involved in fights. The school contacted Mr and Mrs Williams who, although concerned, have been unable to meet with the teachers.

Kathy, an education welfare officer (EWO), a qualified social worker, visits the home and talks first to the whole family, then to Mr and Mrs Williams together and to Dan and Mark individually. From these conversations Kathy starts to develop a sense of how each member of the family sees the situation.

CASE STUDY: DAN AND HIS FAMILY

Dan Williams is 13 and lives with his father Eric, mother Jean, and younger brother Mark, aged ten, on a housing estate in southern England. Dan's father is white and his mother is black. They moved from northern England two years ago to live near Eric's elderly parents. Six months after moving Eric, aged 43, had a stroke. He has some difficulty supporting his own weight and walking so often uses a wheelchair. He has difficulty managing aspects of life that he used to take for granted.

Dan misses his old friends and finds it difficult to settle in his new school. He is the only black child in his class. He has also recently grown quickly and is physically awkward. His classmates tease him about his clumsiness, and some taunt him because he is black. His parents have not been as involved with his activities or schoolwork as they were before they moved. Dan misses going to football matches with his father and to the local football club he ran. Dan has been helping his father wash and dress since he became unwell. He sometimes takes him to the pub at lunchtime. Dan wants to help his father and finds this easier than facing life at school.

He knows his mother has been worried since his father's stroke. She helps Eric when she can but has taken a part-time job in a local library. She seems too busy to spend time with Dan or his brother. Dan tries to steer clear when she gets angry and shouts at his younger brother. She was recently very upset when Mark got into trouble with the police.

CASE STUDY: MR WILLIAMS

Eric used to be a builder and also set up a local football team. Since his stroke he has been unable to work. Eric followed a physical rehabilitation programme in hospital and was provided with some mobility aids and adaptations to the house before discharge. He also received advice about disability benefits.

No personal care services were arranged, as Mrs Williams believed she would be able to cope. However, Eric depends on his eldest son as well as his wife for help and assistance. Mr Williams has little to occupy his time so watches a lot of television, reads the papers, goes to the pub and plays computer games with his younger son in the evenings. He feels frustrated and depressed because he knows Jean is worried about their situation but he feels unable to help.

During her first contact, Kathy demonstrated sensitivity and skill, earning a degree of trust from the family that has helped her assessment. Although Dan was the reason for Kathy's involvement, he is not the only person experiencing difficulties. Dan is possibly the family member who most feels he can do something to help. He does need to improve his school attendance, but that is not the issue most on his mind. Of the two boys, Mark's situation is of most concern. Kathy does not think that he is in immediate need of protection although, he may be at risk of getting into trouble with the law or of being mistreated at home.

The indications are that Mr and Mrs Williams care a great deal about both children but are exhausted by their circumstances. Eric's stroke has had a

---

CASE STUDY: MRS WILLIAMS

Jean is distressed because she feels unable to manage the family's problems. Since her husband's stroke she has worked part-time and is now the family's main earner. The drop in family income worries her constantly as mortgage repayments are hard to meet. She tries keeping these worries to herself and is seeking full-time work despite being unsure how she will find the time.

She is also concerned about Mark who, she thinks, is becoming cheeky and uncooperative. She was upset when the local police suggested Mark might be involved in incidents of stealing from local shops. She says she has punished Mark recently by locking him in his room because she was so angry she thought she might hit him but assures Kathy that she has not.

CASE STUDY: MARK

Mark seems happy and easygoing. He seems to accept his father's situation and says he enjoys playing computer games and likes dad helping him with homework. He agrees that recently his mother has often been angry with him and confirms that he is sometimes shut in his room when this happens. He denies stealing. When Kathy asks what things he would most like to change he says that he wishes his mum would stop shouting at him.

---

significant impact on the family and there is an urgent need to consider how he and they might be helped to manage. In keeping with the Children Act's principle of partnership it will be important to involve all members of the family in discussions about the situation.

Discussing these conclusions with the family Kathy tells them that, although there are ways in which she can help, she will also need to work with other professionals. They all agree she can talk to the teachers, contact the social services child care team and the local primary care trust.

CASE STUDY: DAN

Dan says he is late for school because he helps his father, but he also thinks school is boring. When Kathy asks what things he would most like to change he says he would like to go out and do the things with friends that he used to do before moving.

Kathy contacts the child care team to tell them both Mark and Dan could be considered children in need and asks for a full assessment. She asks the Trust for an assessment of Mr Williams' needs and tells both agencies of her referral to the other and of the plan to contact the schools.

The child care social worker and the Trust's care manager

The referral is seen first by the child care team manager. She sees there is the potential that the family, who have already talked to the EWO, might now be visited separately by a member of her team and a care manager, and asked for the same information. The family are already stressed and it is important not to make this worse. She contacts her colleague in the Trust and they agree their staff should work together and, initially, visit together.

They also arrange for the child care social worker to be a black man and the care manager a white woman. Although they do not know how much this matters to the family, they think this may help them develop trust and confidence in the service (Dominelli 1988). The child care social worker, Darren, and the care manager, Holly, are both qualified social workers. They meet to discuss how they should work together. Legally, they have specific assessment responsibilities:

- under s17 of the Children Act 1989 – an assessment of children in need,

- under s47 of the NHS and Community Care Act 1990 – an assessment of Mr Williams' need for community care services,

- under the Carers and Disabled Children Act (2000) to assess Mrs Williams' and Dan's, and possibly Mark's, needs as carers (although not expected, Dan may feel he wants to help care for his father, and while this should not interfere with his education, it would be easy to overlook this aspect of Dan's needs).

=== **ACTIVITY** ===

- Look up the sections noted of the Acts referred and check exactly what the responsibilities are.

- Which of these responsibilities are unique to social work and which any professional could carry out?

Each worker will have to complete a set of formal documents recording these assessments. Their aim will be to explore with the family how they have managed to make their life together work as well as they have, and what they see as the things that most need to change to help them manage better. This may be helpful, as it could allow them to discuss things they have not talked about before. The workers will have to plan carefully how they will explore these issues and start to form a plan of help.

QUESTION

■ What aspects of the first visit would they need to plan?

Meeting with the family will show they understand that while their responsibilities are to ensure the well-being of the two boys on the one hand, and Mr Williams and his carers on the other, they are better addressed together. Though the two workers may need to make separate visits later, this should help the family see these pieces of work form part of a whole.

CASE STUDY: DAN continued

The family and their networks

The two workers meet with the family and discuss the practical difficulties Mr Williams and the rest of the family have encountered following his stroke, and also how this has affected their relationships and those with the wider community. Talking about these things does help them to see they have been working hard to keep things going, and that they have been a great help to each other. They now see it is time to talk about the changes that have affected them and what changes they may need to make.

Following this meeting, with the full cooperation of the family the workers visit again separately to complete their assessments.

Health care professionals and the community care assessment

The community care assessment is completed by the care manager but draws on advice from the occupational therapist, physiotherapist, and general practitioner who are all part of the primary care trust team. Holly establishes with Mr Williams that his strongest need and wish is to be able to lead a life of his own, and to offer something to his family instead of feeling he is totally dependent. There are financial limits but Eric does meet the eligibility criteria for services. Holly can arrange services to help with: personal care, especially bathing; mobility and transport; housing adaptations; opportunities for training and employment and; benefits and financial advice.

Holly discusses with Eric whether he would like her to arrange these services or whether he would prefer to employ staff with the money that can be paid to him directly. While this might seem complicated to manage, help arranged this way is often more flexible and allows disabled people greater independence.

QUESTION

- What do you think are the advantages and potential problems of service users arranging their own care?

The main effect of the carer's assessment for Mrs Williams and Dan is that it makes clear the help that they have been providing for Eric cannot be taken for granted. The plan agreed with the family is for a male homecare worker to visit weekly to help Mr Williams bathe and take him to the pub. A neighbour has also offered to take Eric out for a drink weekly. In the assessment Mr Williams expresses interest in developing computer skills so Holly investigates the possibility of him joining a project at the local library.

Holly also gives Eric information about a local organisation active in promoting the rights of disabled people. Eric begins to recognise that he does not have to consider the difficulties he has encountered since his stroke as primarily his problem.

Children in need assessment

As part of the children in need assessment Darren contacts Kathy about her discussions with the schools and speaks to a member of the local Youth Offending Team about the police reports.

CASE STUDY: MARK

Mark appears to have settled at his junior school, though he is one of three black children in his year and the only black boy. His teacher is pleased with his progress but observes that he is in a gang of boys who can be very lively in school and sometimes get into trouble. On reflection she remembers a couple of occasions when Mark has been caught misbehaving and blamed for something which has involved others in the gang. She wonders if Mark has been the scapegoat in the shoplifting incident as well.

CASE STUDY: DAN

Dan's teachers remain concerned about his attendance and performance at school. However, in the course of the assessment he talks to his mother about some bullying at school. Both she and Kathy discuss this with his teachers, who agree to look into this further, and confirm the bullying and agree that it seems to relate to his ethnicity.

QUESTION

- Why might Dan have been bullied and how might this relate to his ethnicity?

Case conference

Kathy, Darren and Holly decide there is so much happening that it would help everyone to meet and coordinate plans. This meeting (sometimes called a case conference, or coordinating meeting) brings together Mr and Mrs Williams, the boys' teachers, a Youth Offending Team representative, Kathy, Darren and Holly, and another representative of the primary care trust team. It is chaired by a social services team manager. Dan and Mark decline the offer to attend but their views are represented at the meeting by a children's advocate who had helped them write down their views on what should happen.

QUESTIONS

▓ Why might Dan and Mark have decided against attending the case conference?

▓ If you were invited to such a meeting as a service user or carer what sort of support and preparation would you want?

The proposed solutions

Dan's sports teacher offers to spend some time with him talking about his interest in football and to encourage him to talk to some other boys about a local under-14 football club. Dan is also told about the Young Carers project in the city but decides he prefers to join the football club.

Dan's school also decide to address the issue of potential racism within the school by making it the focus of their next in-service day. Mark's school suggests he enrols in their after school club. It is hoped this will break the link with going home with the gang and allow Mrs Williams make plans for full-time employment. The Youth Justice worker notes Mark may have been unfairly associated with stealing and agrees to discuss this with the police member of the team who will explore this with the local officer. Holly and Darren agree to meet the family again to discuss how the plans are working. A key aspect of this will be whether they have helped Mrs Williams feel less overwhelmed by the family difficulties and more free to think about her financial and employment options.

Conclusion: the contribution of social work to interprofessional working

Social workers often have a key role in situations of this kind, based on a social perspective that seeks to take into account how different aspects of a person's life work together to help them flourish or oppress or overwhelm them. They are not the only professionals who draw on this perspective, but the services they provide are often concerned more with enhancing and developing the networks within which people live, and seek to avoid the more individual focus that may appropriately be taken by other professions.

Social workers are aware of the importance of working with other professionals and are increasingly likely to find themselves working alongside other health and social care professionals in unified interprofessional teams and as part of organisations not dedicated exclusively to social work. Potentially there is a high degree of overlap between the responsibilities, knowledge, and skills of social workers and those of other professions. Exactly what comes to be regarded as the distinctive contribution of social workers will depend partly on how precisely this is prescribed in the way that agencies are set up; and partly on the particular interests and skills of the staff.

References

Adams R., Dominelli L. and Payne M. (eds) (2002) *Social Work: Themes, Issues and Critical Debates* (2ⁿᵈ edn). Basingstoke: Palgrave.

Adoption and Children Act 2002. London: TSO.

Brenton M. (1985) *The Voluntary Sector in British Social Services.* London: Longman.

Butler-Sloss E. (1987) *Report of the Inquiry into Child Abuse in Cleveland 1987.* London: Department of Health and Social Security.

Care Standards Act 2000. London: TSO.

Carers and Disabled Children Act 2000. London: TSO.

Children Act 1989. London: TSO.

Coulshed V. and Orme J. (1998) *Social Work Practice.* Basingstoke: Macmillan.

Dalrymple J. and Burke B. (1995) *Anti Oppressive Practice: Social Care and the Law.* Buckingham: Open University Press.

Davis J. and Sims D. (2003) Shared values in interprofessional collaboration. In Weinstein J., Whittington J. and Labia T. (eds) *Collaboration in Social Work Practice.* London: Jessica Kingsley, pp. 83–99.

DoH (Department of Health) (1991a) *Care Management and Assessment: Practitioners' Guide.* London: HMSO.

DoH (1991b) *Patterns and Outcomes in Child Placement.* London: HMSO.

DoH Health Act 1999. London: The Stationery Office.

DoH *Health and Social Care Act 2001.* London: The Stationery Office.

DoH (2002a) *The single assessment process guidance for local implementation.* www.doh.gov.uk/scg/facs accessed August 2004.

Dominelli L. (1988) *Anti-Racist Social Work.* Basingstoke: Macmillan.

Dominelli L. (2002) Values in social work: contested entities with enduring qualities. In Adams R., Dominelli L. and Payne M. (eds) (2002b) *Critical Practice in Social Work.* Basingstoke: Palgrave, pp. 15–27.

Ferguson H. (2002) *Blame culture in child protection.* The Guardian, Wednesday January 16, 2002.

Glasby J. and Littlechild R. (2002) *Social Work and Direct Payments.* Bristol: The Policy Press.

GSCC (General Social Care Council) (2002) *Code of Practice for Social Care Workers and Employers.* London: GSCC.

Holman R. (1978) *Poverty: Explanations of Social Deprivation.* Suffolk: The Chaucer Press.

IASSW/IFSW (International Association of Schools of Social Work/International Federation of Social Workers (2004) www.iassw.soton.ac.uk/Generic/DefinitionOfSocialWork accessed March 2003.

Millham S., Bullock R., Hosie K. and Haak M. (1986) *Lost in Care: The Problems of Maintaining Links Between Children in Care and Their Families.* Aldershot: Gower.

NHS and Community Care Act 1990. London: TSO.

Rowe J. and Lambert L. (1973) *Children who wait.* London: Association of British Agencies for Adoption and Fostering.

Seebohm F. (1969) *Report of Committee on Local Authority and Allied Personal Social Services (Seebohm Report) Cmnd 3703.* London: HMSO.

Taylor P. (2001) Meeting the needs of older people in the community: an examination of a new generic health and social care role. *Local Governance* 27: 239–46.

Treasury (2003) *Every Child Matters Cm 5860*. Chief Secretary to the Treasury. London: TSO.

Trevithick P. (2000) *Social Work Skills: A Practice Handbook*. Buckingham: Open University Press.

Younghusband E. (1959) *Report of the Working Party on Social Workers in the Local Authority Health and Welfare Services Committee*. London: HMSO.

Youth Work

Billie Oliver and Bob Pitt

Introduction

> The purpose of youth work is to facilitate and support young people's growth
> through dependence to independence, by encouraging their personal and social
> development and enabling them to have a voice, influence and place in their
> communities and society.
>
> (NYA 2001: 1)

Youth work has experienced some well-documented fluctuations in popularity
and has struggled to gain recognition as a profession. At the beginning of
the 21st century the government's modernisation agenda has emphasised the
importance of youth work in Transforming Youth Work (DfEE 2001b). This
transformation of youth services and youth work in England should be viewed
alongside Learning to Succeed (DfEE 1999) which announced the Connexions Service, a new support service for young people aged 13–19. The
Connexions Service and the accompanying role of Personal Adviser is explored
within this chapter because, when launched, it was viewed as a potential threat
to youth work and youth services and led to a re-examination of youth work
values and principles.

Youth workers aim to build relationships of trust, respect and confidentiality
with young people as they move from child to adult. Youth workers develop
these relationships through informal education and voluntary association with
groups of young people outside of the formal school system.

The Connexions agenda relates specifically to the transition from school to post-16 learning and the world of work. The Connexions target group is the individual young person not in education, employment or training (NEET) with an emphasis on participation in education, training or employment, and social inclusion.

This chapter presents the aims and purpose of youth work and the Connexions Service, outlines the roles of youth workers and Connexions Personal Advisers, illustrated with case studies from practice. In addition it offers a flavour of current debates and issues facing youth work as a result of the opportunities and tensions created by the transformations of these services. Opportunities include the integration of services and the challenge of collaborative working with different professionals for the benefit of young people.

What is youth work?

Youth work has both national and local professional qualifications validated by the National Youth Agency (NYA) which lists the areas of competence covering the skills and knowledge required for practice. Key skills for youth work include the ability to:

- build relationships with young people,

- enable young people to organise and take increasing responsibility for activities, events and projects,

- plan, manage and develop youth work, and

- support and develop effective, efficient and ethical practice in youth work.

Youth workers work with young people aged 11–25, those who make most use of the service tend to be aged 13–19. The core purpose of youth work is to provide personal and social education in a variety of informal settings including youth clubs, drop-in centres or on the street.

> Youth work helps young people learn about themselves, others and society, through informal educational activities which combine enjoyment, challenge and learning.
>
> (NYA undated: 1)

According to Smith, youth workers achieve this by 'being friendly, informal, and acting with integrity' (2002: 13), and by being concerned with the education and the general welfare of young people. Smith argues that youth work involves a focus on young people, an emphasis on voluntary participation and relationships, and a commitment to association. Youth work, he suggests, involves the notion of young people coming together in a spirit of companionship to undertake some activity. Williamson (1997) found that what young people want from youth work is the opportunity to meet together and do things. His research highlights the importance of autonomy where young people have their own safe space to meet and make decisions, and of advice providing the opportunity to talk to someone other than their parents or friends about problems or issues in their lives.

One important aspect of youth work is the voluntary nature of activity for young people where they can choose to use the services. This contrasts with the statutory duties of other professionals, such as social workers, who may be required to intervene in the lives of families or individuals. Youth work encourages and supports young people, gives them responsibility, encourages participation, and helps build their confidence and self-esteem during the transition from dependence to independence. Youth work enables young people to become involved with their local communities as active citizens in programmes such as Millennium Volunteers, and with national and local award schemes such as the Duke of Edinburgh's Award.

Youth work is built on establishing trust over time with groups or individuals. This requires youth workers to be non-judgmental and to make use of conversation, chat and activities to engage with young people. The aim is to draw them into informal educational opportunities to explore issues that affect their lives, such as sexual health, drugs or alcohol misuse, bullying, sexism, and racism. In this way youth work offers both spontaneous and planned opportunities for young people to learn about themselves, others and wider society.

Transforming Youth Work sets out the government's view of good youth work that:

- offers **quality support** to young people ...which will help them achieve and progress;

- enables **the voice of young people** to be heard, including helping them to influence decision making at various levels;

- provides a rich diversity of **personal and social development** opportunities and choices to young people, to include voluntary action, peer support and mentoring;

- promoting **'intervention and prevention'** to address the individual, institutional and policy causes of disaffection and exclusion.

(DfEE 2001b: 4)

QUESTIONS

- Why might the opportunity to talk to someone other than friends or family be important?

- How might participation in youth work activities help build confidence and self-esteem?

- Why is it important for the views of young people to be heard?

Transforming Youth Work followed a series of OFSTED reports criticising some local authority youth services for their poor quality of services, recognising variations in levels of funding between authorities, and highlighting difficulties in recruiting, training and retaining youth workers. In addition, reports such as Learning to Succeed (DfEE 1999) and Bridging the Gap (SEU 1999b) identified risks for young people when agencies and professionals work in isolation without effective communication. Reinforcing partnership working between agencies involved with young people is seen by the government as key to achieving the transformation of youth work.

Where does youth work take place?

Local authorities, national and local voluntary organisations and independent groups all offer youth services. Youth work takes place wherever young people meet although it traditionally occurs in youth clubs or community centres, often referred to as centre-based work. Recently there has been an increase in street youth work (detached youth work) in the attempt to contact young people who do not use centres. Youth work might take place in schools or colleges for example, lunch or after-school activities or where the youth worker contributes to personal, social and health education, and the citizenship curriculum in the classroom. Youth work also operates through outreach work where workers develop new provision with and for young people. This might involve setting up specialist projects aimed at particular groups, such as young people in danger of exclusion from school, or dealing with current issues like drug misuse; and through mobile projects where, for example, a converted bus takes youth workers and resources to communities without youth centre or club provision.

As with other public services there has been a move towards partnership working and youth services now commonly work with other services such as housing, youth justice, health, social services and education in order to meet the needs and aspirations of young people. Youth workers may take on a variety of roles such as advocate or mentor to work with young people to gain access to services and to create opportunities.

======= QUESTIONS =======

- What challenges might there be for centre workers to meet the needs of all these different groups?

- In what sorts of situations might youth workers need to work with other professionals?

The professional role, accountability and boundaries in youth work

Youth work is committed to the principle of equality of opportunity and the NYA considers that effective youth work helps to redress disadvantage and discrimination. Key concepts in youth work are choice, freedom, responsibility and justice. Banks has suggested that youth work embodies concerns about 'professional integrity, trustworthiness and honesty in relation to its service users' (1999: 3) underpinned by principles that 'respect young people's rights, respect cultural diversity and work for participatory democracy' (*ibid*: 4).

CASE STUDY: A YOUTH DROP-IN CENTRE

The centre is situated in a small town operating within local authority diversity and accessibility policies so as to appeal to all young people. The local authority pays the running costs and employs a manager and part-time staff who offer seven drop-in sessions a week during the day and evenings for young people. Although not activity-based the centre does have a pool table, television lounge, a computer with free Internet access and a coffee bar run by the young people. The centre operates as an informal place where young people can come for a friendly chat and to chill out.

The priority target is the 13–19 age group. The centre opens for four lunchtime sessions. Those dropping in include young people from the local school; young people without a job; those who have fallen out of the school system or dropped out of college; and former regulars who continue to find it a convenient meeting place, such as young mums. On average about 40 young people use the centre in any week and most sessions have about 25–30 attending.

At lunchtime there tends to be an even gender mix and the young people stay for about an hour. They often have individual queries or issues where other agencies or services such as careers, housing, benefits and health and social services may be involved. One morning each week the local Connexions Service provides an information session.

The centre also operates two sessions a week with pupils from the local comprehensive school. One is focused on a youth award scheme with a group of year ten pupils; the other provides an alternative to school for a group of year 11 pupils identified as disengaged or disaffected. Over several weeks a programme emerged involving music production on computer, a singing performance, band practices, gaining youth award points and credits through cookery, producing CDs, and a pool tournament. The manager feels that as both she and the Connexions Personal Adviser have a youth work background they complement each other's approach to working with this group.

The evening sessions attract a predominantly male group who tend to stay longer giving the centre manager a chance to help the young people to put together their own programme of informal education. Typically this might involve organising trips out to go tenpin bowling, watching a video on misuse of alcohol followed by discussion, planning a residential trip to an outdoor activity centre, decorating the television lounge, or devising a dance night competition.

Youth workers operate according to the following statement of principles of ethical conduct established by the NYA:

Ethical principles
Youth workers have a commitment to:
■ Treat young people with respect …

- Respect and promote young people's rights to make their own decisions and choices ...
- Promote and ensure the welfare and safety of young people ...
- Contribute towards the promotion of social justice ...

Professional principles
Youth workers have a commitment to:
- Recognise the boundaries between personal and professional life ...
- Recognise the need to be accountable ...
- Develop and maintain the required skills and competence ...
- Work for conditions in employing agencies where these principles are discussed, evaluated and upheld.

(NYA 2001: 4)

These ethical principles may create dilemmas for youth such as, a need to betray a confidence or undermine the trust built up with a young person because of an issue of child protection or of a young person's safety.

CASE STUDY: A PROFESSIONAL DILEMMA

The drop-in centre manager, Yvonne, received a letter from an education welfare officer (EWO) based within the local youth offending team. She was asked to co-operate with a truancy sweep organised by the education welfare service, police and local school to identify young people *bunking off* school on a particular day. Rather than use the police station or school, the EWO wanted to use the centre as neutral territory to bring young people picked up on the street.

The dilemma for Yvonne was that she was more interested in why young people play truant rather than who or how many, and she thought that the trust relationships with young people could be undermined if the centre was used in this way. There was a commitment to honesty and on not *grassing them up* to the school authorities. After discussion with centre staff Yvonne believed that to maintain relationships of trust with the young people, it was only fair to let them know that the centre would be used as part of a planned truancy sweep.

Yvonne explained the principles by which the centre operated to the EWO and asked for more details on when, where and why this sweep was happening, and what would happen to the young people picked up. They agreed that Yvonne would let the young people who attended the centre know the week, but not the day, of the planned truancy sweep.

QUESTIONS

- Do you think Yvonne's action appropriate? If so why? If not why not?

- What are the potential advantages and disadvantages of using the centre in this way?

The Connexions Service

In the late 1990s a number of social policy reports identified fragmentation of services and therefore a need for a joined up approach to working with young people. These reports suggested that while agencies continued to operate in traditional ways, there were too many examples of practice where:

- Young people's difficulties had been at the margins of responsibility of different services,

- No service had taken 'ownership' of the full range of issues that young people faced and as a result a large number of young people had not had their needs properly met,

- There had been no one person to co-ordinate responses or provide the support for the needs of young people.

(CSNU 2001: 3)

Research (SEU 1998, 1999a, 1999b, 2000, DoH 1999) indicates, that where young people have a number of agencies working to support them, those agencies do not always communicate effectively. This leads young people to feel they are being 'passed from pillar to post' (CSNU 2002: 113) and frustrated by having to tell their story yet again. Young people's needs were often not met, or being only partially met by the different agencies. Whilst each agency was likely to have delivered its primary responsibility to the young person, it may have lacked 'the time, opportunity, resources and awareness to ensure that all other agencies committed resources in the most efficient and coherent manner' (CSNU 2002: 7). The research also suggested an increased likelihood that young people would slip through the net of service provision and experience greater social and educational disadvantage if professionals and agencies work in uniprofessional ways.

Bentley and Gurumurthy (1999) suggested a need for a new professional grouping (a youth broker or personal adviser) who would maintain an overview of a young person's needs and provide coherence across different agency boundaries. These ideas manifested in the design of the Connexions Service for England, introduced in 2001. The service takes the form of a single national agency, employing staff with a range of professional backgrounds, such as youth workers, careers guidance staff, education welfare officers and social workers, and represents a significant change in the way support is provided to young people (DfEE 1999). The Connexions Strategy has been built around key principles that inform thinking and practice, as well as development and design. These principles are informed by the government's modernisation agenda. Practice principles are aimed at working with young people to help raise their aspirations and enable them to overcome barriers to learning. Central to the strategy are principles of partnership working and community involvement, on the assumption that by working collaboratively agencies can achieve more for young people, parents and communities than by working in isolation.

The Connexions Service operates only in England, and is delivered by 47 local Connexions Partnerships. These partnerships are 'multi-agency bodies, made up of a range of partners – for example, Local Education Authorities, Youth Services, Careers Services, Youth Offending Teams, Social Service Departments, Health Bodies and Voluntary Sector Agencies' (DfES 2002b: 6). By developing the service across organisational boundaries it is intended that Connexions 'will help to develop consistency in the support young people receive, based on a shared understanding of their needs' (*ibid*: 6).

The new role of the Connexions Personal Adviser

At the heart of the Connexions Service is 'an accountable professional – the Connexions Personal Adviser' (DfEE 2001a: 4) whose role is to assess the needs of and broker support to young people. Personal Advisers (PAs) work within a framework of assessment, planning, implementation and review with the aim of working with the young person, and other relevant people and agencies to reduce barriers to social, educational and economic inclusion. Important skills underpinning the role include networking and advocacy. Community involvement is seen as a key driving principle and so PAs are expected to work interprofessionally by brokering access to local welfare, health, arts, sport and guidance networks.

The role of Connexions Personal Adviser involves:

■ engaging with the young person and agreeing her wants or needs,

■ enabling the young person to understand her entitlements,

■ co-ordinating the range of available support to ensure there is cohesion in its delivery,

■ advocating on behalf of the young person with other relevant service providers,

■ supporting the young person and her carers/partners where relevant,

■ working with the young person to secure change,

■ supporting the young person in her transition to independence,

■ brokering relevant services and resources to support the young person to meet her needs,

■ working with other agencies and the community to support the young person.

(DfEE 2001a: 10)

At the time of writing the role of the Connexions PA is relatively new and continues to evolve. Local Connexions Partnerships and PAs are engaged, together with relevant trades unions, in clarifying the role although differences in interpretation are emerging. Davies *et al.* suggest recent challenges to professional identity 'with the blurring of role distinctions and demands for multi-professional collaboration [have forced professionals] to question what they could be in the future' (2000: 287). Some of this lack of clarity is due to the way the Connexions Service replaced the existing careers service. A key factor in understanding the relationship between the PA and other professionals, such as the youth worker, is the recognition of the PA as a new professional role rather than as a new profession. The Connexions Service considers that any suitably qualified professional within any agency can be a PA.

Traditionally, youth work seeks to help young people to develop their potential by offering opportunities through informal education and life skills training to build confidence, self-motivation and self-esteem. This helps young people to make decisions, to take responsibility for their actions and to take control of their lives. Interventions by youth workers do make a positive difference to the lives of young people and this 'vital contribution' (DfES 2002a: 8) is recognised as essential to the success of the Connexions Service. However, recognising that the introduction of the Connexions Service and PA raised concerns about the future of youth work, the Connexions Service National Unit (CSNU) reinforced their support of youth work by suggesting four models of guidance on how youth workers and PAs can work together.

- Model 1: Youth workers and Connexions Personal Advisers remain based in their existing professional contexts both delivering a Personal Adviser service to young people. CSNU anticipate many youth workers will become PAs following PA training.

- Model 2: Youth workers become Connexions PAs in a multiagency Connexions team, for example, in a school or community setting.

- Model 3: Connexions PAs are placed into existing youth service settings such as advice and information centres, youth clubs or community centres.

- Model 4: Youth workers work alongside PAs to deliver specialist support to young people with whom they have regular contact.

Each model requires collaborative working between youth services and the Connexions Service. By adopting the role of PA, youth workers have been able to demonstrate the value of their skills in engaging with young people. At the time of writing, and in light of the Green Paper *Every Child Matters* (DfES 2003), the routes to qualification for professions working with children and young people are under review. These routes include studying at universities and gaining National Vocational Qualifications (NVQs) through the workplace. Each route is informed by the development of national occupational standards and PAs need a professional qualification equivalent to at least NVQ level four in a relevant subject such as careers guidance, youth work or social work. In addition a PA will need a Higher Education Diploma for Connexions Personal Advisers.

Where do Personal Advisers work?

The Connexions Service provides young people aged 13–19 the right to access a PA. Many young people will choose not to use the service and others may simply use it as a source of information. For some young people, PAs may provide advice on post-16 learning options or on information sources. For others, who experience a range of difficulties, PAs might provide intensive one-to-one support, and/or broker access to other specialist support. In other cases, the PA may focus on recognising early signs of social exclusion and preventing escalation of adverse circumstances. Generally speaking, it is the intensive one-to-one role being developed by youth workers.

CASE STUDY: KATE

Kate, a young white teenager, first ran away from home when she was 12: 'I didn't get on with my step-dad' she said. She walked around until after dark and was brought home by the police. She ran away next when she was 13 spending the night at a friend's house. 'No one cared. No one came looking for me.' The third time 'I walked around all night by my mum's house. It was scary and cold.' This time she was careful not to get caught by the police.

It is estimated (SEU 2002) that, by the age of 16, one in nine young people run away for at least one night. Running away increases the risk of entering care and becoming homeless as an adult. The main trigger for running away is family problems. Most runaways return home or are returned but receive little help in sorting out their problems.

The weekend Kate spent sleeping in the bus shelter aged 14, she was returned home by the police. On this occasion the police made a referral to the Connexions PA based at Kate's school. The PA explained to Kate that, if she wanted, they could meet confidentially. They met the following Monday evening at the local youth centre and spent some time exploring Kate's concerns in an attempt to identify options available to her.

The PA, a qualified youth worker, had little experience of working with runaways so made contact with a local voluntary agency specialising in helping young runaways. All parties agreed that, because of the trust built up between them, the PA would continue to work with Kate on this issue. Kate agreed that her mother and stepfather could attend a meeting where all would have an opportunity to talk about the situation as they experienced it. The PA advocated for Kate when it appeared that Kate's mother was not recognising points Kate was trying to make. They agreed on some strategies and boundaries to try to help Kate feel less *pushed out*. For example, they agreed a set amount of time Kate would spend with her mother each week and Kate agreed she would inform her mother where she was going when she left the house.

During the next two months Kate and her PA had weekly meetings either at the school or at the youth centre, where they assessed Kate's progress with her family. Kate's PA provided the emergency telephone number of the young runaways project to use if she felt she wasn't coping well. At school, the PA arranged to organise some personal, social and health education sessions covering the dangers of running away and where to find confidential advice.

Kate has become actively involved at the youth centre in group work around living at home and the dangers of running away. She has made new friends and feels she has a safe place to go, with people she can talk to.

To meet the needs of young people PAs need to work in a variety of settings including schools, further education colleges, one-stop shops, Connexions Centres and community based projects, and initiatives throughout local partnerships, including youth centres. Connexions PAs aim to build on and link existing services across agencies, to ensure provision is not duplicated and young people receive cohesive support. How this is done differs according to local circumstances, but key principles underpinning this interagency approach are outlined below.

- The most appropriate worker will be determined by taking account of the young person's views, their relationship and involvement with existing support workers, their circumstances and needs and the likely length or intensity of worker involvement. Where appropriate, the existing youth worker will take on the PA role.

- The aim is to reduce the number of different professionals working directly with a young person. For this a PA may need to seek advice from specialist colleagues rather than making referrals. Where a specialist intervention is required the PA helps to ensure clarity between the different roles of each professional.

Support for young people offers consistency and continuity, and professional boundaries do not impair the support on offer. For example, if a young person becomes homeless it may be beneficial for a worker based within a youth housing agency to adopt the PA role.

Accountability and professional boundaries

The introduction of the Connexions strategy has highlighted differences between professions and attitudes towards information sharing and confidentiality. The role of the PA as a critical link (DfEE 2001a) bringing together effective support for young people raises important issues of accountability, confidentiality and professional boundaries. Tensions arise concerning the purpose of youth work and the perception that youth workers are being required to perform a policing role through surveillance and record keeping (Smith 2003). What information professionals can or should share without the consent of a young person and what is meant by confidentiality in the different agencies are issues of concern. Some professionals have statutory duties that override confidentiality under certain circumstances, such as child protection. Tensions have also arisen from different practices and attitudes towards health and safety such as lone working and making home visits to young people and their parents or carers.

Following consultation the Code of Practice for Connexions PAs came into effect in October 2003 and provides guidelines on ethical issues and professional practice. It is intended to complement, rather than replace, existing professional practice guidance.

The six key principles of Personal Adviser practice
Personal Advisers must:

- work in the best interests of young people, placing the young people's needs, welfare and interests before their own beliefs and values.
- work to establish and maintain the trust of young people, providing an appropriate and agreed level of confidentiality in all their dealings with young people.
- promote the rights of young people when working with other voluntary, statutory and community organisations, advocating on young people's behalf and ensuring there is a coherent approach to support for young people.
- wherever possible, engage parents, carers and families in supporting young people, upholding their trust in the service.
- uphold the integrity of the profession at all times.
- be responsible for reflecting on their own professional practice and for taking steps to maintain and improve their own knowledge and skills so they are able to continually deliver a quality service.

(CSNU 2003: 2)

QUESTIONS

- What might be the challenges for workers in consistently demonstrating these principles?

- What skills would PAs need to use and develop to work within these principles?

- What support might they need from managers and other professionals?

Conclusion: The future of youth work

One debate that has followed the introduction of the Connexions Service centres on threats to the professional identity of youth workers. Some fear the youth work approach will be lost as a result of an emphasis on formal rather than informal education and by targets set for the number of young people achieving accreditation for personal and social development. In Smith's (2003) view youth workers could become mere employment and training brokers or trainers and tutors concerned with placing individuals in employment rather than with valuing the principles of voluntary associational activity. Smith (2001) has also criticised the narrow objectives of the Connexions strategy, arguing that youth work is being transformed into a means of surveillance, control and containment by central government principally because young people are viewed as being in some way a problem.

Transforming Youth Work asks 'how can youth work be built in to the core of the Connexions partnership activity?' (DfEE 2001b: 17) suggesting one way effective youth work might be undertaken in England. However, youth work continues in Northern Ireland, Scotland and Wales without being embedded into the Connexions Service. The value of devolution for some is the opportunity for innovation rather than imitation. Wales, for example, uses its own policy document Extending Entitlement (NAW 2000) to transform and develop youth work. In Wylie's view, if realistic partnerships are to succeed 'they need to be based on mutual respect – for the values, methods and professionalism of the respective elements' (2003: 24). The challenge facing those involved in youth work lies in how to achieve what Wylie calls a shared vision. Transforming Youth Work: Resourcing Excellent Youth Services 'provides a specification of a sufficient local authority youth service' (DfES 2002a: 4) although it is not clear what is meant by sufficient. Further work is required to establish common understandings between government, youth workers and young people about what constitutes valid and reliable evidence for this.

Debates continue about what counts as youth work and whether the voluntary relationship between youth worker and young person is important. Questions remain about whether youth work should provide a service for all young people, or should target particular groups, take on individual casework and shift towards formal education. Some argue that opportunities for young people to be involved in association, activities and autonomy are being lost due to the decline in traditional settings such as the youth club. Youth work, however, continues both inside and outside the Connexions strategy. A substantial amount of voluntary youth work, independent of government funding and resources, is being maintained and developed, for example, through faith-based youth work. Youth work within the Connexions Service focuses on individual young people rather than on groups and associational activities. However, a wider view of youth work illustrates that young people are for the most part active members of their community achieving transition from child to adult alongside dedicated and well trained youth workers operating to clear ethical and professional principles.

Tucker discusses the challenges to professional identity in youth working, defined as 'shorthand for the occupational activities involved in the fields of health, welfare and education … [arguing that the world of] …youth working appears to be changing at a rapid rate' (1997: 89) and the issue of effective management of change is facing many public services. The socio-political climate for public sector professionals working with young people has changed so fundamentally that there is a need to understand not only the nature of that change, but also how it impacts on the professional work and identities of particular individuals and groups. Successful interprofessional working to benefit young people is likely to result from youth workers gaining more confidence about what they have to offer in terms of their skills, knowledge and practice, and actively seeking to share this with other professions.

References

Banks S. (1999) Ethics and the youth worker. In Banks S. (ed.) *Ethical Issues In Youth Work*. London: Routledge, pp. 3–20.

Bentley T. and Gurumurthy R. (1999) *Destination Unknown: Engaging With the Problems of Marginalised Youth*. London: Demos.

CSNU (Connexions Service National Unit) (2001) *Introduction to Connexions*. Sheffield: CSNU.

CSNU (2002) *Understanding Connexions Module Handbook*. Sheffield: CSNU.

CSNU (2003) *Code of Practice for Connexions Personal Advisers*. Sheffield: CSNU.

Davies C., Finlay L. and Bullman A. (eds) (2000) *Changing Practice in Health and Social Care*. London: Sage.

DfEE (Department for Education and Employment) (1999) *Learning to Succeed: A New Framework for Post-16 Learning*. London: The Stationery Office.

DfEE (2001a) *Introduction to Connexions*. Nottingham: DfEE Publications.

DfEE (2001b) *Transforming Youth Work: Developing Youth Work for Young People*. Nottingham: DfEE Publications.

DfES (Department for Education and Skills) (2002a) *Transforming Youth Work: Resourcing Excellent Youth Services*. Nottingham: DfES Publications.

DfES (2002b) *Working Together, Connexions and the Statutory Youth Service*. Nottingham: DfES Publications.

DfES (2003) *Every Child Matters*. Nottingham: DfES Publications.

DoH (Department of Health) (1999) *Mapping Quality in Children's Services: An Evaluation of Local Responses to the Quality Protects Programme*. London: HMSO.

NAW (National Assembly for Wales) (2000) *Extending Entitlement: Supporting Young People in Wales*. Report by Policy Unit, National Assembly for Wales, September 2000. www.wales.gov.uk/young-people.

NYA (National Youth Agency) (2001) *Statement on Ethical Conduct in Youth Work*. Leicester: NYA.

NYA (undated) *The NYA Guide to Youth Work and Youth Services*. http://www.nya.org.uk/Templates/internal.asp?NodeID=89721 accessed December 2003.

Smith M.K. (2001) *Transforming Youth Work*. http://www.infed.org/youthwork/transforming.htm accessed April 2003.

Smith M.K. (2002) *Transforming Youth Work: Resourcing Excellent Youth Services: A Critique*. the informal education homepage http://www.infed.org/youthwork/transforming_youth_work_2.htm accessed January 2003.

Smith MK (2003) The end of youth work? *Young People Now*. 5–11 February.

SEU (Social Exclusion Unit) (1998) *Truancy and school exclusion*. London: SEU/The Stationery Office, Cm 3957.

SEU (1999a) *Teenage Pregnancy*. London: SEU/The Stationery Office, Cm 4342.

SEU (1999b) *Bridging the Gap: New Opportunities for 16 to 18 Year Olds Not in Education, Employment or Training*. London: SEU/The Stationery Office, Cm 4405.

SEU (2000) *Young People: report of Policy Action Team 12*. London: SEU/The Stationery Office.

SEU (2002) *Young Runaways: report by the Social Exclusion Unit*. London: SEU/The Stationery Office.

Tucker S. (1997) Youth working: professional identities given, received, or contested? In Roche J. and Tucker S. (eds) *Youth In Society*. London: Sage, pp. 89–97.

Williamson H. (1997) *Youth and Policy: Contexts and Consequences*. Aldershot: Ashgate.

Wylie T. (2003) Connexions with youth work. *Careers Guidance Today* 11(1): 22–4.

The Future for Interprofessional Working

CHAPTER 15

Issues for the Future

Judith Thomas

This chapter draws together some of the themes and issues relating to inter-professional working that emerge from this book. The areas considered cover personal issues relating to the impact on individual workers, the local context within which they work and broader issues of policy. The following themes are identified for further consideration.

■ *Continued change and uncertainty.* Policies and practices in health, social care, education, criminal justice and housing are constantly changing and developing. While writing this book major changes have been announced to the structure of some services and the way they are organised. The pace of change means that practitioners now, more that ever, need to have the capacity for critical reflection and the ability to constantly update and review their knowledge and skills.

■ *So what's new about interprofessional working?* This theme explores what is new and different about interprofessional working at the beginning of the 21st century and the implications for workers and service delivery.

■ *Service user and carers.* Here the importance of service users and carers being at the centre of service development, care planning and evaluation, rather than being passive recipients, is identified. However, the challenges of making this a reality are considerable requiring a fundamental rethink of many taken-for-granted practices and assumptions.

- *Roles.* At the beginning of the 21ˢᵗ century roles are becoming increasingly complex and blurred. New roles are emerging prompting questions relating to professional identity, management, support and supervision.

- *Interprofessional and professional identity.* Inherent in initiatives from recent policies are potential mixed messages that need highlighting, one example being, the strengthening of professional identity through protection of titles and registration whilst simultaneously promoting interprofessional working.

- *Professional education and development.* The chapter concludes by offering a format for practitioners to use that promotes critical reflection on interprofessional working.

Exploring the tensions, contradictions and paradoxes within these themes helps identify why interprofessional working is necessary and desirable but also why it can be problematic. In this chapter it is argued that interprofessional working needs to be a conscious and explicit process leading to collaborative working between service users, carers and professionals. Gaps between policy and practice illustrating the complexity of interprofessional working are identified. Questions for practitioners are posed to promote reflective analysis, greater understanding and critical evaluation of interprofessional working.

Continued change and uncertainty

In Chapters 3–14 authors identify how each profession developed, discuss recent trends and consider their continuing evolution. From this it is apparent that interprofessional working is constructed in many different ways. It can be formal or informal, it ranges from different professionals working in separate teams coming together in order to respond to the needs of individual service users to integrated teams that consist of many different professionals.

Perhaps the only thing professionals can be certain of is that practices will continue to change and develop. The changes in policy and legislation articulated throughout the book illustrate how interprofessional working is continuing to evolve. While writing this book significant changes were announced, for example in relation to the organisation of the probation service and also the Children Bill (2004) that brings with it fundamental changes to services for children.

═══════════════════════ **QUESTIONS** ═══════════════════════

- Choose one of the health and social care professions from Part II of this book. Using the relevant chapter and the references provided identify any significant changes.

- What impact might these changes have on service users, carers and the workers involved?

- What additional changes can you identify that have occurred since this book was published?

The extent of interprofessional working in different situations can be seen as a continuum. In straightforward situations, interprofessional working may involve some initial joint planning and shared record keeping. Where people have more complex needs workers, service users and carers will need to engage more actively and consciously in interprofessional working. Each situation is likely to need a different level of interprofessional working the extent of which is likely to change at different points. Professionals need to recognise the level of interdependence required to deliver services effectively and be flexible about how this can best be achieved locally.

So what's new about interprofessional working?

As asserted in Chapter 1 interprofessional working is not new. Some contact between different professionals in their daily work has always occurred but practices that have existed formally and informally for decades as each profession has emerged are being actively constructed, named and defined. Despite attempts for closer definitions different terms describing collaborative practice are often used interchangeably. While there remain subtle differences in terminology, the term interprofessional is gaining common currency and is beginning to replace its predecessor, multidisciplinary working.

Marsh and Fisher (1992) identify the dangers of the DATA (*Do All That Already*) where workers assume they are adopting particular practices. Interprofessional working may have existed for some time but current policy and financial drivers together with well publicised failures mean it needs to be an explicit and conscious activity integrated in the practice of all health and social care professionals. So while interprofessional working may not be new, attempts to define it clearly together with a greater emphasis on doing it actively and consciously, are becoming more widespread.

<hr>

QUESTION

▨ Think of a situation where you have assumed you *do all that already* in relation to interprofessional working. What systems could you use more actively or develop with colleagues to support effective interprofessional working? This might include, for example, reviewing the collaboration within each piece of work you undertake, using team meetings to discuss collaborative working practices or setting up a peer review process with a colleague from another discipline.

<hr>

Chapter 2 considers the difficulties for individual workers and some of the conflicts, stresses and opportunities that interprofessional working may present. There are myriad factors that influence how individual workers feel about interprofessional working. For example, some staff in interprofessional teams may have been seconded with limited choice about working in a different setting alongside other disciplines. The way in which changes have been implemented at local level will effect the enthusiasm or otherwise of the workforce. In interprofessional teams the leader may be drawn from one of a number of disciplines. This can create additional tension for workers who may feel isolated and consider their unique professional skills are not being developed through supervision. They may also feel that their particular professional perspectives are being diffused or eroded. In many situations staff will have made deliberate choices to move from uniprofessional to interprofessional working and embrace the accompanying challenges. Others will have started their careers in integrated teams so be less likely to carry the baggage of old ways of working. Professionals emerging from training will have experienced varying emphasis on interprofessional working in their programmes. In some programmes students will have opportunities to learn with and from other professionals, as can been seen from the examples provided on the CAIPE website (www.caipe.org.uk). These experiences are not yet the norm in professional education and Freeth *et al.* (2002) argue more research is needed to evaluate the impact of interprofessional education on practice.

ACTIVITY

- Develop your knowledge of other professions.
  Identify the professions you are likely to work with in a specified setting, for example a nursing home, a summer play scheme, a community team working with people with learning disabilities.
  Assess your knowledge of the professional roles and boundaries of each one on a basis of a scale of 1–3, where 1 represents very limited knowledge, 2 represents some awareness but gaps in knowledge, and 3 represents very well informed.

Name of Profession	Your score (1–3)
a)	
b)	
c)	

If the professions you have identified are included in part II of this book, read the relevant chapter(s). You could also ask a representative from those professions to talk to you about their roles, responsibilities and professional boundaries and use the opportunity to share information about your own profession.

- Assess your attitudes to interprofessional working.
  Which of the statements below most closely reflects your attitude to interprofessional working:

1	unwilling
2	willing but unsure
3	very willing

If you have identified yourself as category 1 or 2, read the section on willing participation in Chapter 2 of this book and ask yourself whether you can justify a uniprofessional approach to meeting the holistic needs of service users. Also identify what factors make you unwilling or unsure and discuss with colleagues ways of resolving these difficulties.

Policy developments that promote interprofessional working are identified in Chapter 1 but the extent to which these initiatives have filtered down to front-line working is variable. Irvine *et al*, citing reviews of the empirical literature argue that 'relationships between service providers remain variable and complicated' (2002: 199) with Øvretveit (1997) and Miller *et al.* (2001) making similar points. The impact of this for workers and service users is highlighted in Chapter 7 illustrating the sorts of gaps in services that can occur when national policy advocates changes from specialised services to more integrated approaches.

Policy changes take time to permeate everyday practice particularly when the pace and scale of change is as radical as in the late 1990s and the early years of the 21st century. Charlesworth draws attention to the problems associated with the 'possibility of "too much" partnership and consultation which can also slow down organisations' progress on meeting local targets' (2001: 283). She highlights the paradox that can occur:

> the government wants partnership to happen but this, added to the scale and pace of change, targets and performance measures, means there is an element of retreat to core business and it is still too early for organisations to see partnership working itself as core business. Thus there are a number of conflicting tensions and pressures which are potentially proving counterproductive to government policy on joined-up working.
>
> (*ibid*: 285)

Interprofessional working requires new thinking about leadership. The case for non- hierarchical structures has been argued extensively (see Chapter 2). However, the NHS and local authorities, where the majority of health and social care workers have traditionally been employed, are bureaucracies with hierarchical structures. The Primary Care Trusts set up under the NHS Plan (DoH 2000) to provide integrated services show similar hierarchical tendencies. This prompts questions as to whether the argument for fewer hierarchies in interprofessional working is naive and unworkable and whether it is unrealistic to deny real differences between professional practices. Structural differences in status created by pay differentials, entry requirements for training, level of qualification, political power of professional associations and historical standing cannot be denied and all contribute to the maintenance of traditional power relationships. At local level agency policies and team practices may create more equitable ways of working where power differences are minimised and the valuable contribution of all team members, including service users and carers, is recognised. Chapter 2 discusses the complexities of power and provides a useful format for analysing it. An appreciation of power and how this connects with structural inequalities together with the opportunities to openly consider how this potentially and actually permeates relationships may help practitioners and teams toward greater collaboration.

Service users and carers

Improving services for users and carers has been central to arguments for inter-professional working (DoH 1990, 1997, 1998, Audit Commission 2002) and it is argued (DoH 2001) that they are the best judges of whether partnership is working. Barton makes links between human rights, the services that should be available to enable disabled people to live as independent a life as possible and the way in which users should be active agents of their lives. She argues they should be 'treated as partners and be in control [and that their] experience and expertise ... particularly their understanding of their own requirements... should be recognised and valued' (2003: 109). Douek makes similar arguments in relation to carers. She draws attention to the National Strategy for Carers (DoH 1999a) which 'requires service providers to see carers as partners in the provision of help to the person needing care' (2003: 123).

Obviously there are challenges for all professionals in making partnership a reality and ensuring that service users are in control, as illustrated by the case studies in this book. In Chapter 5 the doctor has to determine the degree of risk associated with Mr Fitzpatrick if he stays at home and face a potential public outcry if problems then occur. Chapter 11 identifies motivation as a key factor in the work of probation officers, but service users are offenders so their use of the service may be compulsory with limited choice between using the service or being in prison. Here the notion of the service user being in control is inevitably constrained. One of the criticisms in the Laming Report (2003) (see Chapter 10) was that none of the professionals spoke directly to Victoria Climbié about her life or how she was feeling so, even the basics of user involvement were absent. In Chapter 3 Sofie's mother, as the carer, experienced difficulty challenging professional viewpoints. The obstacles she faced in finding out about options relating to medical procedures and the fight she had to promote the value of sign language so that her daughter was included in communications are typical of the sorts of frustrations that carers can experience.

=== QUESTIONS ===

■ Identify a situation where you have been a service user or a carer.

- To what extent did you feel in control?
- In what ways was the power or control you had in the situation limited?
- How could your involvement have been enhanced?

The way in which health and social care services were set up in 1948 with separate funding streams that translated into different eligibility criteria led to frequent conflict as to whom was responsible for the funding of services. Service users and carers suffered most from this being passed 'from one service to another in the hope that the cost will be met from an alternative source' (Barton 2003: 113). Changes have been made in the way funding is allocated where pooled budgets, made possible by the Health Act (DoH 1999b), have been introduced giving service users access to funding to buy in their own care. The Carers Grant (DoH 2002) allows for funding to be ring fenced by local authorities for needs such as respite care and support groups. Consequently the way in which money can now be allocated is an important step in giving service users and carers more power and control over their lives and professionals have a responsibility to support this process.

Roles

In Chapter 2 the importance of clarity and competence in one's own professional role for effective interprofessional working is discussed, referring to studies showing clarity cannot always be achieved (Bliss *et al.* 2000, Booth and Hewison 2002). Other chapters illustrate different views both within professions and externally about their role and purpose. For example, within social work there has long been a debate about whether social workers are agents of state control whose purpose is to help people fit into existing structures or whether social workers through community and political action should be attempting to change society (Barnes and Hugman 2002). In Chapter 10, Kennison and Fletcher highlight differences between public perceptions of what the police should be doing and the view of the police endorsed in targets set by government that, in turn, determine levels of funding. In Chapter 6 the complexity of the midwife's role and the blend of knowledge and skills needed for competent practice is considered. This may include, for example, detailed physiological knowledge of pregnancy and birthing combined with an understanding of the potential psychological reactions, social conditions and the skills to promote the rights of the woman whilst ensuring the health of the baby. From these discussions we see that the role of each professional is complex and requires a blend of different types of knowledge and skills; roles are not fixed but depend on the context within which the person is working.

QUESTIONS

■ Choose a professional group and identify some of the potential tensions for the workers in that profession, others they may work with, service users and carers in terms of the way in which their role could be perceived.

■ What stereotypes do you have of each profession?
   – how were these formed?
   – how are they perpetuated?
   – what purpose do they serve?

New roles are being created, for example, the role of the Connexions Personal Adviser (PA), as discussed in Chapter 14. Here the PA may be assumed or perceived to be a specific role within the orbit of a distinct professional group, for example youth workers, rather than being an extension of the existing role, for instance, of careers advisor, teacher or social worker. Changes to the role of each professional and the activities they perform are a common feature of modern health and social care services. One example is of prescribing medication, until recently this responsibility rested with doctors but now certain medications can be prescribed by nurses (Chapter 7), with plans to extend this function to physiotherapists (Chapter 9) and radiographers (Chapter 12).

New structures are also emerging within services, for example, a four-tier structure is proposed for radiography setting out the tasks workers at each level would be expected to perform and the level of training required to fulfil these responsibilities. In child and adolescent mental health services different tiers are used to convey the range of workers who may be involved with children and young people (Spender *et al.* 2001). Potentially there is some tension between arguments for non-hierarchical working practices advocated for interprofessional working and the hierarchies emerging within professions. However, the breakdown of services into different tiers can be helpful in enabling service users, carers and workers to appreciate different roles and functions but inevitably there will also be local variations and a degree of overlap between the different tiers.

Professional verses interprofessional identity

Alongside moves towards role flexibility and new ways of working there is also greater emphasis on professional identity. Indications of this include the legal protection of titles of registered nurse, social worker or physiotherapist. While there has been long-standing protection in some cases, such as doctor, others are more recent with provision made for protection of the title of social worker and physiotherapist introduced in 2004. National Occupational Standards, Codes of Practice and academic benchmarks for qualifications have been developed in profession-specific ways. Whilst these documents include reference to collaboration and understanding the contribution of others, they have mainly evolved from within the discipline to which they refer. It could also be argued that they make the distinction between different professions more acute and that this potentially militates against interprofessional working.

Organisations such as NICE (National Institute of Clinical Excellence) and SCIE (Social Care Institute of Excellence) supporting professionals in developing and disseminating research to inform practice have been established. These organisations are government funded and aim to provide information for practitioners on different treatments and working practices. Professional bodies support and monitor standards within each profession, for example the NMC for nursing and midwifery, and the GSCC for social work and social care. These initiatives, together with points about the status of different professions, as argued in Chapter 2, all contribute to a clearer professional identity.

However, Yelloly argues that 'Defining competences, specifying the work to be done, measuring performance against specified criteria (and paying accordingly), combined with opening up the professional market place has further eroded professional autonomy' (1995: 19–20). Arguments presented in Chapter 1 and made by others (for example, Foster and Wilding 2000, Sullivan and Skelcher 2002, Ahmad and Broussine 2003) also warn that increasing levels of centralised government and managerial control, together with the effect of performance targets, undermine professional choice. While the blurring of boundaries in some areas may be positive (for example, assessment no longer being the preserve of social work or probation) it also creates concerns about the demise of professional identity and undermines liberal values.

Professional education and development

Whittington considers

> The ethical responsibility of …care professionals is not only 'to do' as effectively as their skills with allow, but also to 'reflect' as rigorously as possible both on what they do and what is being offered as evidence to justify it.
>
> (2003: 30)

Such views can be traced back to Schön who argues that professionals are consistently faced with problems where one theory or solution cannot easily be applied and suggests skilled professional workers actually draw on a range of theories to help them make sense of their world. He also questions whether 'the prevailing concepts of professional education will ever yield a curriculum adequate to the complex, unstable, uncertain, and conflictual worlds of practice' (1987: 12). So while professional training may help people understand and analyse their role and ensure they have relevant knowledge for practice, it is unrealistic to assume professionals will qualify with all the knowledge they need for each situation they will encounter. This combined with the instability created by the changing nature of policy, partly prompted by political changes, and factors such as variations in demography and social structures means professionals need to be equipped and motivated to critically appraise their working practices regularly.

The questions provided below can be used to consider, explore, analyse and evaluate interprofessional working. They can be used by teams to explore collective practices or by individuals to critically reflect on their own work. However, as interprofessional working takes place in a social context and requires interaction with others discussion with other team members is encouraged. In working through the questions you will need to focus on a particular incident or situation, this way of reflecting on an incident using a structured format is often referred to as a Critical Incident Analysis (see Fook et al. 2000, Taylor 2000 and Thomas 2004). The questions provided are designed to prompt thinking and reflection, consequently some will not have clear, easy answers or solutions.

=========================== **ACTIVITY** ===========================

Critical Incident Analysis:

Start by thinking generally about the context in which you are working and the strengths and limitations of interprofessional working in this setting.

Think of an example of some work either with a specific service user or carer or an event, such as a meeting, where you observed or were part of interprofessional working.

■ What were your first impressions of interprofessional working in relation to the incident?

■ What was effective about the way different professions worked together?

■ What hindered interprofessional working?

■ Where did this happen? (Details of room, setting, physical environment and so on).

■ What did you notice about the way people *communicated* with each other?
  - Did everyone who wanted to, contribute to the discussion?
  - Was anyone excluded or ignored?
  - Did anyone dominate? If so, how and why?
  - What did you notice about the nonverbal communication?
  - What did you notice about the use of language – was it specialised?

■ Was there any profession or person *missing* who could have made a useful contribution?

■ What did you notice about the *relationships* between those involved? Was there any particularly strong connection or rapport between particular people?

■ What were the service user's and carer's views, expertise and strengths?
  - How central were they to the discussion?

■ What was the *atmosphere* like? (Identify conflict, humour, routines, refreshments).

■ What was the main content of the discussion?
  - Diagnosis/identification of problems, progress, future planning?
  - Did any of the discussion consider how professions had or could potentially work together?

■ What was your *role*?
  - How clear were you about this?
  - What role conflicts did you experience or observe?
  - Did you understand the role of others present?
  - If not why not and what can you do about this?

■ Which of the following *skills* did you use and how effectively did you use them?
  - Active listening,
  - Sharing your views,
  - Being aware of other people,
  - Using eye contact,
  - Using silences,
  - Summarising,
  - Asking open questions,
  - Acknowledging other contributions,
  - Challenging.

■ How did *power* and *leadership* operate?
  - Was there a formal leader and if so why did this person take the lead?

- Were there any shifts or changes in leadership during the process if so why?
- What were the power dynamics? (use Figure 2.1 in Chapter 2 to help you analyse these).
- What did you notice about the way in which formal and informal power operated?
- How did you use your power and influence?
- Did you feel able to challenge others?
- Were any viewpoints or contributions ignored or undermined?
- Was there conflict, if so how was this resolved?
- What else did you notice about power?

■ What *learning* occurred?
  - For you?
  - For others?
  - How did this happen? (For example, discussion in group, follow up discussion with practice teacher, mentor, supervisor, clinical educator and so on).

■ Did any new practices or ways of working emerge from the situation?

■ How can you apply the understanding you have gained from this situation in the future?

■ What gaps in your knowledge, understanding and skills can you identify and how can you bridge these? Think about who you may need to talk to, what you might need to investigate further and what skills you might need to practice.

Conclusion

The challenges of interprofessional working need to be recognised, Reason considers that working in multidisciplinary teams is

> very difficult...it requires highly evolved practitioners who are in significant ways non-attached to their paradigms of practice and to their Self. More than this it requires a social setting which supports and encourages such detachment: an evolved multidisciplinary group.
>
> (1996: 245)

Consequently it will not happen unless people are committed to identifying and working through difficulties as they occur. Policy initiatives and the needs of those who use services and resources will continue to steer the interprofessional agenda. In order for new policies to operate effectively they need the commitment of professionals to work collaboratively together with the ability to critically evaluate practices and develop these with service users and carers. The authors have conveyed the complexity of incorporating collaboration within the context of distinct professional roles. The task has stimulated authors to think more deeply about their personal paradigms of practice and the integration of interprofessional identity within their specific uniprofessional culture. It is hoped this book will help readers to think critically about the nature of interprofessional practices and how this can be incorporated into their daily work.

References

Ahmad Y. and Broussine M. (2003) The UK public sector modernization agenda: reconciliation and renewal? *Public Management Review* 5(1): 45–62.

Audit Commission (2002) *Integrated Services for Older People: Building a Whole System Approach.* London: Audit Commission.

Barnes D. and Hugman R. (2002) Portrait of social work. *Journal of Interprofessional Care* 16: 277–88.

Barton C. (2003) Allies and enemies: the service user as care co-ordinator. In Weinstein J., Whittington C. and Leiba T. (eds) *Collaboration in Social Work Practice*. London: Jessica Kingsley Publications, pp. 103–20.

Bliss J., Cowley S. and While A. (2000) Interprofessional working in palliative care in the community: a review of the literature. *Journal of Interprofessional Care* 14: 281–90.

Booth J. and Hewison A. (2002) Role overlap between occupational therapy and physiotherapy during in-patient stroke rehabilitation: an exploratory study. *Journal of Interprofessional Care* 16: 31–40.

Charlesworth J. (2001) Negotiating and managing partnership in primary care. *Health and Social Care in the Community* 9(5): 279–85.

Children Bill (2004) London: The Stationery Office.

DoH (Department of Health) (1990) *NHS and Community Care Act*. London: HMSO.

DoH (1997) *The New NHS: Modern, Dependable*. London: The Stationery Office.

DoH (1998) *Modernising Social Services: Promoting Independence, Improving Protection, Raising Standards*. London: DoH.

DoH (1999a) *Caring about Carers: A National Strategy for Carers*. www.doh.gov.uk accessed April 2004.

DoH (1999b) *Health Act 1999: Modern Partnerships for the People*. London: The Stationery Office.

DoH (2000) *The NHS Plan, A Plan for Investment, A Plan for Reform*. London: The Stationery Office.

DoH (2001) *Health and Social Care Awards 2001*. London: DoH.

DoH (2002) Carers Grant. http://www.carers.gov.uk/grantdetermination.pdf accessed April 2004.

Douek S. (2003) Collaboration or confusion? The carers perspective. In Weinstein J., Whittington C. and Leiba T. (eds) *Collaboration in Social Work Practice*. London: Jessica Kingsley Publications, pp. 121–36.

Fook J., Ryan M. and Hawkins L. (2000) *Professional Expertise: Practice, Theory and Education for Working in Uncertainty*. London: Whiting and Birch.

Foster P. and Wilding P. (2000) Whither welfare professionalism? *Social Policy and Administration* 34(2): 143–59.

Freeth D., Hammick M., Koppel I., Reeves S. and Barr H. (2002) *A Critical Review of Evaluations of Interprofessional Education Learning and Teaching Support Network*: London: Health Sciences and Practice.

Irvine R., Kerridge I., McPhee J. and Freeman S. (2002) Interprofessionalism and ethics: consensus or clash of cultures? *Journal of Interprofessional Care* 16: 199–210.

Laming Lord (2003) *Inquiry into the Death of Victoria Climbié*. London: The Stationery Office.

Marsh P. and Fisher M. (1992) *Good Intentions: Developing Partnership in Social Services*. York: Joseph Rowntree Foundation.

Miller C., Freeman M. and Ross N. (2001) *Interprofessional Practice in Health and Social Care Challenging the Shared Learning Agenda*. London: Arnold.

Øvretveit J. (1997) How to describe interprofessional working. In Øvretveit J., Mathias P. and Thompson T. (eds) *Interprofessional Working for Health and Social Care*. Basingstoke: Macmillan, pp. 9–33.

Reason P. (1996) From conflict to creativity: interprofessional collaboration, education and training. In Patrick C. and Pietroni C. (eds) *Innovation in Community Care and Primary Health.* New York: Churchill Livingston.

Schön D.A. (1987) *Educating the Reflective Practitioner.* San Francisco: Jossey-Bass.

Spender Q., Salt N., Dawkins J., Kendrick T. and Hill P. (2001) *Child Mental Health in Primary Care.* Oxford: Radcliffe Medical Press.

Sullivan H. and Skelcher C. (2002) *Working Across Boundaries: Collaboration in the Public Services.* Basingstoke: Palgrave.

Taylor B.J. (2000) *Reflective Practice: A Guide for Nurses and Midwifes.* Buckingham: Open University Press.

Thomas J. (2004) Using 'Critical Incident Analysis' to promote critical reflection and holistic assessment. In Gould N. and Baldwin M. (eds) *Social Work, Critical Reflection and the Learning Organisation.* Aldershot: Ashgate.

Whittington C. (2003) Collaboration and partnership in context. In Weinstein J., Whittington C. and Leiba T. (eds) *Collaboration in Social Work Practice.* London: Jessica Kingsley Publications, pp. 13–8.

Yelloly, M. (1995) Professional competence and higher education, in: M. Yelloly and M. Henkel (eds) *Learning and Teaching in Social Work: Towards Reflective Practice.* London: Jessica Kingsley Publications. www.caipe.org.uk/publications.html accessed April 2004.

Index